ENGINEERING CYBERNETICS

PRENTICE-HALL INFORMATION AND SYSTEM SCIENCES SERIES

Thomas Kailath, *Editor*

ENGINEERING CYBERNETICS

ROBERT M. GLORIOSO

Department of Electrical and Computer Engineering
University of Massachusetts

Prentice-Hall, Inc.
Englewood Cliffs, New Jersey

Library of Congress Cataloging in Publication Data

GLORIOSO, ROBERT M.
  Engineering cybernetics.

  (Information and system sciences series)
  Includes bibliographical references.
  1. Cybernetics. 2. Information theory. 3. Computer engineering. I. Title.
  Q310.G45   001.53   74–13091
  ISBN 0–13–277335–X

PRENTICE-HALL INTERNATIONAL, INC., *London*
PRENTICE-HALL OF AUSTRALIA, PTY, LTD., *Sydney*
PRENTICE-HALL OF CANADA, LTD., *Toronto*
PRENTICE-HALL OF INDIA PRIVATE LIMITED, *New Delhi*
PRENTICE-HALL OF JAPAN, INC., *Tokyo*

To
Nan and Mickey,
Dee and Scott

CONTENTS

PREFACE

This book was developed for a one semester course given in the Electrical and Computer Engineering Department at the University of Massachusetts, Amherst. This course serves as a senior elective as well as an introduction for both Engineering and Computer Sciences graduate students to advanced work in artificial intelligence, pattern recognition, adaptive control, adaptive communications, and system design. Although some junior level students have successfully completed this course, it has been a popular course for seniors following an introductory course in computers and switching theory. Thus, the prerequisites for this course are switching theory, a reasonable background in probability or random signal theory, and some familiarity with computer programming.

The various disciplines which together are generally referred to as cybernetics, including adaptation, learning, self-organization, self-repair, game playing by machines, pattern recognition, and artificial intelligence have been generating interest for the past two decades. It is one purpose of this book to explore these concepts under one cover and present a framework wherein these topics can be united. Another purpose is to present some of the applications of cybernetics which have emerged thus far. Finally, the student is provided with some of the background necessary to carry out further work in these areas.

This book is organized into roughly three major sections: Motivation, Basic Tools and Definitions, Specific System Examples, and Neural Models and Pattern Recognition. The primary objectives of the first four chapters are to develop motivation and provide background in fundamental computer organization and behavior, symbols and decisions in machines, information, logic and automata. The fifth chapter provides definitions of the concepts which are applied in Chapters Six through Ten. Search techniques are also discussed in this chapter. Chapters Six and Seven are concerned with specific examples of adaptive, learning, and self-organizing systems as applied to control and communications respectively. The principles of redundant design, fault masking, and repair for creating reliable systems are presented in Chapter Eight. A simple introduction to the structure and behavior of neurons and neural models developed in Chapter Nine provide historical perspective and an introduction to threshold logic. The concepts of a separating plane and a hyperspace are put forth in the first part of Chapter Ten. The remainder of Chapter Ten is concerned with single and multilevel threshold logic synthesis and descriptions of the Adaline, Madaline, and the Perceptron. Pattern recognition naturally follows in Chapter Eleven where the various aspects of the problem including input systems for both optical and acoustical pattern recognition, feature extraction, and classification are defined and discussed.

No work of this kind happens spontaneously but grows from one's interest in the subject and from interaction and discussions with colleagues and friends. I would like to acknowledge the following individuals for their special contributions. First, my colleagues at the U.S. Army Electronics Command at Fort Monmouth, N.J., where first thoughts of this book originated, especially Messrs. J. C. Dunn, G. R. Grueneich, W. Huber and W. Rothamel. Messrs. M. A. Arbib, L. E. Franks, L. O. Gilstrap, A. Ginsburg, and W. Kilmer each suggested material which was included in the text. Finally, I thank my wife, Dee, and son, Scott, for their patience and understanding without which this text could not have come to pass.

ROBERT M. GLORIOSO

Amherst, Mass.

1

COMPUTERS AND INTELLIGENCE

INTRODUCTION

Mention the words *cybernetics*, *artificial intelligence*, or *self-organizing systems* and the word computer seems to emerge almost immediately. Since this seems to be the case, this chapter will be devoted to introducing some of the concepts of cybernetic or intelligent systems or one of the other names used to describe these concepts and to relating them to the computer. First, let us examine the nature of the beast—the computer.

1.1 WHAT IS A COMPUTER?

The first thing one usually conjures as his image of a computer is a massive machine capable of reducing or operating on large files of numbers or solving complex scientific equations. This image of a computer is often referred to as the *number cruncher* approach. However, this is not the only framework in

1

which a computer can be and is applied. For example, a general-purpose computer may be used as the controller in a process control environment such as steel and oil refining and manufacturing plants oɪ as an integral part of an automotive ignition-fuel injection system. The areas in which computers are used is growing and will continue to grow. Integrated circuit technology and the growth of MSI and LSI (medium-scale integration and large-scale integration) in both central processor and memory technology are making the computer more attractive as an element or building block in large systems. It is clear that the engineer will soon be using the computer as readily as he now uses an operational amplifier or logic gate. This innovation makes it more attractive to incorporate more esoteric features such as adaption, learning, and self-repair into everyday designs.

A general-purpose computer has certain features and characteristics which are of interest here. The flow of data through a computer is controlled by a device called a control unit which routes data into, out from, and through the machine, as illustrated in Figure 1.1. Internally, the memory and arith-

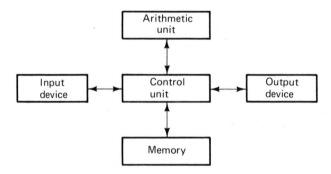

Figure 1.1. Block diagram of a general-purpose digital computer.

metic units are the objects of most of the flow within the machine. The memory may be magnetic core, semiconductors, magnetic tape, disc and drum, or some combination of the above. The arithmetic unit performs the mathematical and numerical operations and logical decisions, necessary to compute the results required in the programs stored in the computer's memory. The nature of these data in their most basic form is, of course, digital or binary numbers. The representation of these data with respect to the user may be other than binary numbers. For example, they may be simple symbols such as mathematical notation or alphanumeric characters. It is the ability of the general-purpose computer as a symbol manipulator that makes this device so unique as a tool of systems engineering. This characteristic plus the ability of the computer to make simple decisions have prompted its exploitation and application in such areas as game playing, theorem proving, and other areas which heretofore were limited to human participation and control.

The computer described thus far is missing the elements which now and even more so in the future distinguish one computer from another [1], namely the input-output (I/O) equipment. Typical I/O equipment includes teletypes, paper tape readers and punches, card readers and punches, and simple switches and lights. These devices are usually, although not always, identified as the trappings of computers used as number crunchers. The I/O equipment for computers which is having an impact on complex systems design includes analog-to-digital and digital-to-analog converters, digital channels and analog and digital multiplexors. These devices provide an easy interface to the sensing and control equipment of many engineering systems.

1.2 SYMBOLS AND DECISIONS

As suggested in the previous section, symbol manipulation is a natural process for the general-purpose digital computer. For example, it is possible, as anyone with some programming experience has observed, to encode natural language text into a computer. It is also possible to provide a simple symbol table for the machine which can be used to look up symbols in one language and translate them into symbols in another language. Thus, the process of language translation, which certainly is not number crunching, can be accomplished with these machines. The specific languages which are involved in the translation process are, of course, very important. The translation which occurs in the compilation of a FORTRAN or other high-level language program into a machine language program is an everyday process for many computers, while the translation from say Russian to English or from some other natural language to another natural language is not. The reason for this difference is that the artificial languages associated with computer processing are specifically designed to avoid the ambiguities and syntax problems associated with natural languages [2].

Another interesting example of symbol manipulation is the graphical processing of information using a cathode-ray-tube (CRT) terminal, light-pen, and push-button man-machine interface. Here the human operator works with man-oriented symbols such as schematic drawings and diagrams and operates on the computer by drawing in usually some restricted man-oriented language using the light pen. Automatic typesetting and machine control systems are other examples of symbol manipulation by general-purpose stored-program digital computers. For example, some of these machines read typed stories from bond paper, format the page, correct spelling, and set newspaper type, all automatically. It should now be abundantly clear that the image of the computer as a mammoth number cruncher which swallows and regurgitates punched cards paper or magnetic tape is in no way a complete picture of the system tool which the computer is now.

The unique capability of the computer to make logical decisions and thence modify its behavior is the heart of the power of this device. These decisions, whether obviously simple or horrendously complex, always can/must be broken down into a series of basic decisions as they must be carried out by conditional jump or branch instructions. For example, the process associated with the typical decision apparently made with some frequency by members of the college population is illustrated in Figure 1.2.

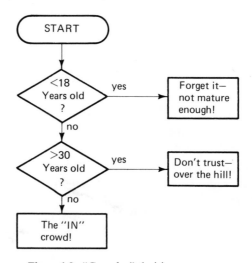

Figure 1.2. "Complex" decision process.

1.3 WHAT IS INTELLIGENCE?

As a first step toward answering the question "What is intelligence?" we shall start with two dictionary definitions of intelligence: (1) capacity for understanding and for other forms of adaptive behavior; and (2) knowledge of an event, circumstance, etc., received or imparted; news; information.

Discussions of the definition of intelligence and artificial intelligence have been in progress ever since computer operations were compared with thinking and the brain. These concepts are also part of the definition presented by Fogel et al. [3]: "the distinction between knowledge and intelligence became clear: knowledge being the useful information stored within the individual, and intelligence being the ability of the individual to utilize this stored information in some worthwhile (goal-directed) manner."

Although some people may argue the point, it is generally assumed that whatever intelligence is, it is a characteristic exhibited by man. The question now is, Can computers think and exhibit intelligent behavior? Can we create artificial intelligence? The following are some of the arguments both pro and con concerning computers, thinking, and artificial intelligence.

First, if one considers thinking to be a uniquely human endeavor and intelligence to be a uniquely human attribute, then, by definition, this process and attribute cannot be associated with a computer or other mechanical or artificial system.

On the other hand, it has been argued that if there is some fundamental physical limitation on the ability to compute, process, decide, judge, and think which applies to the creation of machine intelligence, then these same limitations must also apply to human intelligence. That is, any theoretical limitations based on universal natural laws must be universally applicable to both man and machine. This argument, of course, discounts the precept that the essence of intelligence is mystical or mysterious.

A more scientific approach to this whole question was proposed by Turing [4, 5] in 1950, who suggested that the question can be answered by experiment and observation in which the relative behavior of the computer is compared with the behavior of a system which, by definition, thinks and exhibits intelligent behavior—namely human behavior. To this end Turing proposed a question and answer technique where the trappings of both the machine and a man are hidden and questions are asked and answered via some type of remote terminal such as a teletype. If one could, by asking questions, reliably determine whether the machine or the man is answering the questions, then one would question whether the machine were intelligent or if it exhibited the same intelligence as the man. On the other hand, if one could not tell the difference, then it could be said that the machine is as intelligent as man. This imitation game is an interesting approach which has not yet been fully explored.

Perhaps a more rational approach to this question is to visualize a continuous intelligence space where men, machines, animals, plants, or what have you are positioned in the space based on their relative intelligence. Here, perhaps, a mass of material such as rocks and plants would be at one end and man and other higher animals would be at the other end. Thus, one could consider all things as having some degree of intelligence. This approach side-steps or compromises the question "Are machines intelligent?" rather than truly answering it.

Another common argument against the concept of machine intelligence is that a computer is a dumb machine which does only what it is told by its human programmer. But if one critically examines the nature of human intelligence, one must admit that his biological system along with the adaptive ability of his behavior both endowed by nature and the totality of his experience give him these unique powers of thought and intelligence. Thus, the basic, built-in characteristics of man coupled with the changes in him through experience endow him with the proper "program" for successful performance in his environment. Therefore, Simon [6] has suggested that

"If a computer thinks, learns, and creates, it will be by virtue of a program that endows it with these capacities. Clearly this will not be a program—any more than the human is—that calls for highly stereotyped and repetitive behavior independent of the stimuli coming from the environment and the task to be completed. It will be a program that makes the system's behavior highly conditioned on the task environment—on the task goals and on the clues extracted from the environment that indicate whether progress is being made toward these goals. It will be a *program* that analyzes, by some means, its own performance, diagnoses its failures, and makes changes that enhance its future effectiveness."

The essence of cybernetic systems and artificial intelligence is contained in this statement. The ability of a system to examine and modify its behavior accordingly is necessary if it is to have any of these attributes.

1.4 SOME TECHNIQUES OF ARTIFICIAL INTELLIGENCE

If we can now agree that it is the program stored in a computer that will be crucial if it is to exhibit this behavior, then let us examine the kinds of programs which are used to obtain results which are called learning or intelligence.

The first technique or tool which we shall examine is the algorithm. An algorithm is a specific set of operations, procedures, and decisions which is guaranteed to yield the correct results. Examples of algorithms extend from the simple procedures for finding a square root and synthetic division to learning algorithms for systems which can be described by stochastic transition matrices [7].

A procedure which is often confused with algorithms is a heuristic. A heuristic is a rule of thumb, trick, strategy, simplification, or other method which aids in the solution of complex problems. The heuristic used in many problems of engineering cybernetics generally reduces the size of the space in which one needs to search for solutions to the problem at hand. One of the major differences between a heuristic and an algorithm is that while the heuristic generally aids in finding the solution, it does not guarantee an optimal solution or even a solution at all. Thus, while a heuristic is often helpful, with an algorithm one can be sure of finding the correct result.

There are two kinds of heuristics, special and general. A special heuristic is one which applies to a particular problem, whereas a general heuristic is a process or philosophy which can be applied to a wide range of problems.

For example, a game-playing program (say chess) which identifies sequences of moves which threaten the computer's winning chances is a special heuristic for that particular game.

As anyone who has proved some theorems knows, it is generally easier to work backward from the theorem being proved to known theorems or axioms rather than working forward from known theorems and axioms rather blindly searching for the new theorem. The process of working backward in theorem proving is a general heuristic.

Another general heuristic is the recognition of features in the present problem which are similar to problems solved previously. The critical part of this technique is the recognition of the similarity which itself may be a special heuristic.

A final example of a general heuristic which has been developed is a program called GPS (general problem solver) by Newell and Simon [8]. This process, called means-ends analysis, is related to the process of problem solving employed by humans when performing a specific task. Here, the problem statement is transformed into a target or goal state which represents the solution to the problem. This state provides a means of identifying a proper solution of the problem. The program then identifies the difference between the present state and the goal state and then selects sequentially the operations which reduce the difference between the new present state and the goal state. Another form of means-ends analysis is called planning, wherein a simplified statement of the problem is reduced to a plan by means-ends analysis, which is then used to operate on the full problem.

The techniques of artificial intelligence most often require that the problem be defined in some specific way, for example, the breaking down of a complex decision into a series of simpler subdecisions which lead to the final solution. The representation of a problem in a simple, easily processed form then aids in the development of a solution. Thus, the process of deciding a single move in a game in the context of the overall strategy has developed as an important exposition of some of these techniques.

In Chapter 2 we shall explore games and some of the ways they can be played by machines in an "intelligent" way. These methodologies are not reserved for games only and have been applied to theorem proving, general problem solving, and pattern recognition [9].

Chapter 3 serves as a link from these techniques of artificial intelligence to advanced work in this area and sets the mathematical tone for Chapter 4. Chapter 4 is concerned with computing machines, their abstract representation, and their theoretical limitations. These concepts tell us just how far we can go in the application of cybernetic principles using real machines by providing a basis for analysis. The remainder of the book is devoted to the exposition of cybernetics and its applications in engineering systems.

1.5 SUMMARY

The application of computers in sophisticated problem-solving environments and systems has been suggested here. As technology progresses, the concept of a digital computer as a tool such as an operational amplifier or system element will become more important to the engineer. The incorporation of the computer into cybernetic systems requires an understanding of the principles of artificial intelligence and adaptive, learning, self-organizing, and self-repairing systems. The remainder of this book explores these principles and presents examples of their application.

1.6 EXERCISES

1.1. Discuss the validity of the statement "Computers are dumb machines and do only what they are told."

1.2. Give three examples of symbolic representations in a general-purpose digital computer.

1.3. Give a flow chart for an algorithm which finds the number of the position of the letter closest to z in a sequence of 10 letters. The letters are numbered sequentially from left to right.

1.4. Give a flow chart for a program which orients the four accompanying triangles such that the smallest angle in each triangle points directly up. Assume that there is a subroutine for finding the smallest angle.

REFERENCES

1. COURY, FRED, "A Systems Approach to Minicomputer I/O," in 1970 *Spring Joint Computer Conference*, AFIPS Conf. Proc., Vol. 36, Montvale, N.J., AFIPS Press.

2. GARVIN, PAUL L., ed., *Natural Language and the Computer*, McGraw-Hill, New York, 1963.

3. FOGEL, L. J., A. J. OWENS, and M. J. WALSH, *Artificial Intelligence Through Simulated Evaluation*, Wiley, New York, 1966.

4. FEIGENBAUM, E. A., and J. FELDMAN, eds., *Computers and Thought*, 5th ed., McGraw-Hill, New York, 1963.

5. TURING, A. M., "Can Machines Think?," reprinted in *Computers and Thought*, 5th ed., E. A. Feigenbaum and J. Feldman, eds., McGraw-Hill, New York, 1963.

6. SIMON, H. A., *The New Science of Management Decision*, Harper & Row, New York, 1960.

7. GLORIOSO, R. M., and G. R. GRUENEICH, "A Training Algorithm for Systems Described by Stochastic Transition Matrices," *IEEE Transactions on Systems, Man and Cybernetics*, Vol. 1, No. 1, Jan. 1971.

8. NEWELL, A., and A. SIMON, "GPS, a Program that Stimulates Human Thought," reprinted in *Computers and Thought*, 5th ed., E. A. Feigenbaum and J. Feldman, eds., McGraw-Hill, New York, 1963.

9. NILSSON, NILS J., *Problem Solving Methods in Artificial Intelligence*, McGraw-Hill, New York, 1971.

2

GAME PLAYING AND MACHINES

One of the first areas in which the concepts of artificial intelligence through heuristics and algorithms were applied was automatic game playing by machines. Initially, there was a good deal of speculation that soon a computer would be the world chess champion because computers, by virtue of their tremendous speed and large memory, can examine all possible moves and thus always know exactly which moves lead to a win. Early investigators quickly came to the conclusion that this brute force approach leads directly up the garden path, which is a long way from a chess win.

2.1 DECISION MODELS

In the course of playing most games one generally comes to a point where at least one decision must be made. For example, in the games of tick-tack-toe, checkers, and chess, each move requires that a decision be made by the appropriate player. The simplest decision, a binary decision, can easily be

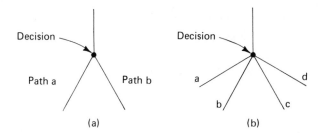

Figure 2.1. (a) Representation of a binary decision.
(b) Representation of a multiple-alternative decision.

represented in the simple graph of Figure 2.1(a). Here, the nodes in the graph represent decision points, and the edges represent the directions in which these decisions lead. The more complex decision illustrated in Figure 2.1(b) has four possible alternative moves. Here, if one reaches a point where only one of several alternatives can be successful, then there is only one course of action. This is called a forced move.

The moves associated with a chess game can also be represented in a tree called a game tree. The initial or opening moves by the first player are given in the first level of the tree, and the first moves by the second player are given in the second level of the tree, as shown in Figure 2.2. Note that only the

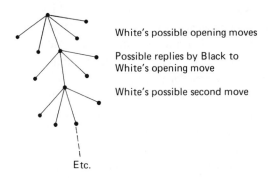

White's possible opening moves

Possible replies by Black to White's opening move

White's possible second move

Figure 2.2. Game tree for chess.

possible moves associated with the particular game being played are illustrated in Figure 2.2 and that all possible moves in all possible games would require branches from every node in the figure. The computer playing in a brute force manner needs only to store all possible paths in a game in its memory. It has been estimated that there are approximately 10^{120} different paths through the chess tree. In contrast, it has been estimated that there are approximately

10^{10} neurons in the human nervous system. Thus, the practicality or even the desirability of storing all paths is questionable. If we could endow a chess-playing program with the ability to disregard the low-likelihood paths by some means of selective, intelligent search, then perhaps it would play a reasonable game of chess. Thus, the searching and processing of trees is an important technique of heuristic programming.

2.2 GAME TREES [1, 2]

The techniques treated in this section can be applied in many areas, however, for illustration, we shall restrict our attention to game trees.

Game trees must be generated, searched, and pruned in order to be handled economically by a computer. There are basically two types of game trees: explicit and implicit trees.

An explicit game tree is one in which the top node represents the starting position, and the shape or color of the node represents the player whose turn is associated with that node. Also, an explicit tree is one in which every move through the tree is included.

An implicit tree contains the starting node together with the rules necessary to generate the remainder of the tree for each particular game. These rules must include the termination criteria, which are needed to determine when the game is over, and the successor rules, which indicate the ways in which the successive positions—nodes—are generated. Naturally, a node for which the termination criteria are satisfied has no successor rule. The rules for most board game moves such as in checkers and chess are the successor rules for generating the tree for these games.

There are two generation procedures for generating implicit game trees called breadth-first and depth-first, respectively. Breadth-first generation proceeds by generating every node in the first position, every node in the second position, and so forth in a fanlike manner. After the generation of three positions, the tree may look as shown in Figure 2.3.

The depth-first generation procedure generally works in a left-to-right manner by first generating all successive positions on the left side of the tree through the termination of the graph or to some intermediate position. It then takes the next leftmost position and generates all its successors through to termination, etc. It is clear that for complete depth-first generation the termination criteria must be exercised at each branch end. Figure 2.4 shows the order of generation of the tree of Figure 2.3 using depth-first search.

There are two basic search procedures which can be applied to game

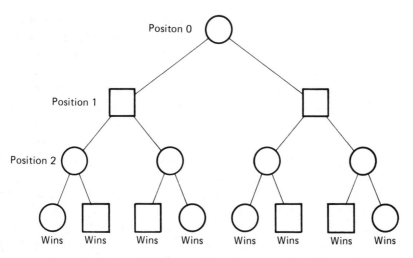

Figure 2.3. Breadth-first procedure after generation of three positions, which terminates the game.

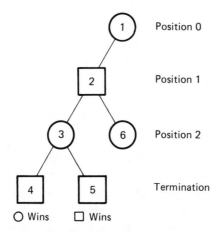

Figure 2.4. Depth-first generation after six steps.

trees, namely the depth-first minimax and the alpha-beta procedures. These procedures, however, require that each move, and hence each position, be evaluated. In simple games the tree may be sufficiently small so that the terminal moves themselves can be evaluated, and therefore the intermediate moves may easily be determined by examining their relationship to a final winning move. On the other hand, the final moves may be accessible only (because of finite computer time and storage) in the end game of larger games such as chess or checkers. For these larger games, then, the opening and middle game moves must be evaluated with respect to some intermediate nodes rather than with respect to the end or terminal nodes. It is possible, of course, to formulate an evaluation procedure which operates on the present and next lower-level nodes alone; however, it is generally desirable to look as far ahead into the game tree as possible when evaluating the present move. The evaluation of either the terminal or some intermediate nodes must be projected back to the present node in order to determine the "best" move. In a game it is desirable to program the computer such that it will move to the position which has been evaluated as having the largest value where the evaluation function assigns a value to the position which is directly related to the chances of winning in that position. A terminal state will, therefore, generally have a probability of winning of either 1, if the game is won, or zero, if the game is lost. Thus, the machine always moves to try to maximize the value of the present position and as such is sometimes called the MAX player. The opponent is generally forced to play in a minimizing position with respect to his game and is called the MIN player. Note that the game trees which are of concern here are for the MAX player only. The MIN player must generate his own tree by these or some other method.

The evaluation function is a particular relation which is used to evaluate the relative attributes of a particular position in a tree. The simplest and most often applied type of evaluation function is a linear weighted sum of all the characteristics associated with a particular position, j,

$$B_j = C_j \cdot Y_j = \sum_{i=1}^{N} c_{ij} y_{ij} \tag{2.1}$$

where C_j is a $1 \times N$ weight vector and Y_j is a column vector associated with the parameters in the system. Thus, we can evaluate each position in a game tree with respect to the particular position itself. This, however, does not provide us with the means for evaluating the paths through the tree which necessarily lead to a win. To do this each position must be examined with respect to the other positions which are possible in that chain.

Next, let us examine a method whereby these positions can be evaluated with respect to a machine win. This process assumes that we begin at the end of a tree or at some predetermined intermediate position by applying the evaluation function. We then project back up the tree by using a minimax backing-up procedure. Here, the value of a max position (computer move) is obtained by making it equal to the maximum of its successor moves. Thus, the value of the max position given by the square in Figure 2.5 is 0.6. The value of a min position is found by projecting the minimum value of

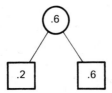

Figure 2.5. Finding the value of a max position from its successors.

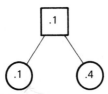

Figure 2.6. Finding the value of a min position from its successors.

the successor moves back to the min position. For example, the value of the min position given in Figure 2.6 must be 0.1. This is called the minimax procedure, as it tends to maximize the winning chances for the machine while minimizing the winning chances of the opponent. The specific search procedures which are used to operate on game trees can now be examined.

The depth-first minimax search results from a combination of the minimax backup procedure and the depth-first generation procedure. The first step in this search is to generate the leftmost section of the tree and evaluate the last or some intermediate position; the next position is then generated and evaluated. These numbers are then backed up, and the process continues until the values of the positions associated with the next move can be determined. For example, if the final backed-up values are as shown in Figure 2.7, then the computer decides to make the move associated with the highest value, in this case 0.6.

Another search procedure which can be used to operate on game trees is

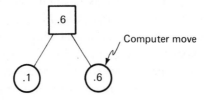

Figure 2.7. Selection of next move after tree has been evaluated.

called the alpha-beta or backward pruning procedure. The pruning which is possible with this process can reduce the number of computations (with respect to the depth-first minimax procedure) by several orders of magnitude. One of the advantages of the alpha-beta procedure accrues by combining the tree generation and position evaluation procedures. In this way, if one finds the best path in the initial branch generation and evaluation, then it is not necessary to generate and evaluate the remainder of the tree. For example, consider the tree in Figure 2.8, where the square represents the machine's

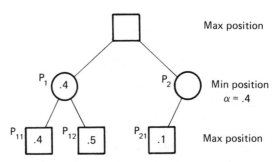

Figure 2.8. Alpha cutoff application to a min position.

moves. Here, three branches have been generated and the terminal nodes evaluated. Notice that the leftmost min position has been evaluated and has a value of 0.4. Thus, we say that the alpha cutoff $\alpha = 0.4$. Now, since projections back to a max position are the maximum value of the min position, and the value of P_{21} is less than α, there is no need to generate P_{22}. Thus, the next branch of the tree, say P_3, and its terminals P_{31} and P_{32} are generated and evaluated with respect to the alpha cutoff.

Similarly, the game tree in Figure 2.9 can be examined using the inverse of the alpha cutoff on max positions, namely the beta cutoff procedure. In this case, the projection back to min position 1 is the minimum value of max position 2 and the beta cutoff is set at 0.4. Thus, finding $P_{121} = 0.8$, which is greater than the cutoff, immediately eliminates the value of P_{12}, which will be at least 0.8. (Note that a max position picks the maximum value.) Here there is no need to generate P_{122}, and P_2 and its associated terminal nodes are then each generated and evaluated with respect to the beta cutoff. Thus, alpha is the maximum of a min position, and beta is the minimum of a max position. It should be obvious from the above examples that the alpha-beta search procedure generally requires fewer operations than the depth-first minimax procedure.

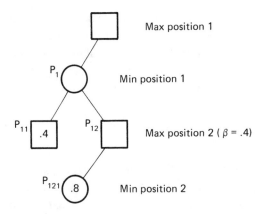

Max position 1

P_1 Min position 1

P_{11} .4 P_{12} Max position 2 (β = .4)

P_{121} .8   Min position 2

Figure 2.9. Beta cutoff application to a max position.

2.3 GAMES

Now that we have studied some ways of representing and playing games in general, let us examine some simple games. The first game is the beloved tick-tack-toe. The process which we shall go through in analyzing tick-tack-toe, albeit not too involved, does demonstrate the principles involved in formalizing a game for machine play.

The first thing done when formalizing board-type games is to label the positions on the board in a nonambiguous way. Thus, the tick-tack-toe board can be labeled as in Figure 2.10. It is clear that there are nine initial moves

11	12	13
21	22	23
31	32	33

Figure 2.10. Board labeling for tick-tack-toe.

which the first player can make, eight moves which the second player can make, etc. Thus, there are $9! = 362,880$ different possible sequences of nine moves in the course of a game. Does this make the computerization of tick-tack-toe as difficult as the computerization of chess? The answer, of course, is no—the complete tree here is large, 362,880 nodes, and brute force computing is quite lengthy, but the structure of this game is such that it can be quickly reduced to a simple game-playing algorithm. For example, it is possible to win a game in five plays where an average game may be six plays. This reduces the number of possible sequences to

$$\frac{9!}{3!} \simeq 60,000$$

A first approach might be directed toward taking advantage of the symmetry of the board to reduce the number of tree branches to be searched. Note that the corner positions are equivalent and that the alpha-beta search generally reduces the total number of branches which must be searched. This then reduces the number of branch combinations which must be searched by the computer if it makes the second move to 1700 for that move and 40 for the fourth move [3]. The remaining moves would require a miniscule number of searches.

Another approach to computerizing this game is to use heuristic techniques which optimize each play. To do this, we must define a win matrix, $\mathbf{W}$, which contains all the winning positions and conditional win matrices which contain only two of the columns of the win matrix. Thus, w_{23} contains the second and third column of the win matrix $\mathbf{W}$:

$$\mathbf{W} = \begin{bmatrix} 11 & 12 & 13 \\ 21 & 22 & 23 \\ 31 & 32 & 33 \\ 11 & 21 & 31 \\ 12 & 22 & 32 \\ 13 & 23 & 33 \\ 11 & 22 & 33 \\ 13 & 22 & 31 \end{bmatrix}$$

A procedure for playing the game can now be defined as shown in Figure 2.11.

At this point, let us examine the game of tick-tack-toe in terms of the minimax search procedure presented previously. It should be clear, however, that it is not desirable to search the 9! nodes in the tick-tack-toe tree in order to find the first move. Therefore, it is necessary to evaluate moves with respect to intermediate positions in the tree as well as to take advantage of the sym-

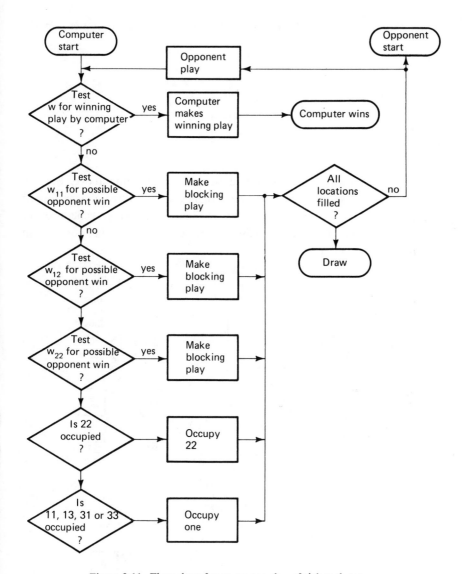

Figure 2.11. Flow chart for computer play of tick-tack-toe.

metry of the game. The evaluation function which shall be applied here is

"Number of winning rows remaining—if j is not a winning position."

$$E_j = \begin{cases} N\text{—if } j \text{ is a winning move for the computer} \\ 0\text{—if } j \text{ is a winning move for the opponent or a draw} \end{cases}$$

Thus, the evaluation of the *j*th position, where X is the computer's mark,

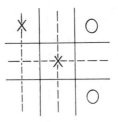

is $E_j = 3$, as indicated by the three dash lines in the game above. For the first move, because of board symmetry, there are only three alternatives to consider. These alternatives are shown in Figure 2.12, where generation of the tree to a depth of 2 is shown. Also, the evaluation of the final positions in

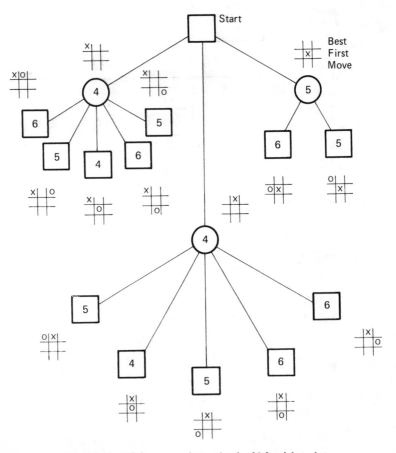

Figure 2.12. Minimax search to a depth of 2 for tick-tack-toe.

the tree shown have been calculated and backed up by the minimax procedure to the other nodes. The results indicate that the move to square 22 is the best one for this evaluation procedure. The remaining moves can also be determined in this way by generating the tree from the opponent's move down two more levels, evaluating these nodes, backing up the values, etc., until the game ends.

2.4 LAST ONE LOSES: G-1A [4]

The game to be described in this section provides a simple illustration of an algorithm which appears to exhibit "learning" behavior, although we shall define learning more formally later.

The game material consists of 12 chips, a pair of dice, or a deck of cards labeled sequentially from 1 through 12. A board labeled as shown in Figure 2.13 is also needed.

Chips placed on board →

A	B	C	D	A	B	C	D	A	B	C	D
0	0	0	0	0	0	0					
1	2	3	4	5	6	7	8	9	10	11	12

Figure 2.13. Board for last one loses where the die or card picked is 7.

The game proceeds as follows: The dice are thrown or a card is picked and that number of chips are placed on the board. Each player in succession then removes from one to three chips from the board, and the player who removes the last chip loses the game.

2.5 THE G-1A CUP MACHINE

Game G-1A is simple enough, and most people can learn the winning strategy after playing a few games. The following machine using Dixie cups and cards can also learn to play G-1A. The G-1A cup machine illustrated in Figure 2.14 consists of four cups labeled A through D with three chips in each labeled 1 through 3.

Figure 2.14. Cup machine for G-1A.

Initially, the machine makes its moves by randomly selecting one of the three chips in the cup associated with the present chip on the board and removes the number of chips indicated by that choice. For example, cup C is used for the position indicated in Figure 2.13. The machine then discards the last card drawn in a game which the machine loses—this includes the card drawn prior to encountering an empty cup. If the same cup is selected on two successive machine moves, the same card may be used again. A singleton card in a cup is used each time that cup is selected. An empty cup indicates a location where the machine forfeits the game.

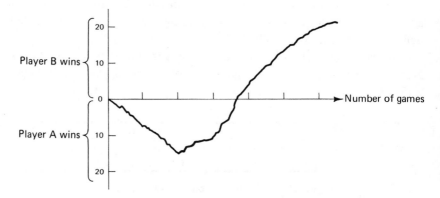

Figure 2.15. Learning curve for G-1A.

The learning curve shown in Figure 2.15 indicates the rate of learning for the cup machine. It is suggested that one trying this game plot learning curves for both human and machine players and compare them. It will be found that after several games the cup machine will converge to the configuration given below:

2.6 THEORY OF G-1A

First, consider the case where there are five chips left on the board and it is player B's turn. Here, if player A knows the optimum strategy, then player B can only lose—for, if he takes one chip, then player A takes three, leaving player B the last chip, and so forth, as tabulated below:

Player A	1	2	3
Player B	3	2	1

Further examination reveals that the same situation will occur if there are 9, 13, 17, ... chips on the board. Thus, the winning strategy is clear; each player tries to leave 1 modulo 4 chips on the board. Here 1 modulo 4 means that 4 is divided into the number of chips remaining and that 1 is the remainder. A player facing that remainder is in a losing state.

The player that has the first move has a predetermined probability of winning provided he makes the correct moves. For example, an initial move with 1, 5, or 9 chips on the board are losing states and therefore the probability of drawing or throwing 1, 5, or 9 on the initial play determines the probability of getting into a losing state provided the opposing player knows the winning strategy.

If cards are used to determine the number of chips for the game, there are 3 losing cards in the deck of 12, and the probability of losing is

$$P(\text{first player loses}) = \tfrac{3}{12} = \tfrac{1}{4}$$
$$P(\text{first player wins}) = 1 - \tfrac{1}{4} = \tfrac{3}{4}$$

A converged machine will then win three quarters of the games in which it has the first move.

For dice, there are only two losing numbers which can occur: 5 and 9. Since there are six possibilities for each die, there are $6^2 = 36$ different possible states for the dice.

The losing throws are

$$\left.\begin{array}{l} 1, 4 \\ 2, 3 \\ 3, 2 \\ 4, 1 \\ 5, 4 \\ 6, 3 \\ 3, 6 \\ 4, 5 \end{array}\right\} \quad \text{eight losing throws}$$

and the probability that the machine wins on the first move is

$$P(\text{machine loses}) = \tfrac{8}{36} = \tfrac{2}{9}$$
$$P(\text{machine wins}) = 1 - \tfrac{2}{9} = \tfrac{7}{9}$$

2.7 SUMMARY

Some techniques for playing games by machine have been examined in this chapter. Heuristic search procedures for searching trees and choosing moves have been explored. It is important to note that, although these techniques were presented in the context of games, these processes can also be applied in other areas such as theorem proving, pattern recognition, and learning.

2.8 EXERCISES

2.1. Find the backed-up values and the best initial move for square for all the positions in the following trees:

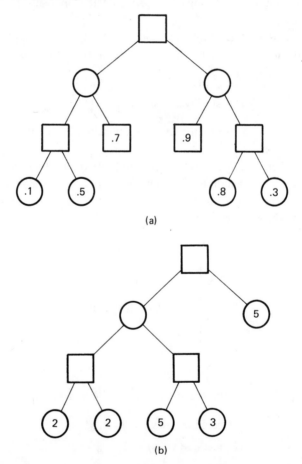

(a)

(b)

2.2. Are there any ways in which the computer play of tick-tack-toe given above can be improved? If so, how?

2.3. Generate the game trees for two games of tick-tack-toe with different first moves which you have played with a friend.

2.4. Generate three levels of a game tree for G-1A with seven chips initially on the board. What is the width of the tree at this point?

2.5. Using the number of winning rows remaining as the evaluation function, generate a game tree for alpha-beta search for tick-tack-toe's first move.

REFERENCES

1. SLAGLE, J. R., *Artificial Intelligence—The Heuristic Programming Approach*, McGraw-Hill, New York, 1971.

2. NILSSON, NILS J., *Problem-Solving Methods in Artificial Intelligence*, McGraw-Hill, New York, 1971.

3. CARNE, E. B., *Artificial Intelligence Techniques*, Macmillan, New York, 1965.

4. BLOCK, H. D., "Learning in Some Simple Non-Biological Systems," *American Scientist*, Vol. 53, No. 1, March 1965.

3

REASON, LOGIC, AND MATHEMATICS

INTRODUCTION

In Chapter 1 the definitions of intelligence and the arguments surrounding the concept of machine intelligence were considered. In Chapter 2 we were concerned with the process of game playing by machine with algorithmic and heuristic techniques. Thus far we have been examining specific methods for obtaining desired machine behavior. It is the purpose of this chapter to present some of the more formal approaches associated with some of the processes of logic and reason which underlie the areas of artificial intelligence and computing. We shall use some specific mathematical systems to illustrate these processes.

3.1 LOGIC

Logic has been called the "grammar of reason" [1] and as such is concerned with making generalizations and, ultimately, abstractions by a system of orderly thinking. Thus, logic may be applied to the relationship between mathematics and physics or between the behavior of an electrical network and the nervous system. Simply, the goal of logic is progressive systemization and generalization, and the aim is the discovery of abstract forms. The process of logic generally takes one of two forms, deduction and induction, which then may extend to the process of abstraction. We shall first examine the process of deduction.

3.2 DEDUCTION

Deduction is the process of reasoning from one truth value to another, and a system wherein a small number of propositions determines all the other propositions is called a deductive system. A mathematical system is a class of propositions arranged in accordance with a sequence of logical deduction.

For example, Euclidean geometry begins with a set of basic assumptions or postulates, such as

1. A line may be extended indefinitely in both directions.
2. Through two distinct points one, and only one, straight line can be drawn.

Other original propositions which are self-evident are called axioms, such as

1. The whole is greater than any of its proper parts.
2. Things equal to the same thing are equal to one another.

Thus, based on postulates, axioms, and a collection of definitions of terms such as "A line has length but not breadth," Euclid deduced 465 propositions in a logical chain.

Another device associated with mathematical systems is the theorem, which is different from a postulate. First, a theorem must contain nothing that cannot be proved. It must be entirely implied by propositions other than itself, and it may contain no assumptions not made in the postulates.

Further, no two theorems deduced from the same postulates can be contradictory, for if this were true, then the postulates would be inconsistent.

In the process of proving a theorem, it is often necessary to prove an auxiliary proposition. This auxiliary proposition is called a lemma. The logical process is used to develop the connection between a postulate and a theorem where true premises and a valid deduction always yield a true theorem.

3.3 BOOLEAN ALGEBRA OF CLASSES

To illustrate a deductive system [2], we shall examine the Boolean algebra of classes. This particular vehicle has been chosen because it is a good example and is of particular value in computers and logic design. In this discussion, the concept of class refers to a class of objects such as students, faculty, computers, programs, and systems. The Boolean algebra of classes is concerned with the class of all objects to which the algebra applies. This class of all elements associated with the algebra is referred to as the universe class, $U = 1$. On the other hand, the class which contains no elements is called the null class, $N = 0$. Any combination of elements from the universe class is itself a class. Therefore, if there are n elements in the universe class, then there are 2^n different possible classes, as that is the total number of combinations of n elements. Thus, an algebra of $n = 2$ elements x_1, x_2 has four possible classes, 0, x_1, x_2, and both elements in the class, $x_1 + x_2 = 1$.

Before we formally examine the Boolean algebra of classes, it is useful, although not required in the formal development, to review the three fundamental Boolean operations. First, the *union* operation, designated by $A \lor B$, indicates the class which includes all elements in both class A and class B. Second, the *intersection* of two classes, designated by $A \land B$, defines the class which consists of the elements common to both class A and class B. Finally, by the complement of a class A, given by $\bar{A}$, we mean all elements of the universe class, 1, which are not in the class A.

The following development of the Boolean algebra of classes proceeds from a set of primitive, undefined symbols, one basic definition, and a set of nine postulates.

The complement sign (the overbar) together with 0, 1, $\in$ (contained in), $\land$ (intersection), and $\lor$ (union) are the primitive, undefined symbols. Next, we can define identity or equality:

Definition 1: $a = b$ iff (if and only if) $a \subset b$ and $b \subset a$.

The following are the postulates which will be used in this mathematical system.

Postulate 1: $a \subset a$, which is read "a is contained in a" and means that every class includes itself.

Postulate 2: If $a \subset b$ and $b \subset c$, then $a \subset c$: Every class includes the subclass of its subclasses. This is also referred to as transitivity.

Postulate 3: $a \subset b \wedge c$ iff $a \subset b$ and $a \subset c$, which is read "*a* is contained in the intersection of *b* and *c* if and only if *a* is contained in *b* and *a* is contained in *c*." This postulate defines the product of classes.

Postulate 4: $a \vee b \subset c$ iff $a \subset c$ and $b \subset c$, which is read "the union of *a* and *b* is contained in *c* if and only if *a* is contained in *c* and *b* is contained in *c*." This postulate defines the sum of classes.

Postulate 5: $(a \vee b) \wedge (a \vee c) \subset a \vee (b \wedge c)$ indicates that the system is distributive.

Postulate 6: $0 \subset a$ means that every class includes the null class (the class containing no elements).

Postulate 7: $a \subset 1$ means that every class is included in the universe class (the class containing all the elements to which the algebra applies).

Postulate 8: $a \wedge \bar{a} \subset 0$ indicates that every class and its complement are mutually exclusive.

Postulate 9: $1 \subset a \vee \bar{a}$ means that the universe class is all the elements in class *a* or not in class *a*.

As stated before, theorems concerning a mathematical system may be proved by combining postulates in a logical sequence. Thus, we can now begin to prove theorems in the Boolean algebra of classes. In actual practice, however, one often has a specific theorem in mind and proceeds from the postulates and previously proved theorems toward the theorem of interest. This process is similar to means-ends analysis, referred to in Chapter 1.

Theorem 1: $a \subset a \wedge a$.
Proof: From Postulate 3, $a \subset a \wedge a$ iff $a \subset a$ and $a \subset a$ by substituting *a* for *b* and *a* for *c*, and from Postulate 1, $a \subset a$.   Q.E.D.

Theorem 2: $a \vee a \subset a$.
Proof: As in Theorem 1, but use Postulate 4.

Theorem 3: $a \wedge a \subset a$.
Proof: 1. $a \wedge a \subset a \wedge a$ iff $a \wedge a \subset a$ and $a \wedge a \subset a$ by substituting $a \wedge a$ for *a*, *a* for *b*, and *a* for *c* in Postulate 3.
    2. But $a \wedge a \subset a \wedge a$ also is true by substituting $a \wedge a$ for *a* in Postulate 1.
    3. $a \wedge a \subset a$.   Q.E.D.

Theorem 4: $a \subset a \lor a$.

Proof: As in Theorem 3, but use Postulate 4, and then use Postulate 1.

It should be clear that more theorems can be proved in this mathematical system. Additional theorems to be proved are given in the Exercises. This is a generalized Boolean algebra in that there is no restriction on the number of elements in the universe class. We may, however, impose a limit on the number of elements, say k, which results in 2^k classes, where the order of the Boolean algebra is the number of classes in it. For each value of k, a different Boolean algebra results where one Boolean algebra is different from another if and only if some law valid in one is not valid in the other. The well-known binary Boolean algebra is of order 2^1. However, let us first examine some of the higher-order algebras.

The Boolean algebra of order 2^3 has three elements, which may be denoted by a, b, and c, and eight distinct classes, given by 0, a, b, c, $a + b$, $a + c$, $b + c$, and 1, where the plus sign (+) indicates the inclusion of both terms on either side of the sign in that class. The algebra of order 2^2 has two elements, say a and b, and four distinct classes, 0, a, b, and 1. Also, the algebra of order 2^1 consists of the element x and two distinct classes, 0 and 1. Finally, the algebra of order 2^0 is rather trivial as there are no elements and only one class, namely the null class, 0.

When dealing with these algebras, it is often useful to use a schematic representation as an aid in visualizing these systems. The representation which will be used here is called the Venn diagram (Figure 3.1). The rectangular

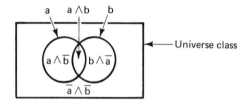

Figure 3.1. Venn diagram for Boolean algebras.

area in the figure represents the universe class, all the elements under consideration, and each circle represents a class in the system usually denoted by some literal, say a or b. The space in Figure 3.1 which is common to both a and b is $a \land b$. The spaces belonging to a and not b and b and not a are $a \land \bar{b}$ and $b \land \bar{a}$, respectively. The space which is not in either a or b is $\bar{a} \land \bar{b}$.

Now, to illustrate the difference between algebras of different orders, we shall consider the following statements: $a \wedge b = 0$ or $a \wedge \bar{b} = 0$ or $\bar{a} \wedge b = 0$, where elements in the algebra are contained in a or b. We shall now represent elements in the algebra as dots on the diagram. Thus, if there are two elements in the system, the above statement can be satisfied as shown in Figure 3.2, where all placement combinations of two dots, elements in the

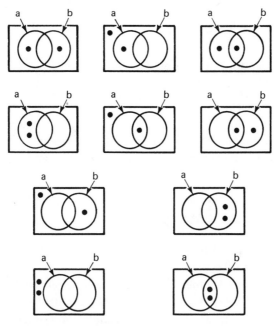

Figure 3.2. Dot placement in Venn diagrams for Boolean Algebra of classes with two elements.

classes, have been used. The above statement is not true for an algebra of order 2^3 since three dots cannot be placed in the Venn diagram such that the statement is satisfied for all possible dot placements. This is shown in Figure 3.3, where the statement is not satisfied for at least one dot placement and we can conclude that it is not true in general for algebras of order 2^3.

It should now be clear that laws for specific Boolean algebras are different; however, any law in the generalized Boolean algebra of classes is a law in any other Boolean algebra. Theorems in these algebras can be deduced from previously discovered theorems in a logical chain. The incorporation of a deductive logic system in a machine is but one of the steps towards artificial intelligence.

This concludes our introduction to deductive systems as a specific method

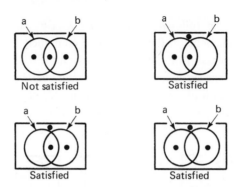

Figure 3.3. Dot placement for Boolean Algebra of classes with three elements showing that the statement $a \wedge b = 0$ or $a \wedge \bar{b} = 0$ or $\bar{a} \wedge b = 0$ is not satisfied for at least one dot arrangement.

of reason and thought. The Boolean algebras of classes are an especially good example of these principles, as the title of Boole's treatise is *An Investigation of the Laws of Thought* [3].

3.4 PROPOSITIONAL CALCULUS

A system in which there is some definite class of elements and definite rules which describe the ways in which members of the class may be combined either with one another or each of the members with itself is called a logical system. The class which is of interest here is any class of propositions where there are two types, specific and general. A specific proposition is concerned with a subject which may be specified by a proper name, while a general proposition is concerned with members of a certain class. The propositions "A boy ran home" and "Every man is mortal" are examples of specific and general propositions, respectively. Some other examples of propositions are "4 is greater than 3," "*a* is contained in the universe class," and "A triangle has three sides." The only significant aspect of any proposition, however, is its truth or falseness. The concept of a proposition is similar to an element, and the truth and falseness of a proposition are similar to the null and universe classes, respectively, of the binary Boolean algebra of classes. Thus, these two systems are isomorphic.

Thus, for the representation of propositions, p, by classes, false propositions are the null class, $p = 0$, and true propositions are the universe class, $p = 1$. It is clear then that binary Boolean algebra is appropriate here and that Venn diagrams can be used to represent propositions, as shown in Figure

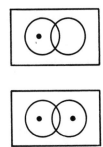

Figure 3.4. Venn diagram for propositional calculus with two propositions p and q where, if a proposition is true, it encloses a dot.

3.4. Here, the areas enclosing the dot represent true propositions, and other areas represent false propositions. It can be seen from this diagram that, among other things:

1. The union of two false propositions is a false proposition, as no dot can be included in the union.
2. The intersection of a true proposition and a false proposition is a false proposition because the region of commonality cannot include a dot or the proposition would be true.
3. A false proposition is contained in a true proposition, as the region of commonality of the true proposition is a false proposition.
4. The union of a true proposition and a false proposition is contained in a true proposition since the union of the two propositions must contain a dot; hence, it contains a true proposition.

The first two statements are obvious from common usage; however, the last two are not.

Let us now adopt symbols which are common to the propositional calculus. The notation "is contained in" is replaced by implies, $\supset$, and the symbol $\equiv$ is used for iff. The statement if $p \supset q$ and $q \supset r$, then $p \supset r$ is read "if p implies q and q implies r, then p implies r." Now, if $p, q, r, \ldots$ are propositions, then other propositions can be formed by means of the following operators: the overbar, $\wedge$, $\vee$, $\supset$, and $\equiv$. The meanings of these operators are given in Table 3.1. Now let $p =$ "it is raining" and $q =$ "the street is wet" and apply these propositions to the relationship

$$p \supset q \equiv \bar{q} \supset \bar{p}$$

which can be written as

It is raining *implies* the street is wet *is a true statement if and only if* the street is *not* wet *implies* it is *not* raining.

Table 3.1. Symbols and Their Meanings in Propositional Calculus

Symbol	Is Read	Meaning
$\bar{p}$	Not p	p is false
$p \wedge q$	p and q	The intersection of p and q, common to both p and q
$p \vee q$	p or q	The union of p and q, either p or q or both
$p \supset q$	p implies q	If p is true, then q is true
$p \equiv q$	p iff q	p is true if and only if q is true; p is equivalent to q

Since we can apply a simple binary value to each proposition, it is useful to be able to operate on propositions which have been reduced to 0, 1 form. The mechanism for doing this is called the arithmetic of propositions and is summarized in Table 3.2.

Table 3.2. Arithmetic of Propositions

$\wedge$	0	1	$\vee$	0	1	$\supset$	0	1	$\equiv$	0	1	$-$	
0	0	0	0	0	1	0	1	1	0	1	0	0	1
1	0	1	1	1	1	1	0	1	1	0	1	1	0
(a)			(b)			(c)			(d)			(e)	

The first identity in Table 3.2(a) means that a false proposition and a false proposition yield a false proposition.

The first identity in Table 3.2(c) means that a false proposition implies both a false proposition and a true proposition. Here the only way an implication can be false is when it is posed that a true proposition implies a false one. Also note that any false proposition can imply either a true proposition or a false proposition. We can evaluate expressions in the propositional calculus which do not contain variables as follows:

EXAMPLES: 1. $1 \vee 0 \vee 0 = (1 \vee 0) \vee 0 = 1 \vee 0 = 1$.

2. $\{(0 \supset 1) \vee 1 \vee 0 \supset \overline{(1 \wedge 0)}\} = \{1 \vee 1 \vee 0 \supset \bar{0}\} = 1 \supset 1$
   $= 1$.

3. $(1 \wedge 1) \supset 0 = 1 \supset 0 = 0$

In these examples, the relationships have a value of 1 or 0 which can be interpreted as valid or not valid respectively.

Now let us return to our first relationship between propositions concerning the weather and the condition of the street and study it with respect to the arithmetic of proposition. First, assume the propositions p and q are true, 1, then we can say

$$1 \supset 1 \equiv 0 \supset 0$$

and from Table 3.2(c) we can reduce this to

$$1 \equiv 1 = 1$$

Because, from Table 3.2(d), we see that 1 is equivalent to 1. Note that 1 cannot imply 0 which means the relationship "it is raining implies the street is not wet" is not valid; therefore, we let $p = 1$ and $q = 0$ which gives,

$$1 \supset 0 \equiv 1 \supset 0$$
$$0 \equiv 0 = 1$$

Now, assume p and q are false, 0, and from the arithmetic of propositions,

$$0 \supset 0 \equiv 1 \supset 1$$
$$1 \equiv 1 = 1$$

Similarly, if we let $p = 0$ and $q = 1$,

$$0 \supset 1 \equiv 0 \supset 1$$
$$1 \equiv 1 = 1$$

Thus, the relationship $p \supset q \equiv \bar{q} \supset \bar{p}$ is valid for all combinations of truth values for p and q.

Boolean algebra and propositional calculus provide a means by which we can examine the relationships between any statements in a particular mathematical system. For example, the end or goal of a problem may be to examine some aspect of a particular statement. The development of the relationship between the given information and the desired goal can be found by examining the function and applying the rules of the system, as was done in the example above. Thus, we have a mechanism for means-ends analysis. This process of determining the validity of a general statement by examining the fundamental relationships in the system is called the process of induction.

3.5 INDUCTION

Whereas the process of reasoning from specific truths to general truths is the process of deduction, the process of reasoning from general observations to specific underlying truths is the process of induction.

Russell [4] has said that there are three methods of arriving at the validity of general propositions: tautologies, complete enumeration, and induction. A tautology is a repetition which in and of itself is obvious and self-evident, such as "All men are male" or "Essential things are necessary."

Complete enumeration is a reasonable method of proof of a general observation if the number of alternatives to be examined is not too large. For example, the statement "There are four blocks on the table" can easily be verified by counting the blocks. Since this method examines all possible combinations—there are no stones left unturned—it is called the method of perfect induction. A systematic approach to this method makes use of truth tables, as illustrated in the following example.

EXAMPLE: Verify the following relationship, known as De Morgan's theorem, by perfect induction:

$$\overline{a \wedge b} \equiv \bar{a} \vee \bar{b}$$

Applying the arithmetic of propositions with a truth table which lists all possible truth values for the propositions yields

a	b	$\bar{a}$	$\bar{b}$	$a \wedge b$	$\overline{a \wedge b}$	$\bar{a} \vee \bar{b}$
0	0	1	1	0	1	1
0	1	1	0	0	1	1
1	0	0	1	0	1	1
1	1	0	0	1	0	0

We now note that the last two columns of the table which represent both sides of the above statement are the same, and De Morgan's theorem is now proved.

The final method for determining the truth or falseness of a general observation is induction. Induction vis-à-vis perfect induction requires that one deal with less conclusive evidence than the complete enumeration of all possibilities. Thus, given the statement "All A is B" and a *relation of intentions* which exist to justify the statement, if the statement seems probable, we have an induction. For example, given the following:

$$1 + 3 = 2^2, \quad 1 + 3 + 5 = 3^2, \quad 1 + 3 + 5 + 7 = 4^2, \quad \text{etc.}$$

we induce the specific truth that the sum of the first n odd numbers is always n^2, which can now be proved.

Theorem: $1 + 3 + 5 + \ldots + r = n^2$, for all $n > 0$ with r odd, where n is the number of terms in the sum.

Proof: The first step in the proof by induction is to show that the theorem is true for $n = 1$:

$$1 = 1^2 = 1$$

Next we note that $n = (r + 1)/2$, thus, $r = 2n - 1$ and

$$1 + 3 + 5 + \ldots + 2n - 1 = n^2$$

Now, we assume that the theorem is true for some n,

$$1 + 3 + 5 + \ldots + r = n^2 \qquad (3.1)$$

and show that it is also true for $n + 1$

$$1 + 3 + 5 + \ldots + r + r + 2 = (n + 1)^2 = n^2 + 2n + 1 \qquad (3.2)$$

To do this we subtract the left hand side of (3.1) from the left hand side of (3.2) and do the same with the right sides of each equation which yields,

$$r + 2 = 2n + 1 \qquad (3.3)$$

but

$$n = (r + 1)/2 \text{ and (3.3) is true.}$$

Therefore the difference added to each side of the equation for successive values of n are equal and we induce that the theorem is indeed true.

This process has been described most lucidly by Russell [4], where he calls the last of Peano's five propositions the principle of mathematical induction. These propositions are

1. Zero is a number.
2. The successor of any number is a number.
3. No two numbers have the same successor.

4. Zero is not the successor of any number.
5. Any property which belongs to zero, and also to the successor of any number which has that property, belongs to every number.

Let us consider briefly the kind of way in which the theory of the natural numbers results from these three ideas ("number," "zero," and "the successor of") and five propositions. To begin with, we define 1 as "the successor of 0," 2 as "the successor of 1," and so on. We can obviously go on as long as we like with these definitions, since, by virtue of Proposition (2), every number that we reach will have a successor, and, by virtue of Proposition (3), this cannot be any of the numbers already defined, because, if it were, two different numbers would have the same successor; and, by virtue of Proposition (4), none of the numbers we reach in the series of successors can be 0. Thus, the series of successors gives us an endless series of continually new numbers. By virtue of Proposition (5), all numbers come in this series which begins with 0 and travels through successive successors: for (a) 0 belongs to this series, and (b) if a number, n, belongs to it, so does its successor, whence, by mathematical induction, every number belongs to the series.

The process of induction has been associated with what has been described as intelligent behavior. Man's continued search for new truths requires the ability to induce them from his environment. To incorporate the ability to apply induction on the part of a machine, however, is a difficult problem yet to be solved. Although computerized approaches to automatic theorem proving have been undertaken with some interesting results, these systems deal with the more structured logical methods such as the propositional calculus [5, 6, 7] and not directly with induction.

3.6 ABSTRACTION

As stated at the beginning of this chapter, the aim of logic is the discovery of abstract forms. Thus, we shall now consider some definitions of abstraction and its relation to logic.

Abstraction is a process which is certainly familiar to everyone; algebra is the abstracted form of an arithmetical calculation; block and schematic diagrams are abstractions of some physical system, say a computer or a control system; and a street map is an abstraction of the streets in a particular town or city. In general, abstraction is the act of considering something as a general object apart from any special circumstances. This concept of abstraction is the one which leads to the association of mathematics with the abstract.

Abstract concepts are communicated by language and training which may be education, indoctrination, or even brainwashing, and they are learned by observation and experience. The concept of number is learned by counting, the concept of shape by fitting objects together, the concept of quality by comparing values, the concept of rules of conduct by observing (and judging) the evidence of good or bad behavior, and an algebraic formula by seeing several examples and observing their common formal property. However, we cannot really understand these concepts without the ability to abstract the common form from the instances we have observed. This ability to recognize a common form or a common principle without the specifics has been described as scientific genius [1]. To endow a machine with the power of abstraction such that it could be called a genius is the ultimate goal of many artificial intelligence researchers. The achievement of this goal is certainly not imminent. There is much work to be done.

3.7 LOGIC REVISITED

Logical reasoning, then, is the method of following the rules as postulated in the mathematical system of interest. The Boolean algebra of classes provides one of these systems of rules.

The processes of deduction and induction provide means for generalizing and proving statements in these mathematical systems, which ultimately may lead to an abstraction. A logical system may then be visualized as an abstract form, or a relational pattern, rather than as an array of concrete things. These logical processes are basic in cybernetics where one is interested in developing and exploiting these principles in a physical system. For example, a program which automatically proves theorems must incorporate some logical processes in it. A machine control of a complicated manufacturing process must, at least, be able to "deduce" the fact that something is wrong.

3.8 EXERCISES

3.1. Prove the following theorems in the Boolean algebra of classes:
    (a) Theorem 5: $a = a$.
    (b) Theorem 6: $a = a \wedge a$.
    (c) Theorem 7: $a = a \vee a$.
    (d) Theorem 8: $a \vee a \subset a \wedge a$.

3.2. Prove the following theorems in the Boolean algebra of classes:
    (a) Theorem 9: $a \wedge b \subset a$ and $a \wedge b \subset b$.

(b) Theorem 10: $a \wedge a = a \vee a$.
(c) Theorem 11: $a \subset a \vee b$ and $b \subset a \vee b$.

3.3. Let $1 =$ humans, $a =$ Americans, $b =$ Bostonians, and $c =$ criminals.
(a) What does the class $a \wedge c$ equal?
(b) Does $a \wedge b = b$?
(c) What does $a \wedge \bar{c}$ equal?
(d) What does $a \wedge \bar{b} \wedge c$ equal?
(e) What does $b \wedge c$ equal?
(f) Find a representation for the class of all Bostonians who are not criminals.

3.4. Use a Venn diagram to show whether the following statements are satisfied in the Boolean algebras of order 2^1 and 2^2:
(a) Either $a \wedge b = 0$ or $a \wedge \bar{b} = 0$.
(b) Either $a = 0$ or $a = 1$.

3.5. List all compound propositions that can be formed just from the propositions p and q under the following restrictions:
(a) p and q occur exactly once and in that order in each compound proposition.
(b) No operator can be used more than once.

3.6. Put the following argument into symbolic form: If p and q are true, then r is true. But r is false. Therefore, either p is false or q is false.

3.7. Evaluate the following:
(a) $(((0 \supset 1) \supset 0) \supset 1) \supset 0$.
(b) $(1 \supset 1 \wedge 0) \equiv \overline{(1 \vee 0)}$.

3.8. Prove by perfect induction:
(a) $(A \wedge B) \vee (\bar{A} \wedge \bar{B}) = \overline{(\bar{A} \wedge B) \vee (A \wedge \bar{B})}$.
(b) $(A \wedge B) \vee (\bar{A} \wedge \bar{B}) \vee (A \wedge \bar{B}) = A \vee \bar{B}$.

3.9. Prove the following theorem by induction: $1 + 2 + 3 + \ldots + n = (1/2)n(n + 1)$.

3.10. Show, using the arithmetic of propositions, that the statement "It is raining or I have washed my car implies the weather will be bad is equivalent to the weather will not be bad implies it is not raining and I have not washed my car" is valid.

REFERENCES

1. HILTON, ALICE MARY, *Logic, Computing Machines, and Automation*, Spartan, New York, 1963.

2. CULBERTSON, JAMES T., *Mathematics and Logic for Digital Devices*, Van Nostrand Reinhold, New York, 1958.

3. BOOLE, GEORGE, *An Investigation of the Laws of Thought*, London, 1854, reprinted by Dover, New York, 1959.

4. RUSSELL, BERTRAND, *Introduction to Mathematical Philosophy*, 2nd ed., George Allen & Unwin Ltd., London, 1920.

5. ROBINSON, J. A., "A Machine-Oriented Logic Based on the Resolution Principle," JACM 12, pp. 23–41, January 1965.

6. ANDERSON, R. and W. W. BLEDSOE, "A Linear Format for Resolution with Merging and a New Technique for Establishing Completeness," JACM 17, pp. 525–534, July 1970.

7. MELTZER, B., "Power Amplification for Automatic Theorem-Provers," Machine Intelligence 5, pp. 321–336, (MELTZER and MICHIE, editors) American Elsevier-Publishing Co., New York, 1970.

4

COMPUTERS AND AUTOMATA

INTRODUCTION

Thus far we have identified the computer as a principal element in cybernetic systems. We have also described some of the techniques which can be used to endow the machine with some aspects of this behavior. It has also been demonstrated that, with the proper rules, a simple automaton (the cup machine) can exhibit apparent learning behavior.

It should be clear that the behavior of machines and their fundamental attributes and limitations lie at the heart of this subject. Therefore, in this chapter, we shall examine the overall descriptive behavior of automata and investigate some of its fundamental limitations.

4.1 AUTOMATA [1]

Automata usually refers to the class of systems which operate on discrete data representations in discrete time intervals, and the discipline which is concerned with the overall input-output behavior of these systems is called automata theory. Automata theory has been applied to the description of computers as well as to nerve networks, biological systems, control systems, and aspects of human behavior. Thus, it is appropriate to study automata and automata theory at this point. We shall examine first a model of a sequential machine and proceed from there to a description of general automata.

In general, a sequential machine or automaton consists of the two major elements shown in Figure 4.1, namely combinational logic and memory.

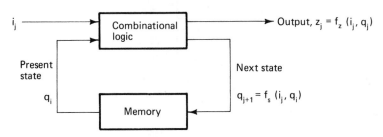

Figure 4.1. General block diagram of sequential automaton.

The combinational logic may consist of AND, OR, NOT, NAND, NOR, or exclusive OR operations or some combination of them all. The memory may be physically magnetic cores, tapes or disc, or simply time delays of a so-called unit length. The input is a sequence of symbols $\{i_j\}$ which occur at finite times j. The output in the jth interval, z_j, is a function of the present input symbol i_j and the present state q_j, which is the present output of the memory. The present input to the memory is called the next state function, which depends on the present input and the present state.

The following example will serve to illustrate the concepts contained in the above description. First, we shall define a unit delay element

$$q_j \longrightarrow \boxed{D} \longrightarrow y_i = q_{j-1}$$

where the delay between the output and input is D seconds. The circuit shown in Figure 4.2 is recognizable as a simple sequential circuit. We can now write a set of next state equations for this machine,

$$q^{(1)}_{j+1} = q^{(2)}_j i_j \tag{4.1}$$

$$q^{(2)}_{j+1} = i_j \oplus q^{(1)}_j \tag{4.2}$$

where $\oplus$ indicates the exclusive OR operation. The output function for this

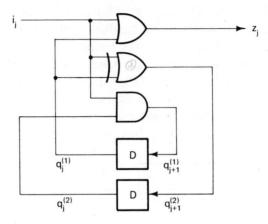

Figure 4.2. Sequential machine using delay memory.

circuit can be written as

$$Z_j = i_j \vee q_j(1) \qquad (4.3)$$

These methods for describing a sequential automaton can now be generalized. This representation takes the form of a 5-tuple,

$$M = \langle I, Q, Z, \delta, \omega \rangle \qquad (4.4)$$

where

1. Q is a set of states.
2. I is a finite set of input symbols.
3. Z is a finite set of output symbols.
4. δ is a mapping $I \times Q$ into Q called the next state function.
5. ω is a mapping of $I \times Q$ onto Z called the output function.

Here the symbol $\times$ indicates the cartesian product. For example, if

$$I = \{0, 1, 2\} \quad \text{and} \quad Q = \{a, b\}$$

then

$$I \times Q = \{(0, a), (0, b), (1, a), (1, b), (2, a), (2, b)\}$$

4.2 TURING MACHINES

Although the general description of sequential machines is of value as a tool in understanding the overall behavior of these systems, its use as a model of a digital computer is certainly limited. One reason for this is the fact that memory in even the simplest digital computer is not small and the number of expressions required to describe the machine immediately becomes prohibitive. Thus, a new model is needed.

The model which is used to describe the fundamental behavior of the modern digital computer was developed by Turing in 1936 [2]. This model, called the Turing machine, which was described before the development of today's computers, was developed as a mechanism for studying the fundamental relationships involved in making computations.

A Turing machine has three basic parts, as shown in Figure 4.3: a control element, a read/write head, and an infinite-length tape. The control unit

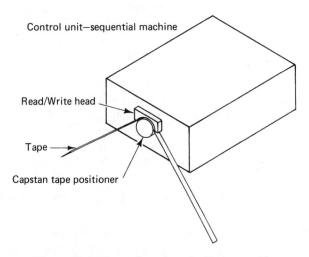

Figure 4.3. Basic configuration of a Turing machine.

which has a drive system which is capable of moving the tape in either direction is a sequential machine. The tape, which may be thought of as any external medium in which information can be stored, read, and changed, is divided into blocks or squares which may contain either a blank or a symbol from a finite set of symbols A. The read/write head can scan on only one square at a time after which one of four possible events can occur:

1. Write a new symbol in the present square.
2. Position the tape such that the head is over the square to the right of the present square.
3. Position the tape such that the head is over the square to the left of the present square.
4. The machine halts.

The operation of the machine is then as follows. A tape is prepared by placing symbols in the proper squares on the tape, the sequential machine is set into its starting state, the tape is positioned on the machine with the proper square placed under the read/write head, and the machine is started.

A complete Turing machine, T, can now be defined as a 6-tuple,

$$T = \langle I, Q, Z, \delta, \omega, q_0 \rangle \tag{4.5}$$

where

1. $I = A \vee b$ is a finite nonempty set of symbols, where b is the blank and A is some alphabet.
2. Q is a set of states.
3. Z is the output set, where the commands move tape right, r, move tape left, l, and halt, h, are included with the alphabet, A, and the blank symbol, b:

$$Z = A \vee b \vee r \vee l \vee h$$

4. δ is the next state mapping of the sequential machine.
5. ω is the output mapping of the sequential machine.
6. q_0 is the initial state of the sequential machine at the start of a computation.

Thus, Q, δ, and ω are the same as defined for the general sequential model, and the difference between the general sequential machine and the Turing machine is the latter's ability to dynamically use the potentially infinite external tape.

It is now of interest to investigate the nature of the sequence of symbols which might appear on a tape. First, the symbols themselves are selected from the set $I = A \vee b$, where A is some alphabet, say $\{a_1, a_2, a_3, \ldots, a_n\}$ and b is the symbol used here to represent a blank square. A sequence of symbols from A (where there are no blanks in the sequence) is called a word. A sequence of symbols consisting of one or more words is called a tape expression and will be so indicated by Greek letters, α, β, $\ldots$. All tape expressions are considered to be of finite length, as we disregard the "infinite" sequence of blanks which precede and follow a tape expression. Thus, a tape expression might be

$$\gamma = b a_1 a_3 b a_2 a_4 b$$

where we include blanks at the beginning and end of tape expressions.

Since the state of this system is determined by the state of the sequential machine in the control unit, it is useful to include this state information in our tape expressions as an aid in analyzing Turing machine behavior. Thus, we

include a bracket within the tape expression which includes the present state
of the sequential machine as well as the present tape symbol being scanned:

$$\alpha a_1[q_j a_1]a_2\beta$$

Here, the present state of the machine is q_j, the present input symbol is a_1,
which is preceded by tape expression α followed by symbol a_1 and followed
by a_2 and tape expression β. This notation is often referred to as the instantaneous description of the Turing machine.

Let us now examine the operation of the Turing machine given in Figure
4.4 with the following tape expression positioned such that the leftmost blank

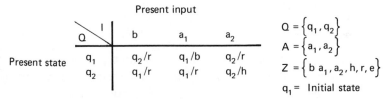

Figure 4.4. Turing machine description.

is under the read/write head:

$$ba_1a_1a_2b$$

The entries in the transition table are

$$q_i/s_i = \text{Next state/Turing machine output}$$

The instantaneous description of the Turing machine described in Figure 4.4
with the above tape expression is

$$[q_1, b]a_1a_1a_2b, \qquad b[q_2a_1]a_1a_2b$$
$$ba_1[q_1, a_1]a_2b, \qquad ba_1[q_1, b]a_2b$$
$$ba_1b[q_2, a_2]b, \qquad \text{Halt}$$

The machine with this input sequence then makes a change in the tape and
halts. Consider now the operation of the machine with the following initial
tape expression, $ba_1a_2a_2b$:

$$[q_1b]a_1a_2a_1a_2b, \qquad b[q_2, a_1]a_2a_1a_2b, \qquad ba_1[q_1a_2]a_1a_2b$$
$$ba_1a_2[q_2, a_1]a_2b, \qquad ba_1a_2a_1[q_1, a_2]b, \qquad ba_1a_2a_1a_2[q_2, b]$$
$$ba_1a_2a_1a_2b[q_1, b], \ldots$$

The Turing machine does not halt with this initial tape expression but continues to run ad infinitum. This kind of initial tape expression has special significance and will be discussed later.

The processes which are performed by a Turing machine may, of course, be concerned with computing functions of a specific kind. The definition of a function here is the one which is common. *A function is a rule or set of rules whereby, given a number called the argument, another number can be computed called the value of the function for that argument.* For example, if x and y are numbers,

$$F(x) = y \tag{4.6}$$

is a function. We can also define a function as "the remainder modulo 2 of the nonnegative integers" and

$$F(0) = 0, F(1) = 1, F(2) = 0, F(3) = 1, \ldots$$

A Turing machine can be used to compute functions, as the argument can be encoded initially in some way on the tape and the resultant tape expression after the machine stops will have the computed function encoded on the tape.

For example, consider the smallest alphabet size $A = \{1\}$ which can be used to code on the tape. Any integer i can be represented by a tape expression with $(i + 1)$ 1s, say

$$5 = b111111b$$

Similarly, the sequence of integers 2, 4, 1 can be represented by

$$b111b11111b11b$$

A Turing machine control which adds two numbers in the above format is given in the accompanying table. The head is initially positioned under the leftmost blank and the initial state of the control is q_1. The machine then proceeds to replace the b between the two numbers with a 1 and replaces the last two 1s with blanks and halts. Thus, the sum of the two numbers is left on the tape in the given format.

Present Input

Q/I	b	1
q_1	q_1/r	q_2/r
q_2	$q_3/1$	q_2/r
q_3	q_4/l	q_3/r
q_4	—	q_5/b
q_5	q_5/l	q_6/b
q_6	q_6/h	q_6/h

Present State: $q_1, q_2, q_3, q_4, q_5, q_6$

$Q = \{q_1, q_2, q_3, q_4, q_5, q_6\}$
$A = \{1\}$
$Z = \{b, 1, h, r, l\}$
q_1 = initial state

4.3 COMPUTABLE FUNCTIONS [3]

Before we examine the class of functions which are called computable, it is necessary to examine some specific properties of functions. The infinite set of all words which may be associated with a function to be computed by a Turing machine is W, and D is defined as a subset of W. A *function whose domain is D* implies a correspondence by which we associate with each $x \subset D$ a $y \subset W$, called the value of the function where x and y are as given in Eq. (4.6). The set

$$Y = \{y \mid f(x) = y, x \subset D\} \tag{4.7}$$

is the range of the function. Here, Eq. (4.7) is read " Y is the collection of elements y such that $f(x) = y$ for x contained in D." A function such as that in (4.6) may also be thought of as a mapping of elements from W into W.

Further, an *r-ary function* is a mapping of a set of r-tuples $(x_1, x_2, \ldots, x_r)$ of elements from W into W:

$$f(x_1, x_2, \ldots, x_r) = y \tag{4.8}$$

An *r*-ary function for $r \geq 1$ is called *total* if its domain corresponds to the set of all *r*-tuples that can be formed from W.

It is now possible to apply these definitions to the concept of functions as applied to Turing machines.

A total function of $f(x_1, x_2, \ldots, x_1)$ defined over the alphabet A will be called *computable* if there exists a Turing machine that will evaluate this function in a finite number of steps.

It is possible that a function is computable for only a subset of all the *r*-tuples that can be formed from W and is not computable for the remainder of the *r*-tuples in W. These functions are called *partially computable*.

Some examples of computable functions, computable in a finite number of steps, are some arithmetic operations. Thus,

$$f_1(x_1, x_2) = x_1 + x_2$$
$$f_2(x_1, x_2) = x_1 x_2$$

are computable. The function

$$f(x) = \sqrt{x}$$

is only partially computable, as the square root can only be found in a finite number of steps if x is a perfect square.

A useful device, then, for use with a Turing machine would certainly be a machine with the appropriate tape (program) that could be used to determine if any given tape will halt when run on any other Turing machine. This is often referred to as the halting problem, and the next sections are needed to develop the answer to this problem. It would also be helpful to be able to evaluate programs for general-purpose digital computers and determine if they will halt or run on forever. Since the Turing machine is our model, the following also applies to general-purpose digital computers.

4.4 CHARACTERISTIC FUNCTIONS

A characteristic function is a device whereby given an element $x \subset G$ we can determine if $x \subset M$, where M is a subset of G. To do this, we evaluate the characteristic function $C_m(x)$, where $C_m(x) = 1$ if $x \subset M$ and we say x is accepted or $C_m(x) = 0$ if $x \not\subset M$ and we say that x is rejected. Now, if we define $C_m(x)$ to be a total function of G which is also computable, then we can use a Turing machine to evaluate the characteristic function.

In the set of words W, if a Turing machine exists that can compute $C_m(x)$ where $M \subseteq W$, then M is said to be *decidable*. If the converse is true (no Turing machine exists), then the set is said to be *undecidable*.

Given a set M and a function f whose range is M, and if unique terms in $f(x)$ can be related to the elements of M, then M is said to be an *enumerable set*. Here we usually let x be the nonnegative integers and define the empty set $\varnothing$ to be enumerable. For example, the set $M = \{x/x \text{ is an even integer}\}$ is an enumerable albeit infinite set given by the function

$$x = 2n \qquad \text{for } n = \text{nonnegative integers} \tag{4.9}$$

Note that Eq. (4.9) is also computable. This leads to another way of defining an enumerable set.

A set M is enumerable if it is empty or if it corresponds to a set of terminal tape expressions that can be generated using a particular Turing machine.

The set of all Turing machines is also enumerable. For example, we know that the alphabet $A = \{1\}$ can be used to code any other set of symbols, as is done in conventional digital computers. Therefore, the transition diagram of the sequential machine control element has two columns corresponding to inputs of 1 and b and n rows, where each row is associated with a state of the machine. The entries in the diagram will be of the form q/z, where $q \subset Q$

and $z \subset Z$ or "don't care" in which case the number of possible Turing machines is [1]

$$N_n = [5n + 1]^{2n}$$

From the fact that there are five elements in $\{Z\}$, n states, the "don't care" and $2n$ positions in the two columns, b and 1. Thus, there is an enumerable number of Turing machines where all the one-state machines are numbered 1 to N_1, two-state machines $N_1 + 1$ to N_2, etc. Thus, we can say that the set of Turing machines is enumerable.

4.5 PREDICATES AND THE PREDICATE CALCULUS

The propositional calculus discussed in Chapter 3 provided a means whereby operations on propositions or statements by logical combinations could be accomplished. In this way, new statements can be deduced from some initial set of propositions. These propositions are declarative sentences which have fixed truth values, namely true or false. The predicate calculus [4] is concerned with propositions in more detail and allows the inclusion of some of the inner structure of the propositions in our analysis. For example, the statement "4 is greater than 3" has a specific truth value in propositional calculus. However, the statement "x is greater than 4" is a form which, of itself, cannot be classified as true or false and must be evaluated with the predicate calculus.

A predicate will be symbolized by $P(x)$ for a single-variable statement and, in general, an r-ary predicate will be denoted by $P(x_1, x_2, \ldots, x_r)$ for $r \geq 1$. A predicate, as with a proposition, is a device for determining the truth or falseness of a statement except that a predicate is concerned with variables— r-tuples of variables. The purpose of the predicate $P(x_1, \ldots, x_r)$ is to generate a mapping of the set of all r-tuples onto the set $\{\text{True, False}\}$, and the characteristic function is a mechanism for computing this mapping:

$$C_p(x_1, \ldots, x_r) = \begin{cases} 1 & \text{for } p(x_1, \ldots, x_r) = \text{True} \\ 0 & \text{for } p(x_1, \ldots, x_r) = \text{False} \end{cases}$$

Thus, the characteristic function associated with the predicate P assigns the r-tuples to the appropriate subset of the set $\{\text{True, False}\}$.

Now, as with the Boolean algebra of classes and propositional calculus, it is necessary to define equality and the logical operations with which we operate on predicates.

Thus, two predicates are equal if and only if their characteristic functions are equal:

$$P_1(x_1, \ldots, x_r) = P_2(x_1, \ldots, x_r)$$
$$\text{if} \quad C_{p_1}(x_1, \ldots, x_r) = C_{p_2}(x_1, \ldots, x_r) \; \forall \; r\text{-tuples}$$

The logical operations are

1. The complement of P:

$$R(x_1, \ldots, x_r) = \bar{P}(x_1, \ldots, x_r)$$

where R is true when P is false and vice versa.

2. Predicate union, $\vee$:

$$R(x_1, \ldots, x_r) = P(x_1, \ldots, x_r) \vee Q(x_1, \ldots, x_r)$$

where R is true if P or Q or both are true.

3. Predicate intersection, $\wedge$:

$$R(x_1, \ldots, x_r) = P(x_1, \ldots, x_r) \wedge Q(x_1, \ldots, x_r)$$

where R is true if and only if both P and Q are true.

4. Quantifiers: $P(y, x_1, \ldots, x_r)$ is an $(r + 1)$-ary predicate, where $y = y_0$, $y_1, \ldots, z$, and

$$R(z, x_1, \ldots, x_r) = \bigvee_{y=y_0}^{y=z} P(y, x_1, \ldots, x_r)$$
$$= P_0(y_0, x_1, \ldots, x_r) \vee \ldots \vee P(z, x_1, \ldots, x_r)$$

means that there is at least one $(r + 1)$-tuple such that $P(y, x_1, \ldots, x_r)$ is true. Also,

$$R(z, x_1, \ldots, x_r) = \bigwedge_{y=y_0}^{y=z} P(y, x_1, \ldots, x_r)$$
$$= P(y_0, x_1, \ldots, x_r) \wedge \ldots \wedge P(z, x_1, \ldots, x_r)$$

means that $P(y, x_1, \ldots, x_r)$ is true for all $(r + 1)$-tuples. The symbols $\bigvee_{y=y_0}^{y=z}$ and $\bigwedge_{y=y_0}^{y=z}$ are called the *bounded existential quantifier* and the *bounded universal quantifier*, respectively.

It should be clear from the above definitions that a predicate is comput-able if its characteristic function is computable. A predicate is called *semi-computable* if there exists a partially computable function whose domain is limited to the subset True.

A mechanism for studying semicomputable functions requires the follow-ing special predicate. One can represent every computable function performed by a Turing machine by a sequence of tape expressions $\alpha_1 \longrightarrow \alpha_2 \longrightarrow \ldots \longrightarrow \alpha_k$, where α_1 is the initial tape expression and α_k is the final tape expression. These expressions are made up of symbols from the finite alphabet $I = A \lor b$, and, because the functions are computable, all computations consist of a finite number of steps. Thus, all possible tape expression sequences form an enumerable set, and a number y can be used to identify a particular sequence. Now, the special computable predicate which we associate with an arbitrary Turing machine M is $T_M(x_1, \ldots, x_r, y)$, which is assigned to the set True if and only if M with the initial tape expression $(x_i, \ldots, x_r)$ generates the sequence of tape expressions associated with the number y.

For example, if the sequence of tape expressions associated with y is $\beta_1 \longrightarrow \beta_2 \longrightarrow \ldots \beta_i \longrightarrow \ldots \beta_k$, we merely start with β_1 in machine M and com-pare the tape expression so generated at the ith step β_i' with β_i. If $\beta_i' = \beta_i$ for $1 \leq i \leq k$, then $T_M(x_1, \ldots, x_r, y)$ is true; and, conversely, if $\beta_i' \neq \beta_i$, then $T_M(x_1, \ldots, x_r, y)$ is false. Since this process is always possible with a finite number of steps, we can conclude that the predicate $T_M(x_1, \ldots, x_r, y)$ is computable.

Given a semicomputable predicate $P(x_1, \ldots, x_r), f_p(x_1, \ldots, x_r)$ is a par-tially computable function which is defined only for those r-tuples for which the predicate is true. Now there must be a Turing machine M_p that can com-pute $f_p(x_1, \ldots, x_r)$ in a finite number of steps for the r-tuples for which the predicate is true and that does not stop for all other r-tuples. From the previ-ous discussion it is clear that there must be a computable predicate $T_{M_P}(x_1, \ldots, x_r, y)$ associated with the machine M_P which will be true only when $P(x_1, \ldots, x_r)$ is true,

$$P(x_1, \ldots, x_r) = \bigvee_y T_{M_P}(x_1, \ldots, x_r, y)$$

where y ranges over all possible values. Thus, $P(x_1, \ldots, x_r)$, a semicomput-able predicate, is defined in terms of the computable predicate $T_{M_P}(x_1, \ldots, x_r, y)$. The remainder of this section is concerned with the predicate associated with the enumeration of Turing machines by a Turing machine and its com-putability.

First, we assume that the predicate P with the associated characteristic function C_p and the complement of C_p, $1 - C_p$, are computable. But $1 - C_p$ is the characteristic function of $\bar{P}$. Thus, both P and $\bar{P}$ are computable, and any function that is computable is also semicomputable. Given the semi-computable predicates P and $\bar{P}$, there must be two computable predicates T_{M_P} and $T_{M_{\bar{P}}}$:

$$P(x_1, \ldots, x_r) = \bigvee_y T_{M_P}(x_1, \ldots, x_r, y)$$

$$\bar{P}(x_1, \ldots, x_r) = \bigvee_y T_{M_{\bar{P}}}(x_1, \ldots, x_r, y)$$

It might appear thus far that all predicates are computable. It will now be shown that this is not true. Assume that the following predicate is computable,

$$P(x) = \bigvee_y T_x(x, y) \tag{4.10}$$

where $T_x(x, y)$ indicates that machine x starts out with a tape expression of machine x. This implies that $T_x(x, y)$ enumerates other Turing machines as it generates tape expressions. The fact that the set of all Turing machines is enumerable was shown earlier in this chapter. Then $\bar{P}(x)$ is at least semicomputable, which implies that there is one machine z which with input x enumerates at least one tape expression which is not a description of a Turing machine.

$$\bar{P}(x) = \overline{\bigvee_y T_x(x, y)} = \bigvee_y T_z(x, y) \tag{4.11}$$

Now assume that we start with machine z; then

$$\bar{P}(z) = \overline{\bigvee_y T_z(z, y)} = \bigvee_y T_x(z, y) \tag{4.12}$$

Now, if we let machine x equal machine z, then from Eq. (4.12)

$$\bar{P}(x) = \bigvee_y T_x(x, y) \tag{4.13}$$

Equation (4.13) then contradicts Eq. (4.10) by implying that $P(x) = \bar{P}(x)$ which says that the predicate which determines if machine x enumerates a Turing machine is equivalent to the predicate which determines if machine x is not a Turing machine. This contradiction does not occur if $P(x)$ is not assumed to be computable. Thus, we conclude that Eq. (4.13) is a semicomputable rather than a computable predicate.

4.6 THE HALTING PROBLEM

A question which must be answered when a tape and machine are mated or if a program is run on a general-purpose digital computer is, Will the machine stop or run on forever? The decision which must be made then is, Given any machine M and an initial tape expression x, find conclusively if the machine will or will not stop. This is called the halting problem. We shall now show that this problem is unsolvable.

Consider a machine that computes

$$\psi(x) = \min_{y} T_x(x, y) \qquad (4.14)$$

which is the minimum value of y for which the predicate $T_x(x, y)$ is true. The domain of (4.14) is those values of x for which $\bigvee_y T_x(x, y)$ is true. But it has been shown that $\bigvee_y T_x(x, y)$ is a semicomputable predicate. Thus, $\psi(x)$ is partially computable, and the halting problem is not solvable in general. This means that there are some machine-initial tape combinations whose halting problem is not uniquely solvable.

It is interesting to note that a program written for a general-purpose digital computer merely describes a particular Turing machine-tape combination. Therefore, the problem of uniquely determining if programs on general-purpose computers will stop or not is also not computable.

4.7 UNIVERSAL TURING MACHINES

A specific Turing machine is designed to carry out the computations associated with a given function by going through the steps indicated by the machine's control element. The universal Turing machine is designed to interpret a tape and then carry out the appropriate computational process. Thus, the transition table for a regular Turing machine would be encoded on a tape to be interpreted by the universal Turing machine. This coding is called a *program*. The function to be computed is also encoded and is called the *data sequence*. The two sequences, program and data, are placed on the tape and form the initial tape expression for the universal Turing machine.

It should be clear from the above description that this process is no different from that used with a conventional stored-program digital computer, the primary difference being that the universal Turing machine has a potentially infinite memory.

4.8 STOCHASTIC AUTOMATA

The machines considered thus far are fixed and deterministic in that their responses to a particular input from a given initial state are always the same. Also, the input sequences which we have been applying to these machines have always had a particular representation associated with them. For example, a program used on a digital computer always has a specific set of symbols in a specific format associated with it. Thus, the output is determined by the program and set of data applied where the same program and the same data always give the same output. A stochastic automaton or probabilistic machine, on the other hand, has an output which is not necessarily the same for every application of the input. Machines which behave this way in practice may have an intermittent component or be subjected to an input sequence which is generated by noise [5].

Stochastic automata have been formulated as models for systems which are made from unreliable components [6], as a representation of a discrete system disturbed by noise [7], as models for psychological learning processes [8], and as a model for adaptive and learning systems [9, 10]. It is therefore of interest here to examine some of the properties of stochastic automata, as they will be of value when we consider applications in later chapters.

There are two methods for representing stochastic automata; however, we shall restrict our attention here to the most general model as given by Booth [7]. A probabilistic machine, as with a deterministic machine, is described by a 5-tuple; however, some of the elements in the representation are different. The 5-tuple is

$$S_p = \langle I, Q, Z, P, \Phi \rangle$$

where

1. I is the input set $\{0, 1, \ldots, J - 1\}$.
2. Q is the state set $\{q_1, q_2, \ldots, q_s\}$.
3. Z is the output set $\{0, 1, \ldots, K - 1\}$.
4. P is a matrix of conditional probabilities $p(z, q_{(j+1)}/i, q_{(j)})$.
5. Φ is the set of all initial state probabilities $\{\psi\}$ associated with the state set Q.

The first three elements above will be recognized as being identical to the terms in the description of deterministic automata given earlier. The last two elements will now be expanded.

The matrix P is the representation of the state transition and output

$$
P = I \times Q
\begin{array}{c}
\\
\\
\end{array}
\begin{array}{c}
0, q_1 \\
0, q_2 \\
1, q_1 \\
1, q_2
\end{array}
\overbrace{
\begin{bmatrix}
.3 & 0 & .4 & .3 \\
.2 & .3 & .4 & .1 \\
.3 & .2 & .1 & .4 \\
.2 & .6 & .2 & 0
\end{bmatrix}
}^{
\begin{array}{cccc}
0, q_1 & 0, q_2 & 1, q_1 & 1, q_2
\end{array}
}
$$

(column header group: Z×Q)

$$I = \{0, 1\} \qquad Q = \{q_1, q_2\} \qquad Z = \{0, 1\}$$

Figure 4.5. Description of a stochastic automaton.

behavior of the stochastic automaton. For example, consider the two-state machine described in Figure 4.5 where the binary input and output formats have been specified. The rows in the matrix correspond to the set formed by the cartesian product of the input and state sets, and the columns correspond to the cartesian product of the output and state sets. Thus, all combinations of states and inputs are represented by the rows, and all combinations of states and outputs are represented by the columns of P. The entries in the matrix represent the probability that the next state and output will occur for the present state and input given by the corresponding row. Therefore in Figure 4.5, the probability of going from input 0 and state q_2 to output 1 and state q_1 is 0.4. Note that the probability of going from one input and state to *any* output and state for *all* possible outputs and states must be certain and that the probability of going from *some* input and state to *some* output and state must be equal to or greater than zero. This is summarized by

$$0 \leq P(z, q(j+1)/i, q(j)) \leq 1 \tag{4.15}$$

and

$$\sum_{z=0}^{k-1} \sum_{q_r(j+1)=q_1(j+1)}^{q_s(j+1)} P(z, q_r(j+1)/i, q(j)) = 1 \tag{4.16}$$

The matrix P gives us the probability of going from one state to another for a corresponding input and output; however, we still do not know how to analyze the behavior of these machines until the element ϕ is defined.

Φ is the set of all initial state probabilities associated with the state set Q, $\Phi = \{\phi = [\phi_1, \phi_2, \ldots, \phi_s]\}$, and a particular element in the set gives us the initial probability of being in each of the s possible states of the machine.

Therefore, in this general formulation, we can know only the probability of being in a given starting state.

It is generally desirable to be able to predict in some way the response of a machine to a particular input sequence. With stochastic automata we can calculate only the conditional probability of an output sequence given a particular input sequence. To do this, we divide the matrix P into submatrices $\Delta_i(z)$ which correspond to particular input-output transition probabilities. Thus, the P matrix in Figure 4.5 can be rewritten as

$$P = \begin{bmatrix} \Delta_0(0) & \Delta_0(1) \\ \Delta_1(0) & \Delta_1(1) \end{bmatrix} \tag{4.17}$$

Now, if we define an s-row column vector of 1s as

$$\mathbf{h} = \left.\begin{bmatrix} 1 \\ \cdot \\ \cdot \\ \cdot \\ 1 \end{bmatrix}\right\} \ s \text{ rows} \tag{4.18}$$

then the conditional probability of an output sequence given an input sequence $i_1, i_2, \ldots, i_v$ is, for one input and one output symbol,

$$P\left(\frac{z}{i}\right) = \boldsymbol{\psi}\Delta_i(z)\mathbf{h} \tag{4.19}$$

and for the sequence is

$$P\left(\frac{z_1, z_2, \ldots, z_v}{i_1, i_2, \ldots, i_v}\right) = \boldsymbol{\psi}\Delta_{i_1}(z_1)\Delta_{i_2}(z_2)\ldots \Delta_{i_v}(z_v)\mathbf{h} \tag{4.20}$$

We shall now examine Eq. (4.20) by means of the following example. Assume that we are given the machine described in Figure 4.5 and that we want to know the probability of the output sequence 011 given the input sequence 010. Now, by (4.17) and the P given, we generate

$$\Delta_0(0) = \begin{bmatrix} 0.3 & 0 \\ 0.2 & 0.3 \end{bmatrix} \qquad \Delta_1(0) = \begin{bmatrix} 0.3 & 0.2 \\ 0.2 & 0.6 \end{bmatrix}$$

$$\Delta_0(1) = \begin{bmatrix} 0.4 & 0.3 \\ 0.4 & 0.1 \end{bmatrix} \qquad \Delta_1(1) = \begin{bmatrix} 0.1 & 0.4 \\ 0.2 & 0 \end{bmatrix}$$

Now applying Eq. (4.20) we have

$$P\left(\frac{011}{010}\right) = \boldsymbol{\psi}\Delta_0(0)\Delta_1(1)\Delta_0(1)\mathbf{h}$$

where

$$\Delta = \Delta_0(0)\Delta_1(1)\Delta_0(1) = \begin{bmatrix} 0.060 & 0.021 \\ 0.064 & 0.032 \end{bmatrix}$$

and

$$\Delta h = \begin{bmatrix} h_1\left(\dfrac{011}{010}\right) \\ h_2\left(\dfrac{011}{010}\right) \end{bmatrix} = \begin{bmatrix} 0.060 & 0.021 \\ 0.064 & 0.032 \end{bmatrix}\begin{bmatrix} 1 \\ 1 \end{bmatrix} = \begin{bmatrix} 0.081 \\ 0.096 \end{bmatrix}$$

Thus,

$$P\left(\frac{011}{010}\right) = \begin{bmatrix} \psi_1 & \psi_2 \end{bmatrix}\begin{bmatrix} 0.081 \\ 0.096 \end{bmatrix} = 0.081\psi_1 + 0.096\psi_2$$

and if we say $\psi = [0.5 \quad 0.5]$,

$$P\left(\frac{011}{010}\right) = 0.0405 + 0.0480 = 0.0885$$

Similarly, if we have no interest in the output sequence, then it is possible to find the probability of being in the different states of the machine after a given input sequence is applied. These probabilities are referred to as the state probability vector. Here, since we are concerned only with the states, we merely lump together the appropriate matrices $\Delta_i(z)$ by

$$\Delta_i = \sum_{z=0}^{k-1} \Delta_i(z)$$

and for the machine of Figure 4.5,

$$\Delta_0 = \Delta_0(0) + \Delta_0(1) = \begin{bmatrix} 0.7 & 0.3 \\ 0.6 & 0.4 \end{bmatrix}$$

$$\Delta_1 = \Delta_1(0) + \Delta_1(1) = \begin{bmatrix} 0.4 & 0.6 \\ 0.4 & 0.6 \end{bmatrix}$$

Now, given the initial state probability vector, we can find the state probability vector after a sequence, say 010, is applied:

$$\psi(i_1, \ldots, i_v) = \psi\Delta_{i_1}\Delta_{i_2} \ldots \Delta_{i_v}$$

and

$$\psi(010) = \psi\Delta_0\Delta_1\Delta_0$$

$$= \begin{bmatrix} \psi_1 & \psi_2 \end{bmatrix}\begin{bmatrix} 0.64 & 0.36 \\ 0.64 & 0.36 \end{bmatrix}$$

$$= 0.64(\psi_1 + \psi_2) \quad 0.36(\psi_1 + \psi_2)$$

It has now been demonstrated that we do not have to deal with deterministic systems but that we can handle systems in a probabilistic or stochastic manner.

4.9 INFORMATION THEORY [11]

The application of a specific input sequence to a stochastic machine gives us the data required to compute only the probability of obtaining some particular sequence. Hence, there is a degree of uncertainty associated with the occurrence of each output sequence. For example, if the probability of obtaining the sequence 101 is 0.4 and the probability of 110 is 0.95 for an input 111, we are more uncertain about getting the former sequence than the latter sequence. Thus, our uncertainty level is inversely proportional to the probability of occurrence of a given event. Similarly, if we know a particular sequence will occur, we learn nothing when in fact it does occur. On the other hand, if we are very uncertain that a particular sequence will occur, we learn more when it does occur. Therefore, we say that the information associated with the occurrence of a sequence or event, E, is an inverse function of the probability of that event, $P(E)$:

$$I(E) = f\left(\frac{1}{P(E)}\right) \tag{4.21}$$

The function $f(\ )$ has been defined as the logarithm to the base 2:

$$I(E) = \log_2 \frac{1}{P(E)} = -\log_2 P(E) \text{ bits} \tag{4.22}$$

Let us now define a "black box" called a source which emits a stream of symbols from a set of q symbols. This source has no memory; that is, the symbol emitted from the source at any time is independent of the symbol emitted at any other time. Therefore, we shall assume that there is a probability associated with the occurrence of each symbol from the source:

$$P(S_1), P(S_2), \ldots, P(S_q)$$

$$\boxed{\text{Source}} \longrightarrow \{S_1, S_2, \ldots, S_q\}$$

The *information* associated with the occurrence of symbol S_i is

$$I(S_i) = -\log_2 P(S_i) \text{ bits} \tag{4.23}$$

and the average information from the above source is the sum of the information per symbol weighted by the probability of that symbol:

$$H(S) = \sum_{i=1}^{q} P(S_i)I(S_i) = -\sum_{i=1}^{q} P(S_i) \log_2 P(S_i) \qquad (4.24)$$

The average information $H(s)$ given by (4.24) is referred to as the *entropy* of the source.

It can be shown that the maximum entropy occurs when all events are equally likely:

$$P(S_1) = P(S_2) = \ldots = P(S_i)$$

For example, consider the binary source $\{0, 1\}$ where the probability of zero is P_0; also

$$P_1 = 1 - P_0 = \bar{P}_0$$

The entropy of this source is

$$H(s) = P_0 \log \frac{1}{P_0} + P_1 \log \frac{1}{P_1}$$

$$= P_0 \log \frac{1}{P_0} + \bar{P}_0 \log \frac{1}{\bar{P}_0}$$

Now define

$$\lim_{P_0 \to 0} P_0 \log P_0 = 0 \log 0 = 0$$

A plot of $H(s)$ as a function of P_0 is shown here where the maximum occurs when the probability of each event is equal, $P_1 = P_0 = 0.5$. Note that if the probability of an event is 1, we learn nothing by the occurrence of that event.

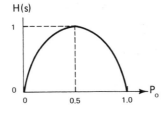

If one is given r symbols in sequence from a source of symbols $q \geq r$, then the maximum information which is contained in that sequence is

$$H_{\max} = \log_2 r \text{ bits}$$

However, if each symbol in the sequence is repeated once, that is, each symbol is transmitted twice, then obviously the information contained in the sequence is reduced:

$$H = \log_2 \frac{r}{2}$$

The ratio of these two terms is used in the following function which defines the *redundancy* in the sequence:

$$R = 1 - \frac{H}{H_{max}} \tag{4.25}$$

This measure is most useful in coding where one deliberately reduces the information in a sequence to overcome a noisy channel.

The concepts of information, entropy, and redundancy have been introduced here to provide the necessary background for the definitions of self-organization and the system performance measures which will be used later.

4.10 SUMMARY

In this chapter we have considered some of the models which can be applied to study the fundamental properties of automata. The limitations of general computing machines were studied via the work of Turing. The concept of a stochastic automaton, which has certain applications in cybernetic systems, has been introduced. Finally, the fundamental definition of information and some of its ramifications have been introduced.

4.11 EXERCISES

4.1. Describe the following sequential machine in terms of a 5-tuple, $\langle I, Q, Z, \delta, \omega \rangle$.

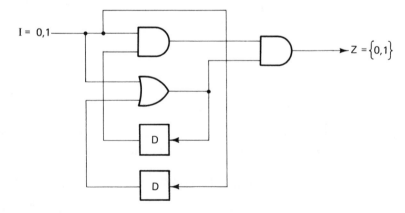

4.2. Describe the computations of the following machine for the following initial tape expressions:

I / Q	b	a_1	a_2
q_1	q_2/r	q_1/b	q_2/l
q_2	q_2/a_1	q_3/r	q_2/h
q_3	q_2/r	q_1/r	q_3/a_1

$A = \{a_1, a_2\}$
$Q = \{q_1, q_2, q_3\}$
$Z = \{b, a_1, a_2, h, r, l\}$
$q_1 = $ initial state

1. $ba_1a_1a_2a_1b$
2. bba_2a_1b
3. $a_1a_2a_2$

The read/write head is placed over the leftmost symbol at the start of the computation.

4.3. Given the following stochastic automaton description, find the probability state vector and the probability of the output sequence 011 for the input sequence 011.

$$Z \times Q$$

$P = I \times Q$		$0, q$	$0, q_2$	$0, q_3$	$1, q_1$	$1, q_2$	$1, q_3$
	$0, q_1$	0	0	0.5	0	0	0.5
	$0, q_2$	0	0.5	0	0	0.5	0
	$0, q_3$	0.5	0	0	0.5	0	0
	$1, q_1$	0	0	0.5	0	0	0.5
	$1, q_2$	0	0.5	0	0	0.5	0
	$1, q_3$	0	0	0.5	0	0	0.5

$$I = \{0, 1\} \qquad Q = \{q_1 \; q_2 \; q_3\} \qquad Z = \{0, 1\}$$
$$\mathbf{\psi} = [\psi_1, \psi_2, \psi_3] = [0.3 \quad 0.3 \quad 0.4]$$

4.4. Calculate the information associated with the output sequence 010 in Problem 4.3 for the input sequence 011.

4.5. Find the entropy associated with each row of the following matrix:

$$\begin{bmatrix} 0.1 & 0.2 & 0.1 & 0.6 \\ 0.25 & 0.25 & 0.25 & 0.25 \\ 0.9 & 0.03 & 0.04 & 0.03 \end{bmatrix}$$

4.6. A teletype unit is capable of encoding 64 characters for transmission down a channel. The encoded sequence uses 8 binary digits. Assuming that each character occurs with equal *a priori* probability, what is the entropy of the teletype source? What is the redundancy of this system?

REFERENCES

1. Booth, T. L., *Sequential Machines and Automata Theory*, Wiley, New York, 1967.

2. Turing, A. M., "On Computable Numbers, with an Application to the Entscheidungs Problem," in *Proceedings of the London Mathematical Society*, Vol. 42, 1936–1937, pp. 230–265.

3. Minsky, Marvin L., *Computation: Finite and Infinite Machines*, Prentice-Hall, Englewood Cliffs, N.J., 1962.

4. Korfhage, Robert R., *Logic and Algorithms*, Wiley, New York, 1966.

5. Booth, T. L., "Random Input Automata," Proc. 1964 International Conference on Microwaves, Circuit Theory and Information Theory, Tokyo.

6. Von Neuman, J., "Probabilistic Logics and the Synthesis of Reliable Organisms from Unreliable Components," *Automata Studies Annals of Mathematical Studies*, No. 34, 1956.

7. Booth, T. L., "Random Processes in Sequential Networks," in *Proceedings of the IEEE Symposium on Signal Transmission and Processing*, No. 4C9, 1965, pp. 19–25.

8. Bush, R. R., and F. Mostellar, *Stochastic Models for Learning*, Wiley, New York, 1958.

9. Shapiro, I. J., and K. S. Narendra, "Use of Stochastic Automata for Parameter Self-Optimization with Multimodel Performance Criteria," *IEEE Transactions on Systems Science and Cybernetics*, Vol. SSC-5, No. 4, pp. 352–360, Oct. 1969.

10. McLaren, R. W., "A Stochastic Automaton Model for the Synthesis of Learning Systems," *IEEE Transactions on Systems Science and Cybernetics*, Vol. SSC-2, No. 2, pp. 109–114, Dec. 1966.

11. Abramson, N., *Information Theory*, McGraw-Hill, New York, 1963.

5

ADAPTATION, LEARNING, SELF-REPAIR, AND SELF-ORGANIZATION

INTRODUCTION

Thus far, we have been concerned with specific techniques and features of "intelligent" systems and characteristics of the automata which may be used to create these systems. In this chapter we shall examine the specific features; adaptation, learning, self-repair and self-organization, which are often associated with these systems. In order to avoid the use of the charged, even nebulous term "intelligent" to describe these systems, we shall define a system which incorporates one or more of these features as a *cybernetic system*.

The first sections of this chapter include definition of the features and models associated with cybernetic systems. The Homeostat, one of the first physical examples of a cybernetic system, is then described. Finally, some techniques used in cybernetic systems are presented.

5.1 ADAPTATION, LEARNING, AND SELF-REPAIR

The word *adaptation* has taken on several meanings in the many disciplines in which it is found. The engineer often equates learning and adaptation, whereas the psychologist makes a sharp distinction between them—and the life scientist is often found somewhere in between. The difference is a function of how broad a definition of learning one is willing to accept. Let us now consider some of the ways in which the words learning and adaptation have been used.

A very broad definition is one given by Wiener [1], who describes learning in such a broad context that it includes the mutation of a species with time. He defines an animal (or system) which learns as "one which is capable of being transformed by its past environment within its individual lifetime. An animal that multiplies is able to create other animals in its own likeness at least approximately, although not so completely in its own likeness that they cannot vary in the course of time. If this variation is itself inheritable, we have the raw material on which natural selection can work." If manifested in some behavior pattern, this change will be continued through the generations if the behavior is not detrimental. Wiener calls this type of change from generation to generation racial or phylogenetic learning, and learning or changes in behavior which take place within a specific individual is called ontogenetic learning. Although both phylogenetic and ontogenetic learning (especially the former) are present in all living organisms, both plant and animal, the degree of the presence of one or the other types of learning is a function of the organism. For example, it is clear that in higher mammals and especially in man ontogenetic learning and individual adaptability are at a high level. And, as Wiener points out, "It may be said that a large part of the phylogenetic learning of man has been devoted to establishing the possibility of good ontogenetic learning." On the other hand, in birds and insects [2] the amount of ontogenetic learning which is possible is limited, and most of their behavior is based on phylogenetic learning. The gross generality of this definition is clear when one considers definitions set forth by others.

Shannon [3] gives a definition of learning which is not so all-encompassing as that of Wiener. Shannon's definition follows: "Suppose that an organism or a machine can be placed in or connected to a class of environments, and that there is a measure of 'success' or 'adaptation' to the environment. Suppose further that this measure is comparatively local in time, that is, that one can measure the success over periods of time short compared to the life of the organism. If this local measure of success tends to improve with the passage of time, for the class of environments in question, we may say that the organism or machine is learning to adapt to these environments relative to the measure of success chosen."

There are several components of Shannon's definition which are more restrictive than Wiener's; also, Shannon's use of the term adaptation in reference to a success measure makes for difficulty when one is trying to communicate with psychologists and some life scientists. This definition considers only the subset of possible learning which can be measured in a time which is short relative to the life of the organism. Thus, the generality of Wiener's definition with respect to that of Shannon is clear. Wiener considers all learning both phylogenetic and ontogenetic, whereas Shannon restricts his attention to a subset of all possible ontogenetic learning.

It is now of interest to consider some of the ways the word learning is used by the psychologist. A thorough treatment of learning is found in Osgood [4], where he describes phylogenetic learning but considers only ontogenetic learning in his definition. His definition is similar to that of other psychologists and is contained in his statement "In repeated situations of similar character, the individual organism varies and multiplies its behaviors, selection among competing responses depending upon their adaptiveness. Selective modifications of this order result from experience of the individual." This definition is similar to that of Shannon, but it points out one facet which is important to the psychologist, that is, that the organism is subjected to repeated situations of similar character. The definitions presented thus far have been relatively consistent, and one may ask, Where do the previously mentioned difficulties in definitions arise? This can be answered when one considers some of the uses of the word adaptation.

In engineering circles the words learning and adaptive are often used interchangeably when referring to systems which are capable of ontogenetic learning; however, the psychologists' interpretation of the word adaptive is likely to be colored by knowledge of the concept of adaptation level theory as used in the classical psychophysical experiments. In this context lie the phenomena of dark adaptation, pain adaptation, and sound adaptation, the ability of an observer to "tune out" one sound source (baby cry) in preference to another [4, 5]. The classic adaptation level theory has been expanded by Helson [6] into the realm of total behavior, both normal and abnormal. For purposes of this discussion three of Helson's postulates are of interest:

1. All behavior centers about the adaptation or equilibrium level of the organism.

2. Behavioral equilibrium depends on the interaction of all stimuli confronting the organism, between present and past stimulation.
3. The adaptation level is approximated as a weighted log mean of all stimuli affecting the organism. (The log relation here accounts for the nonlinear transfer characteristics of the physiological receptors in all living organisms.)

Therefore, one can conclude that the adaptation level can be likened to a behavioral threshold which is a function of the inputs to the organism. The process wherein a persistent stimulus is "tuned out" has also been observed by neurophysiologists when studying human "brain waves" or electroencephalograms (EEG) [7]. For example, when exposed to repeated auditory pulse or click stimulation, the resulting brain wave pulses continue to decrease in amplitude with each stimulus until the response disappears. This physiological equivalent to the adaptation level is called the process of *habituation*.

The fact that confusion exists between the words adaptation and learning was recognized previously by Sklansky [8], who defines learning and self-repair as special forms of adaptation. He considers "a cell, an organ, an organism, or a species to be adaptive if its behavior in a changing environment is 'successful' in some sense." If success by some measure is a requisite, then two properties distinguish an adaptive from a nonadaptive machine: stability and reliability.

In a definition of adaptation given by Ashby [9], the stability requirement of adaptive systems is put forth: "A form of behavior is adaptive if it maintains its essential variables within physiological limits." An example of this property in all living systems is that of homeostasis. Included in this category from a physiological viewpoint are the mechanisms for maintaining the glucose level in the blood and the mechanisms for maintaining body temperature. These mechanisms are essential to physiological survival as well as to the successful performance of any desired task. This discussion suggests a distinguishing property of adaptive systems: persistence of success in a changing environment.

The second property of adaptive systems, as proposed by Ashby and Sklansky, reliability, is also based on observations of physiological systems. If a portion of a system is damaged and the effect of the damage is gradually masked until the system's performance reaches an acceptable level, then the machine is adaptive. Thus, the second property of adaptive machines can be stated as follows: overall functional reliability in the face of unreliability of parts of the machine. In the following discussions, this property with a time constraint is associated with the concept of machine self-repair, discussed later.

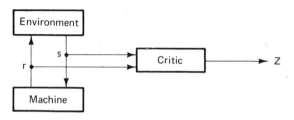

Figure 5.1. MEC configuration.

A functional schema for an adaptive machine is illustrated in Figure 5.1. The machine's input is the "stimulus" s; the machine's output is the "response" r; the measure of success is given by the critic's output or "effectiveness" measure Z. This configuration is called the MEC (machine, environment, critic) configuration. Adaptation is manifested by the presence of either stability or reliability or both.

With respect to the MEC configuration,

1. The system is stable if Z remains within prescribed bounds when E changes.
2. The system is reliable if Z remains within prescribed bounds when M changes.

In this definition, note that none of the requirements for an adaptive system are functions of time.

The definition of learning and the similar effect of self-repair are closely related to time, however. Thus, the effectiveness, the critic's output, is a function of time, $Z(t)$, and we say that M "learns" over a specified time interval $(0, T)$ if the environment changes at $t = 0$ and remains constant over $(0, T)$ and if $Z(T) > Z(0+)$. In other words, a system which learns is one in which, given a change in the state of the environment at $t = 0$, the performance index at time T is greater than the performance index at time $t = 0+$.

A system M undergoes self-repair over a time interval $(0, T)$ if some machine components fail at $t = 0$ and if $Z(T) > Z(0+)$. Self-repair occurs when a system's effectiveness at $t = 0+$ is less than that at $t = T$ when a failure in M has occurred. It is clear that the only difference between the definitions of learning and self-repair is the physical location of the change.

We shall impose one additional constraint on the above definitions, namely, that the performance achieve some predetermined level, $Z(t) = L > Z(0+)$, in time T.

5.2 SOME FORMALIZATION

Zadeh [10] has defined precisely the notion of an adaptive system ("An adaptive system is insensitive to changes in its environment") by characterizing the external manifestations of an adaptive system and couching them in mathematical terms. The following is basically Zadeh's description of adaptive systems, where the input (stimulus) and output (response) sets are not necessarily functions of specific time intervals.

Given a machine A which may be subjected to any one of a specified set of input functions $S_r \triangleq \{\mathbf{u}\}$, where the vector $\mathbf{u}$ may be a function of time. The input $\bar{u}$ may contain components which are both input or stimulus variables and environmental factors and machine failures as well. It is therefore convenient to consider a family of inputs for some given criterion indexed by r. This family of inputs $S_r = \{\mathbf{u}\}$ constitutes a source which may or may not be such that S_r is a stochastic process. It is now possible to define a family of sources $\{S_r\}$, where r identifies a member of the family. The representation here of the machine and its associated input and output functions is similar to the MEC configuration used by Sklansky. The model and the associated terms for this definition are shown in Figure 5.2.

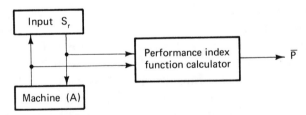

Figure 5.2. Modified MEC configuration.

The performance of a machine A is measured by a performance function **P**, which, when the input is S_r, becomes $\mathbf{P}(r)$. If the output mapping $\mathbf{P}(r)$ is such that $\mathbf{P}(r) \subset W$, where W is a class of acceptable performance functions, then the system is said to meet a criterion of acceptability. For example, if $\mathbf{P}(r)$ is real-valued, then W may be the class of performance functions which exceed in value a prescribed number. The set of all possible input conditions is $r \subset \Gamma$, where Γ is a specified set of values of r. For statistical input information, $\mu \subset M$, where μ is a prior probability distribution on the range of r and M is a specified set of these distributions.

It is now possible to define an adaptive system: A system A is adaptive with respect to $\{S_r\}$ and W if it performs acceptably well. In other words, $\mathbf{P}(r) \subset W$, for every source in the family $\{S_r\}$, $r \subset \Gamma$. More succinctly, A is adaptive with respect to Γ and W if it maps Γ into W.

If the measure of performance for a machine is total distance between the input and output mapping, then A is more adaptive than A' if A' is adaptive relative to Γ' and W, where Γ' is a proper subset of Γ, i.e., A meets the performance criterion for a larger set of inputs than does A'.

The similarity between this definition based on Zadeh and Sklansky's [11, 12] definitions lies in the fact that Zadeh includes changes which may occur as machine failures in his input vector **u**. This has led Sklansky to "suggest that adaptivity, coined by Zadeh, be viewed as the union of stability and reliability, even though Zadeh does not associate adaptivity and reliability explicitly." Also, it is interesting to note that with this definition all systems may be thought of as being adaptive to some Γ and W.

The last statement in the above paragraph offers a link between definitions of adaptive systems in engineering and the concept of adaptation level found in psychology. If the adaptation levels or thresholds encountered are defined to be within an acceptable region of mapping W, then, in a broad sense, any psychological system where the concept of adaptation level is applied is adaptive in the engineering sense.

5.3 A SUMMARY

It is now possible to summarize the definitions of adaptation, learning, and self-repair as they will be used in this book. One can say that a system is adaptive if it responds favorably with respect to a performance function $\mathbf{P}$ in the face of a changing environment or internal machine structure. And one can say that a system learns if it responds acceptably with respect to a performance function $\mathbf{P}$ in time T after a change in its environment. A system undergoes self-repair if it responds acceptably with respect to a performance function $\mathbf{P}$ in time T after a change in its internal structure. Thus, the primary distinction between adaptation and learning/self-repair is that the performance in the face of changes must achieve a given level within a specific time for learning and self-repair and the time constraint is not imposed on an adaptive system. These definitions may appear to ignore the process of habituation; however, if one chooses his performance function properly, the processes of habituation and adaptation will emerge identical.

5.4 SELF-ORGANIZATION

Let us now consider some approaches to the concept of a self-organizing system. Ashby [13] considers first the contradiction of organization, namely separation. Thus, a system which starts with its parts separate, i.e., each part behaves independently, and then acts so that connections are formed and the parts then behave in a more coherent manner is self-organizing in that it changes from "parts separated" to "parts joined." An example of this process is the growth of the nervous system of an embryo where individual cells grow and then the interconnections associated with certain behaviors are formed.

A second approach given by Ashby [13] considers that rather than "changing from unorganized to organized" a system which changes "from a bad organization to a good one" may also be considered a self-organizing system. This approach, however, leads to a definition which is similar to the one given above for adaptation. It is presented here to point out some of the confusion in terms associated with an emerging discipline.

It has been argued by Von Foerster [14] and Ashby [13] that there is no such thing as a self-organizing system in and of itself. The reasoning here is that for a system to become organized, it must extract that organization from its environment. Hence, a system can be self-organizing only if it is defined with respect to some external source of order, because as a system becomes organized, it discards behavior which is not appropriate in a sort of natural behavior selection process in the present environment. Further, if there is no order to the environment, then there is no basis for organization.

This concept was stated by Ashby [15] as the "Law of Requisite Variety: *Only variety can destroy variety.*" This can be described in terms of a system operating in some environment where the success of the system in the environment depends on the ability of the system to cope with the possible states of the environment. For example, as a minimum requirement, the number of different possible states of the system must equal the number of possible states of the environment, although the proper states of the system must be available as well. Thus, to reduce the variety in the environment, the system must be capable of achieving the "requisite variety."

The fundamental principles of self-organizing systems emerge from these arguments. The first is as follows: A necessary condition for a system, A, to be self-organizing in an environment, E, is that the uncertainty in an information-theoretic sense associated with A be equal to or greater than zero:

$$I(A) > 0 \qquad (5.1)$$

Now, consider the contradiction to (5.1), $I(A) = 0$, which implies that the system is deterministic and rigid in its behavior; hence, it can be successful only in a narrower range of environments than a machine with $I(A) > 0$, as there can be no change in organization in the former. This can be extended to the necessary condition for organization that $I(A) \geq I(E)$.

The second principle is associated with a definition of a self-organizing system given by Von Foerster [14] and concerns the redundancy (as defined in information theory) associated with a system. For example, if a system is totally disorganized, then the uncertainty of behavior associated with the system is maximum. One does not know what the system response to a particular input will be. However, as the system learns of its environment and organization has taken place, then one is more certain about its behavior and the system is more redundant. Therefore, the requirement placed on a self-organizing system where R is redundancy is

$$\frac{dR}{dt} > 0 \qquad (5.2)$$

Applying the above operation to the definition of redundancy gives

$$\frac{d}{dt}\left[-\frac{H}{H_{\text{max}}}\right] > 0 \qquad (5.3)$$

If both H and H_{max} are functions of time, the criterion for a system to be self-organizing is

$$H\left(\frac{dH_{\text{max}}}{dt}\right) > H_{\text{max}}\left(\frac{dH}{dt}\right) \qquad (5.4)$$

The rather complex processes that are inferred in Eq. (5.4) can be more easily understood by considering a few special cases. For example, assume that the maximum entropy of the system H_{max} is constant:

$$\frac{dH}{dt} < 0, \qquad H_{\text{max}} \text{ constant} \qquad (5.5)$$

This means that the rate of change of entropy must be negative if the system is to be self-organizing. Also consider the case where the entropy of the system, H, is constant but the number of states in the system is growing. The criterion for self-organization now is

$$\frac{dH_{max}}{dt} > 0, \qquad H \text{ constant} \tag{5.6}$$

Here the only manner in which the entropy can remain constant while the system is growing is for the added states to be incorporated into the system such that Eq. (5.6) is satisfied.

Finally, consider the case where both H and H_{max} are functions of time and therefore the criterion is given by Eq. (5.4). Here the system is said to be self-organizing if the product of the system entropy and the rate of change of the maximum entropy is greater than the product of the maximum entropy and the rate of change of system entropy. This is the situation where the system states are growing and the system organization is faster than that required to incorporate the new states.

It is now possible to summarize our definition of a self-organizing system with respect to the previous definitions. From the above, it is clear that we must have disorganization before organization can occur. Thus, we shall assume that the initial uncertainty is at or near maximum, max,

$$H \approx \text{max}$$

and a *self-organizing system is defined as an adaptive or learning system in which the initial state of the system is unknown, a random variable, or a "don't care."*

5.5 SOME SYSTEM MODELS

There are two basic models of interest here. Each one contains the same basic elements, but their configurations are different. The elements are the forward transfer element, the performance evaluation element or critic, the system parameter transformation element, and the input and output functions. One of the configurations of these elements is given in Figure 5.3.

The forward transfer element (FTE) maps the input function, I, into some output function, Ω. Here, I is some function of the system input, or driving function i, the environment E in which the system exists and must interact with and may or may not be a specific function of time $I = f(i, E, t)$. For example, the forward transfer element may be as simple as a passive electrical network, a complex hybrid (analog-digital) system, or a network of computer

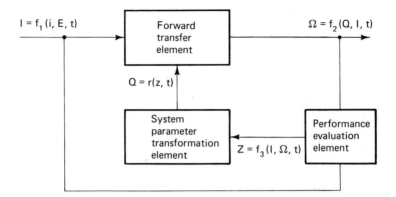

Figure 5.3. Closed self-organizing or adaptive system.

systems. The output function Ω is a function of the input function I and the state Q.

The nature of the performance evaluation element (PEEL) determines the character of the system, as it contains the goal orientation of the system. For example, the goal or goals contained within the PEEL may be "Reduce the error between the input and output functions" as in a simple feedback system or "Extract all sequences of symbols from the input function which make up words from Russian" or "Keep a $3G$ force on the system while expending no more than x pounds of fuel." The PEEL then is said to contain the goals and constraints of the system's operation and maps the input and output functions into a set of measures Z which indicate the performance of the system. The PEEL or critic is often called the teacher, as its function is to provide an input to the system which tells it whether its behavior is proper or not.

In some applications the PEEL makes statistical estimates or measurements of the input signal in order to "learn" what state the system should be in. This kind of system is called learning without a teacher. Thus, a system in which the PEEL is some external observer such as an executive computer or human critic who "teaches" the system how to behave is sometimes called "learning with a teacher," and a system in which the teacher or critic is built in is called "learning without a teacher." Tsypkin [16] has argued that there is no such thing as learning without a teacher, as the essence of teaching is contained in the goals and constraints of the PEEL which are specified by the designer, the teacher. In many systems, especially control systems, this is in fact the case. However, some systems developed lately have certain restricted abilities to independently derive subgoals within the PEEL.

The system parameter transform element (SPTE) transforms the performance measure Z into a system state such that the system behavior tends to fall into a range where the performance improves.

The second model merely places a switch between the FTE and the SPTE and isolates the SPTE and PEEL as an element separate from the rest of the system. Thus, with the switch open, the state of the system cannot change, as there is no feedback or state change information supplied. This is the model for learning with a teacher and is illustrated in Figure 5.4. The philosophy of operation for this system is that the switch is closed during what is called the learning phase and, after the performance reaches some acceptable level, the switch is opened (operate mode) and the system "freewheels" until the switch is closed again.

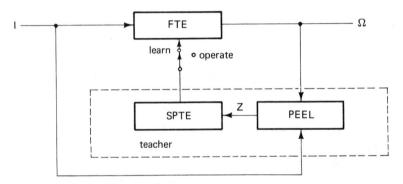

Figure 5.4. Model of learning with a teacher.

It is now possible to consider a formal definition of a cybernetic system as a 6-tuple $S = \langle I, \Omega, \alpha, Z, \gamma, Q \rangle$, where

1. I is an input set or function and includes the environment E and may or may not be a specific function of time.
2. Ω is an output set or function which operates on the environment E and may or may not be a specific function of time.
3. α is a forward transfer mapping or function where the range of the mapping or function determines the domain of behavior of the system.
4. Z is a performance evaluation mapping or function which operates on the input and output to indicate the behavior of the system with respect to the goals and constraints of the system.
5. γ is a system parameter mapping or function which transforms the performance measure into appropriate system parameters generally in a manner such that the future behavior improves in some sense.

6. Q is a state set or function whose value selects a subset of the domain of behavior of the system.

5.6 HOMEOSTAT

The homeostat is one of the first physical realizations which encompassed the concepts of learning without a teacher and was developed by Ashby as an example of an ultrastable system. The word homeostat was derived from the word homeostasis, which describes a process which is stabilizing, such as the physiological process of temperature control.

The homeostat developed by Ashby [9] contains four identical interconnected units where each unit has a magnetically deflected pointer or indicator on top with an appropriate sensing mechanism to determine the relative position of the pointer. The position of the pointer is controlled by several internal parameters; Ashby used the sum of three magnetic fields to provide energy to deflect the pointer. A diagram of one unit of the homeostat is given in Figure 5.5. The deflection of the pointer, M, is proportional to the algebraic sum of the currents in A, B, and C. D is a feedback sensor which through potentiometer P and reversing switch X provides some feedback into the system. The magnitude and direction of the currents in coils A, B, and C are determined by the positions of the three 25-position stepping switches U_1, U_2, and U_3, respectively. The magnitude and direction at each switch position is determined a priori from a table of random numbers. New positions for

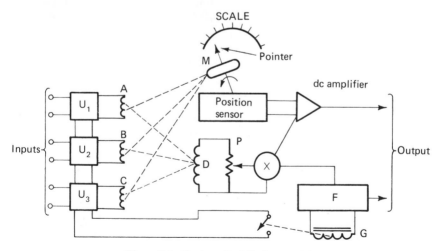

Figure 5.5. Single unit of the homeostat.

the three selectors U_1, U_2, and U_3 are initiated by the closure of relay G, which is governed by the value of the essential variable F. The relay G is energized when the output current exceeds some preset value. Also, the position sensor is adjusted to provide an output of 0 volts of direct current when the pointer is deflected to half-scale.

Four units identical to the unit illustrated in Figure 5.5 are interconnected such that the output of each unit is connected to an input on each of the other units. Thus, when the system is turned on, the pointers are moved by the currents from the other units, which in turn change the currents, etc. The system operates as follows: The essential variable is sampled at specific intervals, say every T seconds, and if the essential variable is within acceptable limits, the stepping switch positions are not altered, and, conversely, if the essential variable is not within acceptable limits, the stepping switch positions are changed.

Thus, the goal of the system is to maintain the essential variables within acceptable limits. This is accomplished by changing the system parameters when one or more of these variables are exceeded until the value of the essential variables are within acceptable limits. This process can be thought of as a search for an acceptable set of system parameters in the n-dimensional space of all possible solutions, as illustrated in Figure 5.6 for a two-dimensional solution space. Note that the homeostat must search a four-dimensional space. Here, the initial state of the system is not in an acceptable region, and the stepping switches are moved seven times until the essential variables are within acceptable limits. Note that the nature of the homeostat forces the search of the space to be random and that it is possible for all but one state of the system to be tried before the acceptable state is found. For the complete homeostat with four sets of stepping switches (one set in each

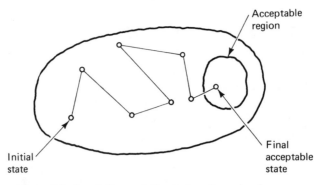

Figure 5.6. Search for a solution in two-dimensional space.

unit), there are 390,625 possible states; thus, it is possible to require that 390,624 states be tried before the acceptable one is found. It is also clear that if the range of perturbation of the collection of pointers is within the range of selection by the stepping switches (a state of the system exists which will control all possible pointer conditions), the system will be ultrastable.

The homeostat can now be examined with respect to the models presented earlier. The input or environment of the system is represented by the positions of the pointers. The forward transfer element consists of the amplifiers, the present position of the stepping switches, and the coils. The output is the magnetic fields which deflect the individual pointers. The performance evaluation element includes the collection of F units, which sense the four essential variables. The output of the PEEL is the position of the relay G, which is transformed into appropriate changes in the state of the stepping switches, which are an embodiment of a system parameter transform element.

5.7 GILSTRAP'S MULTINOMIAL FORWARD TRANSFER ELEMENT

The forward transfer element realization of the homeostat is quite restrictive and certainly difficult to generalize to other systems. A unique and powerful approach to this problem has been expounded by Gilstrap [17]. The objective of his work was to create a method of generating a sufficiently large number of mappings from a set of inputs to a set of outputs such that a "requisite variety" could be realized. In many problems there is a large set of interacting variables which must be combined to create the proper output mapping. Thus, the input variables and the output mappings define non-linear hypersurfaces. These hypersurfaces in turn are described by high-degree multinomials.

Before we can examine Gilstrap's realization, it is necessary to define the three basic forms for multinomials: multilinear, homogeneous, and complete multinomials.

The first class of multinomials forms the basis for this approach and is as follows: A *multilinear multinomial* is a polynomial in m variables in which all possible product pairs, product triples, . . . , and m-way products appear and no variable appears to a degree higher than the first.

The second class of multinomials is needed before we can define the third class: A *homogeneous* multinomial of degree d in m variables is a polynomial where the exponents of the variables in each term sum to d.

The third class is the complete multinomial: A *complete multinomial* of degree n in m variables is the sum of all homogeneous multinomials from zero degree through the nth degree.

For example, the multilinear multinomial in two variables is

$$y = w_0 + w_1 x_1 + w_2 x_2 + w_3 x_1 x_2$$

and the homogeneous multinomial of second degree in two variables is

$$y = w_1 x_1^2 + w_2 x_2^2 + w_3 x_1 x_2$$

where the coefficients w_i are varied to adjust the mapping achieved. Thus, since each coefficient must be adjusted, it is important to know the number of terms which must be handled. For the complete multinomial of degree n in m variables, there are

$$N_c = \frac{n + m}{n! \, m!} = \binom{n + m}{n}$$

possible coefficients. Thus, a complete multinomial of 3^d degree in four variables has

$$N_c = \binom{7}{3} = 35$$

coefficients, which is a significant number of adjustments for a rather simple polynomial. Further, there are $N_M = 2^m$ possible coefficients for a multilinear multinomial in m variables. And for an eight-variable multinomial there are $N_M = 256$ possible coefficients, which is a rather unwieldy number of terms to accommodate.

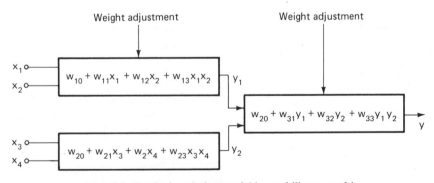

Figure 5.7. Synthesis of four-variable multilinear multinomial with two-variable blocks.

Gilstrap's forward transfer element, which can be used for high-degree multinomials, uses the simple multilinear multinomial in two variables as a building block which can be interconnected to approximate the desired hypersurface of m variables. For example, the four-input multilinear multinomial is developed with the three-building-block interconnection illustrated in Figure 5.7. Here,

$$y_1 = w_{10} + w_{11}x_1 + w_{12}x_2 + w_{13}x_1x_2$$
$$y_2 = w_{20} + w_{31}x_3 + w_{22}x_2 + w_{23}x_3x_4$$

and

$$
\begin{aligned}
y &= w_{30} + w_{31}y_1 + w_{32}y_2 + w_{33}y_1y_2 \\
&= w_{30} + w_{31}(w_{10} + w_{11}x_1 + w_{12}x_2 + w_{13}x_1x_2 \\
&\quad + w_{32}(w_{20} + w_{21}x_3 + w_{22}x_2 + w_{23}x_3x_4) \\
&\quad + w_{33}(w_{10} + w_{11}x_1 + w_{12}x_2 + w_{13}x_1x_2) \\
&\quad \cdot (w_{20} + w_{21}x_3 + w_{22}x_4 + w_{23}x_3x_4) \\
&= v_0 + v_1x_1 + v_2x_2 + v_3x_3 + v_4x_4 + v_5x_1x_2 \\
&\quad + v_6x_1x_3 + v_7x_1x_4 + v_8x_2x_3 + v_9x_2x_4 \\
&\quad + v_{10}x_3x_4 + v_{11}x_1x_2x_3 + v_{12}x_1x_2x_4 + v_{13}x_1x_3x_4 \\
&\quad + v_{14}x_2x_3x_4 + v_{15}x_2x_3x_4x_1
\end{aligned}
\tag{5.7}
$$

which is the fourth-order multilinear multinomial, where

$$v_0 = w_{30} + w_{31}w_{10} + w_{32}w_{20} + w_{33}w_{10}w_{20}$$
$$v_1 = w_{31}w_{11} + w_{33}w_{11}w_{20}$$
$$v_2 = w_{31}w_{12} + w_{33}w_{12}w_{20}$$
$$v_3 = w_{32}w_{21} + w_{33}w_{10}w_{21}$$
$$v_4 = w_{32}w_{22} + w_{33}w_{10}w_{22}$$
$$v_5 = w_{31}w_{13} + w_{33}w_{13}w_{20}$$
$$v_6 = w_{33}w_{11}w_{21}$$
$$v_7 = w_{33}w_{11}w_{22}$$
$$v_8 = w_{33}w_{12}w_{21}$$
$$v_9 = w_{33}w_{12}w_{22}$$
$$v_{10} = w_{33}w_{23} + w_{33}w_{10}w_{23}$$
$$v_{11} = w_{33}w_{13}w_{21}$$
$$v_{12} = w_{33}w_{13}w_{12}$$
$$v_{13} = w_{33}w_{11}w_{23}$$

$$v_{14} = w_{33}w_{12}w_{23}$$
$$v_{15} = w_{33}w_{13}w_{23}$$

It is important to note that a four-variable multinomial requires 2^4 independent coefficients, whereas Eq. (5.7) has 12 independent coefficients. Thus, there are some surfaces which cannot be generated with this interconnection of second-order blocks. The interactions of these coefficients must generally be accounted for in the system parameter transform element. The triangular configuration in Figure 5.7 is not the only way in which multinomials can be realized. For example, an $n \times m$ matrix of two-variable building blocks can be interconnected in a random manner to realize an n-variable $(m-1)$-degree multinomial. The basic requirement to realize a large number of the possible n-variable $(m-1)$-degree multinomials is that there be a *sufficiently rich* interconnection between the blocks. The network of Figure 5.8 can be used to realize a large number of functions since there are a large number of interconnections between the blocks. This network can have cross-product terms of all 8 variables appearing in the output. In practice, larger networks (up to 24 variables) are often used to assure the requisite variety for the problem at hand.

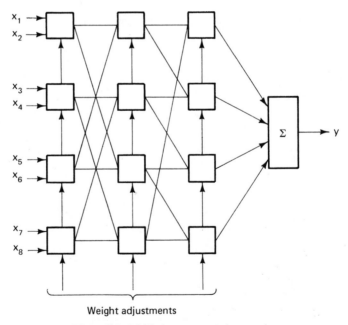

Figure 5.8. Richly interconnected network.

5.8 ADAPTATION AND LEARNING IN STOCHASTIC AUTOMATA [18]

The discussion of stochastic machines given in Chapter 4 showed that the behavior of these machines is determined by a stochastic state transition matrix, and the resulting probabilistic behavior provides a mechanism for achieving variety in the system. The basic implementation of an adaptive or learning system which utilizes this variety can easily be defined in terms of stochastic automata. Now, if we provide information to the machine which causes changes to be made in the values of the entries in the transition matrix, then we have a mechanism for dynamically modifying the machine's behavior, as in the block diagram in Figure 5.3. Models for these systems which are similar to the one given in Chapter 4 will now be examined.

A stationary stochastic automaton [19] is a machine with a finite number of input symbols $I = \{i_1, \ldots, i_m\}$ and a finite number of internal states $Q = \{q_1, \ldots, q_n\}$. The inputs and states are considered at discrete instants of time $t = 1, 2, \ldots$. Now, for each state input pair there exists a probability p_{ij}^k of transfer from state q_i to state q_j with input k, where for any present state q_i

$$\sum_{j=1}^{n} p_{ij}^k = 1 \tag{5.8}$$

For the first representation, it is necessary to define m state transition matrices, one for each input symbol. And, for binary input sources, we need only two matrices, $P(0)$ and $P(1)$, where these matrices generally constitute the forward transfer element of the system. The input 1 is called a penalty and the input 0 is called a nonpenalty (sometimes reward). Now, assume that there is some output or action, z, which corresponds to one or more states of the automaton and that the input, i, at each instant of time is a function of the output during the preceding instant of time,

$$i(t) = C[z(t - 1)] \tag{5.9}$$

where the function $C[\ ]$ is associated with a performance evaluation element. A measure of the behavior of the automaton, A, called the expediency, is the average number of penalties which appear at its input:

$$M(A, C) = \lim_{T \to \infty} \frac{1}{T} \sum_{t=1}^{T} i(t) \tag{5.10}$$

If we now assume that the automaton is operating in a stationary random medium where the behavior associated with state q_v produces a penalty with probability π_v and a nonpenalty with probability $\theta_v = 1 - \pi_v$, then the probability P_{vu} of transferring from state q_v to state q_u is given by

$$P_{vu} = \pi_v P_{vu}^1 + \theta_v P_{vu}^0 \qquad (5.11)$$

where $P_{vu}^1 = 1 - P_{vu}^0$.

Next, let us consider a stochastic automaton in which the transfer probabilities can vary in time. For example, if the transfer from state q_i to q_j results in a nonpenalty input, then it is reasonable to increase the probability of making that transition again. Thus, we increase P_{ij} by some amount and decrease the other probabilities P_{il}, to satisfy Eq. (5.8). Similarly, if the behavior results in a penalty, we decrease P_{il} and increase the other terms P_{ij}. This process provides the basic mechanism for adaptation in a stochastic automaton and constitutes the system parameter transform element of the model given previously. Let us now consider the nature of parameter changes and adaptation in these structures.

Let us assume that we have a set of parameters $\{\alpha\}$ which may be associated with the states of a machine that we would like to vary with respect to some performance function $\Phi(\alpha)$. In most cases one is interested in finding the parameters which optimize, in some sense, the performance of the system, $\Phi(\alpha_{opt})$. And, in general, these parameters describe a multidimensional performance surface much like those described in the previous section. This search for an optimum set of parameters in a multidimensional performance space lies at the core of the problem. In the simplest case this space $\Phi(\alpha)$ is unimodal (only one maximum or minimum and no inflection points) and is free from random fluctuations. A general model [20], however, must include random changes in the description,

$$\Phi(\alpha) = E\{g(\alpha, \rho)\} \qquad (5.12)$$

where $g(\alpha, \rho)$ is a real-valued function on the n-dimensional space α and on a random quantity ρ. The function $E\{\ \}$ is the expectation operator with respect to ρ, which implies that $\Phi(\alpha)$ in Eq. (5.12) is the average of an ensemble of noisy performance surfaces. The latter property coupled with a rather complex system generally make it difficult to handle analytically, and we must resort to so-called on-line adaptive optimization techniques. Now, let us associate a particular parameter α_i with a particular state q_i where the present state is known only in a statistical sense, namely the probability state vector $\psi(\ )$ as defined previously. If we have no a priori information concerning the nature of $\Phi(\alpha)$, then we assign equal probabilities to each state of the system. This corresponds to the maximum entropy condition given in Chapter 4.

The operation of the automaton gives an output which is either punished or rewarded, which then causes changes in the probability of a state transition. The goal of these changes is to minimize the function

$$e = \Phi(\alpha) - \Phi(\alpha_{opt}) \tag{5.13}$$

The succession of state probability vectors $\psi(\ )$ is given by the relationship

$$\psi(t+1) = \psi(t)\mathbf{P} \tag{5.14}$$

where $\mathbf{P}$ is a stochastic transition probability matrix.

Next, we shall assume that we are searching for a maximum in the space $\Phi(\alpha)$. Then *expediency* is said to have occurred if

$$\Phi(\alpha_i) > \Phi(\alpha_j), \qquad \forall\, j \neq i \tag{5.15}$$

in the limit as $t \to \infty$ and the probability of state i at time t is greater than that of state j at time t, $\psi_i(t) > \psi_j(t)$. If there exists one state probability vector for which the system behavior is optimum, then *optimality* is said to have occurred if

$$\lim_{t\to\infty} \psi_i(t) = 1, \qquad \text{if } \Phi(\alpha_i) > \Phi(\alpha_j),\, \forall\, j \neq i$$

and

$$\lim_{t\to\infty} \psi_j(t) = 0, \qquad \forall\, j \neq i \tag{5.16}$$

These concepts can also be defined by considering the limit of the expected value of the performance index:

$$\lim_{t\to\infty} E\left[\sum_{i=1}^{r} \Phi(\alpha_i)\psi_i(t)\right] \begin{cases} = \Phi(\alpha_{opt}), & \text{optimality} \\ < \Phi(\alpha_{opt}), & \text{expediency} \end{cases} \tag{5.17}$$

It might appear then that optimum behavior is the most desirable. However, let us now examine the behavior of an optimum system. The probability of being in some optimum state becomes unity as given in Eq. (5.16), and if there is a change in the environment which requires a new set of optimum parameters, the system cannot change to this new set. On the other hand, if we use an expedient system and limit each state to some less than optimum solution by letting $\psi_i(t) < 1$, $\forall\, i$, then we can always move to some new set of parameters.

5.9 SEARCH TECHNIQUES

One of the central issues in the design of a cybernetic system is the search for the proper parameters. The character of the system often determines the method of search applied. For example, if the system is described by a discrete tree structure such as in games, theorem proving, and problem solving, then it is advantageous to apply heuristic procedures such as those given in Chapter 2. On the other hand, the area of search may be the space of real numbers in a single dimension, the complex plane, or some multidimensional hyperspace. In these instances, we must resort to other techniques in order to find the appropriate parameters.

In the general formulation of search techniques which follows, it is convenient to assume that the environment is relatively constant over the period of time necessary to perform the search. Further, we shall restrict our formulations such that the goal of the search is to find either a maximum or a minimum in our function with respect to the system parameters.

First, consider functions of a single variable, $f(x)$, defined over some domain of x. The *absolute* or *global maximum* of $f(x)$ occurs at a point x_m if $f(x) \leq f(x_m)$ over the domain over which the function is defined. Conversely, the *global minimum* occurs at a point x_m if $f(x) \geq f(x_m)$ over the domain of definition. A maximum which is maximum for only some fraction of the domain of definition is called a *relative* or *local maximum*. A *relative* or *local minimum* can be defined similarly. The single-dimension function in Figure 5.9 illustrates a global maximum and minimum and a local maximum and

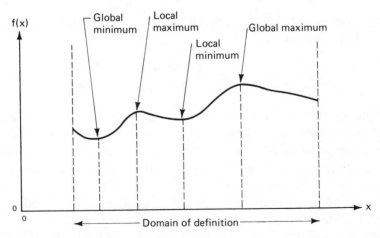

Figure 5.9. Illustration of local global maxima and minima.

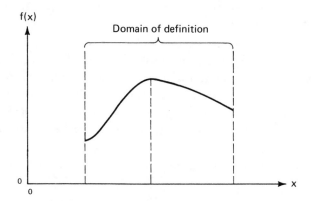

Figure 5.10. Unimodal function—only one maximum.

minimum. Search procedures are greatly simplified if the function of interest is unimodal—having only one maximum or minimum over the domain of definition, as shown in Figure 5.10.

It should be clear that if the function is known explicitly, the maximum or minimum point can easily be found by solving the following expression:

$$\frac{df(x)}{dx} = 0 \qquad (5.18)$$

If this is the case, then of course there is no need for a search. However, in systems which must operate in an unknown or nonstationary environment, this function is not known, and one must search for the proper operating point.

5.10 UNIMODAL SEARCH

A brute force approach to the general search problem divides the x axis into equal intervals, measures the value at each point, and picks the point associated with the maximum value found. The number of search computations with respect to an *exhaustive search* can be reduced for unimodal functions by using the *dichotomous search* procedure. The first step here is to evaluate two points separated by some interval ε in the center of the domain of definition. The half of the domain in which the maximum or minimum lies can now be determined, and two new points can be placed in the center of this interval and so forth until the value of the interval approaches ε. The value of ε clearly establishes the precision of our estimate, and procedures which modify the value of ε as the search progresses have also been developed [21, 22, 23].

A procedure which is similar to the dichotomous procedure but which requires even fewer searches is based on a series of numbers called the *Fibonacci numbers*. The Fibonacci numbers provide an approximation to the *Golden section*, which has some interesting implications in nature and esthetics as well as in search procedures. A discussion of the Golden section is beyond the scope of this text, but the reader will find some interesting discussions in the references [24, 25, 26].

The Fibonacci numbers are generated by the following recursive relationship

$$F_n = F_{n-1} + F_{n-2}, \qquad n > 1 \tag{5.19}$$

where $F_0 = F_1 = 1$ and the sequence is 1, 1, 2, 3, 5, 8, 13, ... To illustrate the Fibonacci search, let us assume that the domain of definition of the function to be maximized (or minimized) is the interval [0, 1], which is given by L_1. The first two points evaluated can now be found by

$$x_1 = 0 + \Delta_2 = \Delta_2$$
$$x_2 = 1 - \Delta_2 \tag{5.20}$$

where Δ_2 is an interval given by

$$\Delta_2 = L_1 \frac{F_{n-2}}{F_n} \tag{5.21}$$

and the ratio $1/F_n$ is equal to or less than the precision with which we wish to estimate the maximum point. For example, if the desired precision is $\leq 5\%$, and $L_1 = 1$, $F_0 = 1$, choose $n = 7$, where $F_0/F_7 = 1/F_7 = 1/21 < 5\%$. After the two initial points, $f(x_1)$ and $f(x_2)$, are evaluated, one of the intervals $(0, \Delta_2)$ or $(1 - \Delta_2, 1)$ will be eliminated and a new interval $L_2 = L_1 - \Delta_2$ will be defined (note that one end of this interval will be either x_1 or x_2):

$$L_2 = L_1 - \Delta_2 = L_1 - L_1\left(\frac{F_{n-2}}{F_n}\right) = L_1\left(\frac{F_{n-1}}{F_n}\right) \tag{5.22}$$

A new interval Δ_3 can be defined with respect to the ends of L_2, say a_2 and b_2:

$$\Delta_3 = L_2 \frac{F_{n-3}}{F_{n-1}} \tag{5.23}$$

The new test points depend on the results of the first evaluations:

$$\left.\begin{array}{l} a_2 = a_1 = 0 \\ b_2 = x_2 \\ x_3 = a_2 + \Delta_3 \end{array}\right\} \quad \text{for } f(x_1) \geq f(x_2) \qquad (5.24)$$

$$\left.\begin{array}{l} a_2 = x_1 \\ b_2 = b_1 = 1 \\ x_3 = b_2 - \Delta_3 \end{array}\right\} \quad \text{for } f(x_1) \leq f(x_2) \qquad (5.25)$$

Evaluation of $f(x_3)$ will eliminate another interval, and the process continues until n iterations are completed where

$$L_n = L_1\left(\frac{F_0}{F_n}\right) \qquad (5.26)$$

This procedure has been shown to be optimum in that it requires fewer evaluations of the function than any other procedure.

Thus far, we have restricted our attention to functions of a single variable. The reasons for this are clear if one considers the problems associated with multidimensional search. For example, consider a two-dimensional function $f(x_1 x_2)$ defined over the domain $0 \leq x_1 \leq 1$, $0 \leq x_2 \leq 1$, where the maximum is to be found within 0.1 in each dimension. A one-dimensional search has 10 different intervals in which the maximum can lie, whereas a two-dimensional search has 10^2 different areas in which the maximum can lie. Also, note that if a one-dimensional search locates the maximum in an interval of 0.1, a two-dimensional search which is reduced to an area of one tenth of the original area locates each dimension only to within $\sqrt{0.10} \simeq 0.316$. Additional dimensionality makes the problem increasingly difficult and costly with respect to computation time. Techniques which are analogous to the single-dimensional methods described earlier and below can also be applied to multidimensional search problems.

The final unimodal technique which is of interest here is the *gradient search* or method of *steepest ascent* or *descent* for maximization and minimization, respectively. Fundamentally, this method measures two points separated by some increment ε and estimates the slope, moves accordingly, estimates the slope again, and stops when the slope reaches some small prespecified value. One problem with this method is immediately evident. Namely, it is possible to move in increments which cause successive points to oscillate about the maximum such that the search never converges. Despite this and other drawbacks, the straightforward formulation and simple implementation of the gradient search method makes it an important and useful cybernetic tool.

Consider a multidimensional continuous differentiable function $f(x)$ $= f(x_1, x_2, \ldots, x_n)$ for which we wish to find the maximum by gradient search. First, define the gradient vector:

$$\nabla f(\mathbf{x}) = \left(\frac{\partial f(\mathbf{x})}{\partial x_1}, \frac{\partial f(\mathbf{x})}{\partial x_2}, \ldots, \frac{\partial f(\mathbf{x})}{\partial x_n} \right) \tag{5.27}$$

The direction of the gradient vector indicates the way in which one must move the vector $\mathbf{x}$ to find the maximum. Since the direction of the maximum* from some present point is known, all one needs to find the maximum is an orderly procedure—an algorithm:

1. Start at some initial point in the domain of definition which is a "best guess" of where the maximum is. Note that in the case where one has no a priori information, any guess is a best guess. (The remaining steps in the algorithm are iterative; that is, one repeats these steps in sequence until the last step is satisfied.)
2. Compute $\nabla f(\mathbf{x}_i)$, where i indicates the ith iteration.
3. Move in the direction of the ith gradient vector, $\alpha_i \nabla f(\mathbf{x}_i)$. α_i is the *step size* of the process and affects both the rapidity of convergence and the precision of the search:

$$\mathbf{x}_{i+1} = \mathbf{x}_i + \alpha_i \nabla f(\mathbf{x}_i) \tag{5.28}$$

4. Terminate the computation and designate $\mathbf{x}_{i+1}$ as the maximum point if $f(\mathbf{x}_{i+1}) - f(\mathbf{x}_i) \leq \varepsilon$, where ε is some a priori specified precision. Otherwise go to step 2.

The criterion given in step 4 is called a *stopping rule* and is just one of many which can be applied [22, 23]. The value of the step size, α_i, used in step 3 is important in gradient search. A value of α_i which is "too" large may cause the search to oscillate about the maximum, thereby inhibiting convergence, while a value of α_i which is "too" small may force many iterations to occur before convergence. An alternative to fixed step size gradient search is an adaptive procedure in which α_i depends on the value of ε calculated in step 4 of the previous iteration. It is important to note that the feasibility of gradient search is a function of dimensionality because the gradient vector computation time increases quickly with increasing dimensionality.

---

*$\mathbf{x}_{i+1} = \mathbf{x}_i - \alpha_i \nabla f(\mathbf{x}_i)$ is used in step 3 when searching for a minimum.

5.11 RANDOM SEARCH

Another approach to search in multidimensional spaces employs a randomization of the points where measurements are made. These *random search* techniques will be examined in four parts: true random search, creeping random search, random search with recalculation, and accelerated random search.

The true random search procedure divides the domain of definition into some finite number of multidimensional cells, say 1000, where the size of the cells and the number tested satisfy the required precision. Next, assume that one of the best 100 cells will satisfy our specifications. Then, if we choose one cell at random, then the probability that it is one of the 100 best is 0.1 and the probability that it is not is 0.9. Since each cell to be measured is chosen independently at random, the probability of finding at least one cell in the best 10% in n samples is

$$P(10\%) = 1 - (0.9)^n$$

Thus, after 44 samples the probability of finding at least one cell which satisfies the search is 0.99. First, the chances of finding a cell which satisfies the search procedure increase rapidly with the number of samples, although there is still a finite probability 0.01 that a cell will not be found. A distinct advantage of true random search is that it is independent of the modality of the space being searched.

A modification of the random search uses a nonuniform distribution from which the sample points are selected as the search continues. The initial point is chosen by making a guess and a nonuniform probability density function is centered on this guess. The consequent samples are then chosen from this distribution, and a cluster of measurements is created. The best of this initial set of samples is then used as the center of a new set of measurements where the same kind of distribution but with a smaller variance is used to generate a new cluster of points. This process is repeated until the search specifications are satisfied. Thus, the search "creeps" toward the maximum (or minimum) with increasing precision. This process is aptly named creeping random search.

A modification of the creeping random search procedure which requires the capability of remembering and comparing the present value with the previous value is random search with recalculation. Here, if the result of a random trial is closer to the maximum/minimum than the previous trial, the center of the search distribution is moved to the new point, and random trials are reinitiated. If no point closer than the present center is found in some number of trials, the search is terminated.

The final search technique of interest here is accelerated random search [27], which combines the best characteristics of the previous methods. It is faster than the other search techniques and is especially suited for multimodal as well as unimodal search. This method also requires an initial guess to start the search. However, in this case if a random trial is closer to the maximum/minimum, another step in the same direction is taken, and if this is a better point, another step in the same direction is selected, etc., until no further improvement occurs. Then, the process moves back to the last point to cause improvement and commences a random search again. The normal distribution is usually used to select the random points. Also, it is possible here to use steps of increasing length while the search is successful, thereby speeding up the search even more.

5.12 SUMMARY

The general formulation of functional models of adaptive, learning, self-organizing, and self-repairing systems has been presented in this chapter. Also, some specific definitions of these terms have been considered.

The homeostat provides us with some historical perspective and a most interesting vehicle for studying the concepts of stability and reliability with respect to our general functional models.

Also, some variations of the stochastic automaton, which lends its consideration within the framework of our functional models of Cybernetic Systems, have been offered.

Several different techniques for searching a parameter space for a maximum or minimum have been presented. Systems in which these techniques are used are covered in later chapters.

These definitions, models, and search techniques provide us with an excellent basis for studying applications in control, communications, and pattern recognition.

5.13 EXERCISES

5.1. Classify the following behaviors and systems with respect to the definitions presented in this chapter:
   (a) A star fish loses a "point" and then grows a new one.

(b) A dual braking system in an automobile.

(c) An antiskid braking system for a vehicle.

(d) The AGC (automatic gain control) in a radio.

(e) A position control for a TV antenna which maintains $\pm 5°$ in winds to 100 miles per hour.

(f) A computer which operates over a temperature range of 0–100°C.

(g) A child who at age 2 can recite the alphabet.

(h) A football player who after a serious accident in which he loses a limb returns as a coach of the team.

5.2. Given the following stochastic automaton, find the probability state vectors $\psi(1)$, $\psi(3)$, $\psi(10)$, and $\psi(11)$ and discuss $\psi(\infty)$:

$$\mathbf{P} = \begin{bmatrix} 0.1 & 0.9 \\ 0.8 & 0.2 \end{bmatrix} \qquad \psi(0) = [0.6 \quad 0.4]$$

5.3. Find the minimum of $f(x) = 3x^2 - 4x + 1$ over the domain of definition $0 \le x \le 1$, where we want 1/32 precision by

(a) Dichotomous search.

(b) Fibonacci search.

5.4. Divide the interval $0 \le x \le 1$ into 32 equal parts. Next take five coins and lay them out to form a binary register. Thus, if all coins are tossed, we can get a random sample in the above domain of definition. Perform a random search on the function $f(x) = 3x^2 - 4x + 1$ and compare this technique with the techniques in Problem 5.3.

5.5. Discuss the relative advantages and disadvantages of expedient and optimum systems. Describe environments in which each of these systems is particularly suited.

REFERENCES

1. WIENER, NORBERT, *Cybernetics*, M.I.T. Press, Cambridge, Mass., 1965.

2. HUXLEY, J., *Evolution: The Modern Synthesis*, Harper & Row, New York, 1943.

3. SHANNON, C. E., "Computers and Automata," *Proceedings of the I.R.E.*, Vol. 41, pp. 1234–1241, 1953.

4. OSGOOD, CHARLES, *Method and Theory in Experimental Psychology*, Oxford University Press, Inc., New York, 1953.

5. KIMBLE, GREGORY A., *Principles of General Psychology*, Ronald, New York, 1956.

6. HELSON, HARRY, "Adaptation Level Theory," in *Psychology: A Study of a Science, Vol. I*, Sigmund Koch, ed., McGraw-Hill, New York, 1959, pp. 565–610.

7. WOOLDRIDGE, DEAN E., *The Machinery of the Brain*, McGraw-Hill, New York, 1963.

8. SKLANSKY, J., "Adaptation, Learning, Self-Repair, and Feedback," *IEEE Spectrum*, Vol. 1, No. 5, pp. 172–174, May 1964.

9. ASHBY, W. R., *Design for a Brain*, 2nd ed., Wiley, New York, 1960.

10. ZADEH, L. A., "On the Definition of Adaptivity," *Proceedings of the IEEE*, Vol. 51, pp. 469–470, March 1963.

11. SKLANSKY, J., "Adaptation Theory—A Tutorial Introduction to Current Research," *RCA Engineer*, pp. 24–30, April–May 1965.

12. SKLANSKY, J., "Threshold Training of Two-Mode Signal Detection," *IEEE Transactions on Information Theory*, Vol. IT–11, No. 3, pp. 353–362, July 1965.

13. ASHBY, W. ROSS, "Principles of the Self-Organizing System," in *Principles of Self-Organization*, H. Von Foerster and G. Zopf, eds., Pergamon, Elmsford, N.Y., 1962.

14. VON FOERSTER, H., "Environments of Self-Organizing Systems," in *Self-Organizing Systems*, M. Yovitts and S. Cameron, eds., Pergamon, Elmsford, N.Y., 1960.

15. ASHBY, W. R., *An Introduction to Cybernetics*, Wiley, New York, 1956.

16. TSYPKIN, YA Z., "Self-Learning—What Is It?," *IEEE Transactions on Automatic Control*, Vol. AC-13, No. 6, pp. 608–612, Dec. 1968.

17. GILSTRAP, L. O., Jr., "Keys to Developing Machines with High-Level Artificial Intelligence," presented at 1971 Design Engineering Conference and Show, ASME, N.Y., April 1971, ASME publication 71-DE21.

18. GLORIOSO, R. M., "Learning in Stochastic Automata," *Proceedings of the 1971 Asilomar Conference on Circuits and Systems*, Sidney R. Parker, ed. Western Periodicals, N. Hollywood, California, 1971.

19. VARSHAUSKII, V. I., and I. P. VORONTSOVA, "On the Behavior of Stochastic Automata with a Variable Structure," *Automatika i Telemekhanika*, Vol. 24, No. 3, pp. 353–360, March 1963.

20. SHAPIRO, I. J., and K. S. NARENDA, "Use of Stochastic Automata for Parameter Self-Optimization with Multimodal Performance Criteria," *IEEE Transactions on Systems Science and Cybernetics*, Vol. SSC-5, No. 4, pp. 352–360, Oct. 1969.

21. COOPER, L., and D. STEINBERG, *Introduction to Methods of Optimization*, Saunders, Philadelphia, 1970.

22. WILDE, D. J., *Optimum Seeking Methods*, Prentice-Hall, Englewood Cliffs, N.J., 1964.

23. MENDEL, J. M., and K. S. FU, *Adaptive, Learning and Pattern Recognition Systems, Theory and Applications*, Academic Press, New York, 1970.

24. GARDNER, M., *Second Scientific American Book of Mathematical Puzzles and Games*, Simon and Schuster, New York, 1961.

25. DANTZIG, T., *Numbers, the Language of Science*, Free Press, New York, 1954.

26. COXETER, H. S. M., *Introduction to Geometry*, Wiley, New York, 1969.

27. GILSTRAP, L. O., JR., H. J. COOK, and C. W. ARMSTRONG, "Study of Large Neuromime Networks," *Final Technical Report AFAZ-TR-316, AD 824470*, Adaptronics, Inc., McLean, Va., Dec. 1967.

6

ADAPTIVE,
LEARNING,
AND
SELF-ORGANIZING
CONTROLLERS

INTRODUCTION

We shall now examine the application of the concepts presented in Chapter 5 in the area of automatic control. Automatic control systems usually incorporate feedback as a means of modifying the present input as some function of the present output. Thus, from the discussion in Chapter 5, the simplest of these systems is adaptive and all automatic feedback control systems are sometimes called cybernetic systems. In this chapter we shall be concerned with control systems which must operate in a class of environments which precludes the use of a simple feedback control system. Some of the systems which we shall study here have been used extensively in the control of high-performance aircraft where the dynamics of the aircraft control problem change with altitude, speed, etc. Also, the basic control systems for the rockets used in the space program make use of adaptive principles in their implementation.

Much of the work in this area makes use of time domain analysis; therefore, we shall first review briefly the basic state variable formulation. Next, the basic types of adaptive control systems will be examined, and their operation will be compared. The class of self-organizing controllers which have been used in both aircraft and industrial control will then be introduced. A new approach to large systems which makes use of a hierarchy of control will then be studied.

6.1 STATE VARIABLE APPROACH

The systems which we wish to control can generally be described by *n*th-order, constant coefficient, linear differential equations of the form

$$\frac{d^n y}{dt^n} + a_{n-1}\frac{d^{n-1} y}{dt^{n-1}} + \ldots + a_1\frac{dy}{dt} + a_0 y = u(t) \tag{6.1}$$

where $y(t)$ is the system output and $u(t)$ is the system input. The n variables in Eq. (6.1),

$$y, \frac{dy}{dt}, \frac{d^2 y}{d+2}, \ldots, \frac{d^{n-1} y}{dt^{n-1}}$$

are called the *state variables* of the system. The *state* of the system is a set of numbers such that given these numbers for some time, the input or forcing functions, and the equations describing the dynamics of the system, one can determine the future state and output of the system. A set of state variables $x_1(t), \ldots, x_n(t)$ can be defined further for the system given by Eq. (6.1) as

$$x_1(t) = y(t)$$
$$x_2(t) = \dot{x}_1(t)$$
$$\vdots$$
$$x_n(t) = \dot{x}_{n-1}(t)$$

This set of state variables can easily be used to write the high-order differential equation as a set of *first*-order differential equations:

$$\dot{x}_1(t) = x_2(t)$$
$$\dot{x}_2(t) = x_3(t)$$
$$\vdots$$
$$\dot{x}_n(t) = -a_0 x_1(t) - a_1 x_2(t) - \ldots - a_{n-1} x_n(t)$$
$$\qquad + u(t) \tag{6.2}$$

These equations can also be written in matrix form as follows:

$$
\begin{bmatrix} \dot{x}_1 \\ \dot{x}_2 \\ \cdot \\ \cdot \\ \cdot \\ \dot{x}_{n-1} \\ \dot{x}_n \end{bmatrix} =
\begin{bmatrix} 0 & 1 & 0 & \cdots & 0 & 0 \\ 0 & 0 & 1 & \cdots & 0 & 0 \\ \cdot & \cdot & \cdot & & \cdot & \cdot \\ \cdot & \cdot & \cdot & & \cdot & \cdot \\ \cdot & \cdot & \cdot & & \cdot & \cdot \\ 0 & 0 & 0 & \cdots & 0 & 1 \\ -a_0 & -a_1 & -a_2 & \cdots & -a_{n-2} & -a_{n-1} \end{bmatrix}
\begin{bmatrix} x_1 \\ x_2 \\ \cdot \\ \cdot \\ \cdot \\ x_{n-1} \\ x_n \end{bmatrix} +
\begin{bmatrix} 0 \\ 0 \\ \cdot \\ \cdot \\ \cdot \\ 0 \\ u \end{bmatrix}
$$

$$(6.3)$$

For example, consider the following second-order differential equation describing the behavior of the simple *RLC* circuit in Figure 6.1:

$$u(t) = Ri(t) + L\frac{di(t)}{dt} + \frac{1}{C} \int_0^\tau i(t)\,dt \tag{6.4}$$

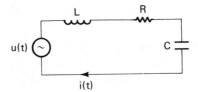

Figure 6.1. *RLC* circuit with forcing function $u(t)$ and no initial energy storage.

We can, of course, consider Eq. (6.4) in terms of charge, q, where

$$i(t) = \frac{dq(t)}{dt} = \frac{dq}{dt} \tag{6.5}$$

and Eq. (6.4) becomes

$$u(t) = L\frac{d^2q}{dt} + R\frac{dq}{dt} + \frac{1}{C}q \tag{6.6}$$

which is a second-order differential equation. Further, we can let $q = x_1$ and

$$\frac{dq}{dt} = x_2 \tag{6.7}$$

and we can rewrite (6.6) as

$$u(t) = \frac{dx_2}{dt}L + Rx_2 + \frac{1}{C}x_1 \tag{6.8}$$

But, from Eq. (6.8) we can write another first-order differential equation:

$$\frac{dx_2}{dt} = \frac{u(t)}{L} - \frac{Rx_2}{L} - \frac{1}{LC}x_1 \tag{6.9}$$

Therefore, Eqs. (6.7) and (6.9) describe the second-order system given by Eq. (6.6) with two first-order equations. Now, as in (6.3), we can write a matrix representation for this system where $\dot{x}_i = dx_i/dt$:

$$\begin{bmatrix} \dot{x}_1 \\ \dot{x}_2 \end{bmatrix} = \begin{bmatrix} 0 & 1 \\ \frac{-1}{LC} & -\frac{R}{L} \end{bmatrix} \begin{bmatrix} x_1 \\ x_2 \end{bmatrix} + \begin{bmatrix} 0 \\ \frac{1}{L} \end{bmatrix} u(t) \tag{6.10}$$

In general, though, there may be one or more forcing functions associated with each of the state variables, and the matrix form is

$$\begin{bmatrix} \dot{x}_1 \\ \dot{x}_2 \\ \vdots \\ \dot{x}_n \end{bmatrix} = \begin{bmatrix} a_{11} & a_{12} & \cdots & a_{1n} \\ a_{21} & a_{22} & \cdots & a_{22} \\ \vdots & \vdots & & \vdots \\ a_{n1} & a_{n2} & \cdots & a_{nn} \end{bmatrix} \begin{bmatrix} x_1 \\ x_2 \\ \vdots \\ x_n \end{bmatrix} + \begin{bmatrix} b_{11} & \cdots & b_{1m} \\ & & \\ \vdots & & \vdots \\ b_{n1} & \cdots & b_{nm} \end{bmatrix} \begin{bmatrix} u_1 \\ \vdots \\ u_m \end{bmatrix} \tag{6.11}$$

The column vector **x** is called the state vector and is similar to the state probability vector **ψ** used in stochastic automata. We can now define a matrix notation for the *system vector differential equation* by

$$\dot{\mathbf{x}} = \mathbf{Ax} + \mathbf{Bu} \tag{6.12}$$

We shall now examine the desired results from our example. The current $i(t)$ is the objective of our analysis; therefore the final equation for the state variable representation is,

$$i(t) = x_2 \tag{6.13}$$

In general, however, the output may be a multivariable response given by the vector **C**, which is a function of both the state variables and the input signals:

$$\mathbf{C} = \mathbf{Dx} + \mathbf{Hu} \tag{6.14}$$

It is now of interest to examine the solution to the vector differential equation (6.12). First, take its Laplace transform

$$s\mathbf{x}(s) - \mathbf{x}(0) = \mathbf{Ax}(s) + \mathbf{Bu}(s)$$

and

$$\mathbf{x}(s) = [s\mathbf{I} - \mathbf{A}]^{-1}\mathbf{x}(0) + [s\mathbf{I} - \mathbf{A}]^{-1}\mathbf{B}\mathbf{u}(s) \qquad (6.15)$$

where $\mathbf{I}$ is the identity matrix. It can be shown [1] that $[s\mathbf{I} - \mathbf{A}]^{-1} = \boldsymbol{\phi}(s)$ is the Laplace transform of $\boldsymbol{\phi}(t) = e^{\mathbf{A}t}$, where, $e^{\mathbf{A}t} \equiv I + (\mathbf{A}t/1!) + ((\mathbf{A}t)^2/2!) + \cdots$ and

$$\mathbf{x}(t) = \boldsymbol{\phi}(t)\mathbf{x}(0) + \int_0^t \boldsymbol{\phi}(t - \tau)\mathbf{B}\mathbf{u}(\tau)\, d\tau \qquad (6.16)$$

The matrix $\boldsymbol{\phi}(t)$ is called the fundamental or transition matrix and describes the natural or unforced response of the system, $\mathbf{u} = 0$:

$$\mathbf{x}(t) = \boldsymbol{\phi}(t)\mathbf{x}(0) \qquad (6.17)$$

The relationship between Eq. (6.17) and the transition matrices used for stochastic automata should now be clear: They are the same.

Now if we consider the unforced or natural response expression from Eq. (6.15) with $x(0) = 0$, i.e., zero initial conditions,

$$s\mathbf{x}(s) = \mathbf{A}\mathbf{x}(s)$$

and

$$[s\mathbf{I} - \mathbf{A}]\mathbf{x}(s) = 0 \qquad (6.18)$$

It can be shown [2] that Eq. (6.18) has a nontrivial solution if and only if

$$p(s) = \text{determinant } [s\mathbf{I} - \mathbf{A}] = 0 \qquad (6.19)$$

Further, the matrix

$$\mathbf{K} = s\mathbf{I} - \mathbf{A} \qquad (6.20)$$

is called the *characteristic matrix* of the matrix $\mathbf{A}$ and the determinant of Eq. (6.19) is called the *characteristic function* of $\mathbf{A}$. The function $p(s)$ is, in general, a polynomial of degree n, where $\mathbf{A}$ is an $n \times n$ matrix. The n roots of Eq. (6.19) are called the *eigenvalues* of the matrix $\mathbf{A}$, and the substitution of each of these values into Eq. (6.18) yields the eigenvectors of the matrix $\mathbf{A}$.

For example, find the eigenvalues and eigenvectors of the following matrix:

$$\mathbf{A} = \begin{bmatrix} 1 & -1 \\ 3 & 1 \end{bmatrix} \qquad (6.21)$$

First, form the characteristic function of $\mathbf{A}$,

$$p(s) = \det \begin{bmatrix} s-1 & +1 \\ -3 & s-1 \end{bmatrix} = s^2 - 2s + 4 = 0$$

and the eigenvalues of $\mathbf{A}$ are

$$s_1, s_2 = 1 \pm j\sqrt{3}$$

The eigenvectors can now be found by first substituting s_1 into (6.18),

$$\begin{bmatrix} +j\sqrt{3} & +1 \\ -3 & +j\sqrt{3} \end{bmatrix}\begin{bmatrix} x_1 \\ x_2 \end{bmatrix} = 0 \tag{6.22}$$

which gives $x_2 = -j\sqrt{3}\,x_1$, and values of $x_1 = 1$ and $x_2 = -j\sqrt{3}$ are a solution of Eq. (6.22) and the eigenvector is

$$\mathbf{x}(1 + j\sqrt{3}) = c\begin{bmatrix} 1 \\ -j\sqrt{3} \end{bmatrix}$$

Similarly, the eigenvector for $S = 1 - j\sqrt{3}$ is

$$\begin{bmatrix} -j\sqrt{3} & 1 \\ -3 & -j\sqrt{3} \end{bmatrix}\begin{bmatrix} x_1 \\ x_2 \end{bmatrix} = 0 \tag{6.23}$$

and $x_2 = j\sqrt{3}\,x_1$ and the eigenvector is

$$\mathbf{x}(1 - j\sqrt{3}) = c\begin{bmatrix} 1 \\ j\sqrt{3} \end{bmatrix}$$

The factor c in the eigenvectors above indicates that these values are solutions for any value which multiplies each element by an arbitrary constant. Consideration of Eq. (6.23) gives

$$-j\sqrt{3}\,cx_1 + cx_2 = 0 \tag{6.24}$$

Substituting the terms in the eigenvector into (6.24),

$$-j\sqrt{3}\,c \times 1 + c(j\sqrt{3}) = 0$$

which is satisfied for all c.

6.2 ADAPTIVE CONTROL SYSTEMS

An adaptive control system has two principal functional elements: a plant to be controlled and a controller where the controller design is based on a nominal but inexact mathematical model of the plant and/or its environment, and a method for altering the controller structure in a dynamic manner. A functional block diagram of an adaptive controller is given in Figure 6.2,

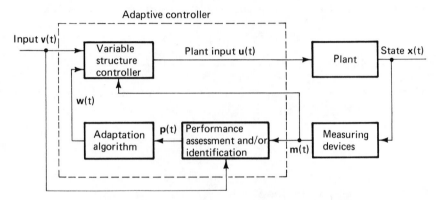

Figure 6.2. Functional block diagram of an adaptive control system.

where the fundamental system variables may be state vectors as defined in the previous section. The goal of the adaptive system is to achieve satisfactory response of the plant state $x(t)$ to an input $v(t)$, where the input is not normally known a priori. A set of inputs is applied to the controller, which generates an input to the plant. The measuring devices then make either direct or indirect measurements on the plant state. These measurements are compared with the input $v(t)$ to determine the present performance vector $p(t)$, which is mapped by the adaptive algorithm into a weighting input $w(t)$. The inputs, $m(t)$ and $w(t)$, to the variable structure controller provide the driving functions for modifying the relation between the command and plant inputs. Thus, the nominal design is dynamically changed to improve system behavior.

This functional model of an adaptive control system is, of course, similar to the general models given in Chapter 5. The variable structure controller and plant make up the forward transfer element; the measuring devices and the performance assessment/identification functions correspond to the performance evaluation element; and the adaptation algorithm corresponds to the system parameter transfer element. Different forms of the model in Figure 6.2 will be considered in the remainder of this chapter.

6.3 PARAMETER ADAPTIVE CONTROL SYSTEMS

Consider the feedback control system shown in Figure 6.3 where the gain of the amplifier, A, can be varied by some external control from an adapta-

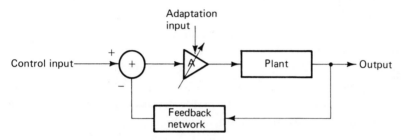

Figure 6.3. Feedback control system with adaptive gain.

tion algorithm, for example. Control theory provides techniques for studying the behavior of these systems with respect to gain, plant dynamics, and the feedback network. Another configuration places the adaptive gain element in the feedback loop and will be considered later in an example. The total system behavior in many cases can be varied over a wide range by changing the gain element. Thus, many systems can be adapted to perform properly over a range of environmental conditions by changing only the gain parameter. This type of control is called a parameter adaptive control system [3], which can be defined as follows:

A *parameter adaptive control system* is an adaptive system in which the controller structure contains elements of a set of adaptive elements that are adjusted according to a specified adaptation algorithm.

These systems have been used extensively for controller realization [4] and form an important class of adaptive controllers. The operation of these systems generally assumes that the environment is stationary for some fixed interval in time, and the plant and its environment are usually described by linear differential equations. The starting point in the design also requires that there exists some a priori information about the plant structure and the range of the change in coefficients which might be expected. Thus, the initial plant structure is tested and evaluated by the performance assessment system for the first time interval of operation, and appropriate changes in the system gains are made by the adaptation algorithm. These gains are used over the next interval, and the process is repeated during each interval.

The performance assessment/identification element is given the task of identifying the state of the plant and the environment in order to initiate changes in the system parameters. Thus, the process of identification is crucial in adaptive controller designs. There are two methods of plant identification [3] which have been defined: explicit and implicit.

The *explicit identification* schemes are directed toward determining the equations of state directly from observations of the system's behavior. Continuous determination of the system's state equations allows the controller gains to be updated to the proper values with as few as one iteration of the gain computation. Thus, explicit plant identification techniques have the advantage of being able to adapt rapidly to changes in the plant environment.

Next, let us examine the explicit identification problem for a system described by the following first-order equation,

$$\dot{x}(t) = a(t)x(t) + u(t) \tag{6.25}$$

where $a(t)$ is assumed to be slowly varying with respect to the response time of the system. Hence, we consider Eq. (6.25) to have constant coefficients. Also, $u(t)$ is the plant input and is given by

$$u(t) = v(t) - k(t)x(t) \tag{6.26}$$

where $k(t)$ is an adaptive gain in the feedback loop and $v(t)$ is the system input function. Now, some mechanism must be provided for determining the exact value, $a(t)$, or an estimate of the coefficient $\hat{a}(t)$.

This value is then used to adjust the feedback gain, and, in this case, according to the criterion,

$$\hat{a}(t) - k(t) = b \tag{6.27}$$

where b is the fixed gain value which produces some a priori designated desirable behavior. Solving Eq. (6.27) for $k(t)$ and substituting the result into Eq. (6.26), we obtain the plant input as a function of the system input, $v(t)$; the system parameter estimate, $\hat{a}(t)$; and the plant state, $x(t)$:

$$u(t) = v(t) - [\hat{a}(t) - b]x(t) \tag{6.28}$$

The final system equation for the closed-loop control system is

$$\dot{x}(t) = [a(t) - \hat{a}(t) + b]x(t) + v(t) \tag{6.29}$$

and if the estimate is correct, then $\hat{a}(t) = a(t)$ and Eq. (6.29) reduces to

$$\dot{x}(t) = bx(t) + v(t) \qquad (6.30)$$

which is the desired system response. The resulting adaptive control system with explicit identification is shown in Figure 6.4.

One of the important considerations when analyzing an adaptive control system is its convergence to the desired behavior. Here, two questions must be answered: (1) Does the system converge at all? (2) Does the system converge rapidly enough to assure stability through the convergence interval? The answer to the first question is that, in general, one can assure so-called asymptotic stability, namely, for $v(t) = 0$,

$$x(t) \longrightarrow 0 \quad \text{as} \quad t \longrightarrow \infty \qquad (6.31)$$

For example, the system described by Eq. (6.3) has as a solution for $v(t) = 0$

$$x(t) = ce^{bt} \qquad (6.32)$$

and one can guarantee asymptotic stability by specifying $b < 0$ in the system design. This design specification can easily be extended to general n-input systems [1].

The answer to the second question is not quite as straightforward as the

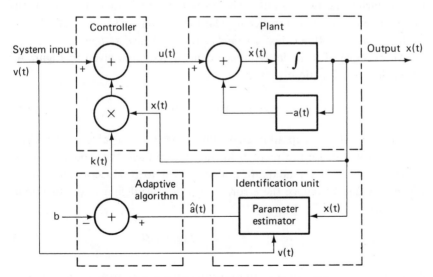

Figure 6.4. Adaptive control system using explicit identification.

first, as there are several generally unknown factors which must be considered. First, the parameter estimation process may not be error-free, thereby causing incorrect adaptation. Also, the rate at which identification errors go to zero initially determines the stability or potential instability of the system. Finally, the delays associated with gain adjustment contribute to the fact that a temporary instability in the system may exist until the parameters have converged and the gains are adjusted.

The process of explicit plant identification has tacitly assumed that a parameter estimator can, in fact, be designed. In general, identification can be accomplished if enough output variables of the system are measured such that the status of the unknown parameters can be determined. If this is true, the parameters are said to be *observable*. There are several techniques which have been developed for identifying plant parameters; however, a detailed study of these techniques is beyond the scope of this text. Certain aspects of this problem are similar to the pattern recognition problem which will be treated later.

Now, consider a system in which some or all of the plant parameters cannot be identified. In this case, we must use an *implicit identification* [3] technique in which specific output variables are compared with the desired performance. This comparison is easily made by driving both the system and a model of the system with unknown parameters. The model produces the proper output for the given input functions, and an error can be generated by comparing the two outputs. The error function is then used to modify the parameters of the controller to adapt the system. This kind of adaptive control system is often called a *model reference control system*.

An example of a model reference control system is given in Figure 6.5 where the error function is given by

$$e(t) = y(t) - y_m(t) \tag{6.33}$$

The objective of the adaptation algorithm is to form a variable feedback gain $k(t)$ which will cause the plant behavior to approach the model behavior.

The function of the adaptation algorithm is to produce a function $\dot{k}(t)$ which will tend to reduce the error. To do this, we define a cost functional of the form

$$J[e(t)] = J = \int_t^{t+T} L(e(\lambda))\, d\lambda \tag{6.34}$$

A functional depends on the time history of its argument rather than on a single value of the argument as with functions. The term $L(e(\lambda))$ is a known,

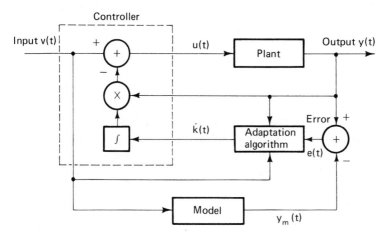

Figure 6.5. Model reference adaptive control system.

scalar, positive, differentiable function with the following properties:

$$L(0) = 0$$
$$L(e) > 0 \qquad \text{for } \bar{e} \neq \bar{0}$$

(6.35)

The function usually chosen is

$$L(e) = \tfrac{1}{2}e^2$$

(6.36)

where the error signal is generally a scalar rather than a vector. The interval $t \leq \lambda \leq t + T$ is a critical parameter in the determination of system adaptation. For example, if the interval is too short, then there is insufficient information concerning the error to make appropriate changes in the controller parameters. One generally tries to make T large enough to include the influence of all the plant parameters on the error functional. As a lower limit one can use the settling time of the model:

$$T > \tau_M$$

The objective of the changes which we make in the gain parameter is to minimize the value of the functional given by Eq. (6.34). However, the relationship between the gain and the functional is not generally known a priori. Thus, we must rely on search techniques to find the value of gain which minimizes the functional, J. To do this, a small change is made in the gain; the error change is observed; and if the value of the functional increases, we reverse the direction of the gain change; and if the value of the functional decreases, we continue to change the gain in the same direction. This process, a realization of the *gradient search or steepest descent technique*, considers a gain change, Δk, which is given by

$$\Delta k = -\alpha \frac{\partial J}{\partial k} \qquad (6.37)$$

where α is a positive constant which specifies the step size of the gain change. The value of α is chosen such that several integration intervals T are needed before the final value of gain k is achieved, thereby causing the system adaptation time, T_A, to be much greater than τ_M:

$$T_A \gg \tau_M$$

There are several specific algorithms for performing gradient search in adaptive control systems [1, 5]; however, further pursuit of them is beyond the scope of this text.

It should now be clear that with implicit identification control systems, one may not know what the ideal values of the gains are; only the direction of change is indicated within these systems. Thus, unlike the explicit schemes, it usually takes several iterations for the gains to converge and, hence, for the system to adapt to plant changes. Further, since adaptation is usually slow, it is often difficult to assume that the plant parameters are constant over the adaptation interval, T_A. This, compounded by the fact that the adaptation algorithm is nonlinear, makes analysis of implicit identification adaptive controllers a difficult task indeed and often makes the prediction of stability much more difficult than for explicit systems.

6.4 LEARNING CONTROL

The control systems considered thus far have been limited to making controller changes based on the instantaneous present performance measure or the performance averaged over some interval just before the present time, and they do not make extensive use of the results of previous measurements in the computation of the new parameters. It then seems reasonable that, for example, if the gradient in an implicit system is in the same direction and improves performance for some n measurements, an increase in the value of α may speed up the convergence process. On the other hand, as one approaches a minimum, a large α would cause the system to overshoot the minimum, and a decrease in α would seem appropriate. The addition of these features to an adaptive control system requires the following changes:

1. The performance resulting from a controller *change* must be classified as "good" or "bad" and the system must be "rewarded" or "punished," respectively.
2. The system must be capable of using the results of past behavior in determining present behavior; i.e., it must have memory.

Therefore, a *learning control system* has been defined as an adaptive controller with the additional properties given above [3, 6, 7]. This definition of a learning control system is not consistent with the definitions given in Chapter 5. Change 1 above merely adds another constraint to the PEEL and change 2 gives the PEEL memory. No specific time constraint on performance, a necessary condition for a learning system as defined in Chapter 5, is applied explicitly. On the other hand, most control systems in a real environment have an implicit time constraint in that performance must be acceptable in some "reasonable" period of time for the system to be useful. Learning control systems generally exhibit performance which gradually improves with time (expediency) and learning usually refers to the fact that either an improvement in the estimate of some information has occurred or some system parameters have been properly identified (learned). The amount of memory in a learning controller will determine how much past experience can be used to estimate present conditions and, hence, the extent of past experience which can be used in learning is a function of memory length. For the remainder of this chapter, we shall use the term learning·controller to refer to an adaptive controller with the changes given above.

The relative behavior of a learning controller with respect to an adaptive controller can easily be seen by examining the optimization of the cost functional given in Figure 6.6 with respect to the gain k. Examination of Figure 6.6 indicates that the point of *optimum* behavior for this system corresponds to the gain k_{opt}, where the cost functional is minimum. Here, *expedient* behavior occurs if the system gain becomes arbitrarily close to k_{opt} and gets closer asymptotically as the system operation progresses. The optimum gain is k_{opt}, where the cost is minimized, and if we are at gain k_i initially, it is desirable to choose a gain k_j such that

$$J(k_j) < J(k_i) \tag{6.38}$$

This assures at least expedient system behavior. Now, if the value of α is

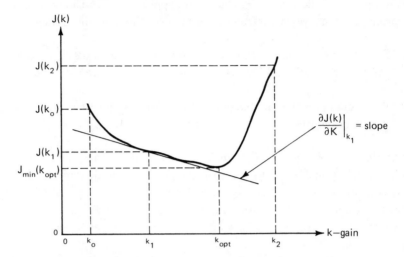

Figure 6.6. Gradient optimization of cost functional.

large, then, starting with gain k_1, it is possible for the new value of gain to be

$$k_2 = k_1 - \alpha \frac{\partial J}{\partial k}\bigg|_{k_1} \qquad (6.39)$$

where $J(k_2) < J(k_1)$. This behavior is typical of implicit adaptive systems. On the other hand, a learning system might remember $J(k_1)$, compare it to $J(k_2)$, *punish* the system by reducing α, go back to gain k_1, and try again. Similarly, given an initial gain of k_0 and a new gain k_1 which satisfies Eq. (6.38), the system would be *rewarded* and the value of α increased.

The additions to an adaptive control system in order to make a learning control system certainly increase the complexity and cost of the control system, and one may ask why one would use a learning rather than an adaptive controller. First, one may say that the learning controller constructs a "model" of the plant by building a set of input-output relationships in its memory and by using this set of data to compute each new set of gains. Thus, less a priori information concerning the behavior of the plant is needed to design a learning controller than to design an adaptive controller, and cost and complexity must be balanced against the available a priori information concerning the plant dynamics. The concept of a self-organizing controller includes many of these features; therefore, we shall reserve study of examples of these processes for the next section.

6.5 SELF-ORGANIZING CONTROLLERS

The definition of a self-organizing system is an adaptive or learning system in which the initial state is either unknown, a random variable, or a "don't care." Thus, it is of interest to look at the simple system given in Figure 6.7, which makes use of probability state variable (PSV) encoding [8, 9]. PSV encoding associates a probability distribution with the system

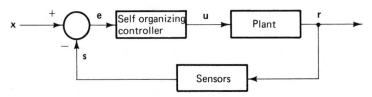

Figure 6.7. Self-organizing controller configuration.

parameters which are to respond to performance evaluation. This is contrasted with the deterministic values of the system parameters used in adaptive and learning controllers. PSV encoding is accomplished by a PSV module located in the self-organizing controller. The function of the PSV is to identify one of the plant parameters, and multiple parameter identification can be accomplished with a combination of PSV units. The identification which takes place in the PSV, however, results in a signal which is related to the parameter being identified only in a statistical sense. In general, these PSV identifications may be described as implicit stochastic identification without the use of a model. An interesting aspect of the configuration given in Figure 6.7 is that the performance assessment takes place within the self-organizing controller, which is in the forward loop. The input **x** and the sensor feedback **s** are compared to form an error vector **e**, which is applied to the self-organizing controller. The output of the controller **u** drives the plant, which in turn acts on the environment, causing the reaction **v**, which is measured by various sensors in the system to form the feedback vector **s**. The sensors in these systems must be chosen such that the performance measured is appropriate to the system goals and constraints. In other words, we must ensure that the sensors do measure the "essential" variables.

Now, if we assume that the sensors can be defined correctly, it is of interest to examine the structure of a self-organizing controller in greater detail. A self-organizing controller for a single variable error vector is given in

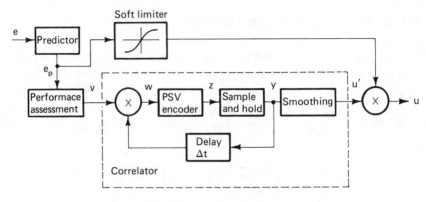

Figure 6.8. Self-organizing controller.

Figure 6.8. The predictor, which has the transfer function

$$\frac{e_p}{e}(s) = 1 + Ts \tag{6.40}$$

provides lead compensation, which can also be described as an augmented derivative of the error signal. Note that here we consider the system variables as scalars rather than vectors. This simple first-order linear predictor has been used successfully in several controllers with both low- and high-order plants. The error function e_p is then processed by the performance assessment module to produce an output which corresponds to a "reward" or "punishment" of the system's behavior. Before we describe the remainder of the controller, let us examine the performance assessment module in some detail.

Since the performance assessment must be based on the predicted error, e_p, let us now define the requirements placed on this function. The augmented derivative representation of Eq. (6.40),

$$e_p = e + T\dot{e} \tag{6.41}$$

provides clues to these requirements. First, the objective of the system is to reduce the predicted error to zero, which corresponds to the condition

$$e = -T\dot{e} \tag{6.42}$$

where the error equals minus the error rate times the prediction time constant T. Equation (6.42) defines a switching line in the phase plane given in Figure 6.9. Now, if we assume that initially the system error e_p corresponds to the point A, then the perpendicular distance from A to the switching line

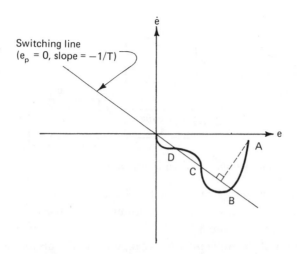

Figure 6.9. Phase plane and switching line for $e_p = 0$.

is a measure of the predicted error e_p. Thus, from A the error is driven toward the switching line, and when e_p changes sign by crossing the switching line at B, the control actions must be reversed and so forth at C and D, as shown in Figure 6.9. Once the switching line is acquired, the error behavior is given by the solution to the homogeneous differential equation (6.43), which is

$$e(t) = e^{-t/T} \tag{6.43}$$

and the error exponentially decreases to zero. Thus, the primary task of the self-organizing controller is to assure acquisition of the switching line, and minimization of the integral of predicted error over each assessment interval, Δt, is a reasonable performance criterion:

$$P(t) = \int_{t_i}^{t_i + \Delta t} |e_p| \, dt \tag{6.44}$$

It can be shown [8] that a simple performance value function for second-order systems which produces a reward, $+1$, and punishment, -1, and satisfies the essential requirements of Eq. (6.44) is

$$V = -\text{sgn} \, e_p \, \text{sgn} \, \ddot{e}_p \tag{6.45}$$

Thus, when the error and error acceleration have opposite signs, indicating that the predicted error is moving toward the switching line, the system is rewarded. Conversely, if e_p and $\ddot{e}_p$ have the same sign, indicating a trajectory

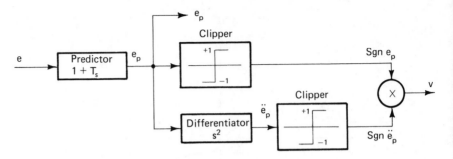

Figure 6.10. Performance assessment module.

away from the switching line, the system is punished. A block diagram of a performance assessment module which implements the function given in Eq. (6.45) is given in Figure 6.10.

The location of the differentiator breakpoints in the performance assessment module must be related to the delay interval in the correlator in order to minimize the effects of noise common to differentiator circuits [10]. Although the performance assessment module given in Figure 6.10 was designed for second-order systems, it has been used effectively in higher-order systems by decreasing the time interval of the correlator. The increased number of correlations per unit time allows the second-order assessment to follow the higher-order responses of the plant.

The correlator compares the previously coded output with the reward or punishment associated with the system. The duration of the correlator delay Δt is from 10^{-4} to 10^{-2} times the closed-loop system response time depending on the order of the plant and the band pass of the performance assessment module.

The actual correlation process occurs in the following manner. The output, $y(t - \Delta t)$, is multiplied by $+1$ or -1, the performance assessment, and the average of several of these individual correlations is derived in the smoothing filter in the first stage of the PSV encoder, as shown in Figure 6.11.

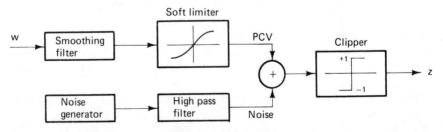

Figure 6.11. Probability state variable (PSV) encoder.

The main purpose of the PSV encoder is to provide a drive signal for the plant, which is decoupled from the high-frequency system components and noise in the sensors. The PSV signal also provides a drive which allows "experimentation" and hence the opportunity to find better system parameters by a guided random search. Thus, the smoothed, correlated signal is passed through a soft limiter which merely constrains its dynamic range to correspond to the magnitude of the noise signal to produce the probability control voltage (PCV). This limiting action does not allow the probability of any one value of the PCV to become unity or zero, thus assuring expedient behavior. The PCV is then corrupted by additive noise, thereby creating a signal where the sign of the output is a stochastic process. The noise signal is carefully tailored by a high-pass filter in order to eliminate low-frequency energy within the plant passband from the plant actuating signal, u, which may excite low-frequency oscillations in the system. The high-frequency noise added to the PCV also tends to decrease the statistical correlation between the controller output signals and the sensor noise, thus allowing the use of high-gain controllers without the usual concomitant instabilities. Finally, the hard limiter in the PSV encoder is used as a decision device, which has an output of $+1$ if the PSV plus noise signal is greater than zero and -1 if this summed signal is less than zero. The relative probability of a $+1$ or -1 PSV output is a direct function of the PCV and hence of w.

Referring to Figure 6.8, the output of the PSV encoder, z, is sampled periodically and held constant at either $+1$ or -1 for a time interval Δt by the sample and hold element. Thus, plant responses to random experiments generated by the PSV encoder can be evaluated over the finite interval Δt, which allows the plant sufficient time to respond to the experimental control signal. Since the sample rate is greater than the response rate of the plant, it is necessary to smooth the correlator output with a low-pass filter or digital register to produce a final correlator output u', which will not excite instabilities in a quick-reaction plant.

The plant-driving signal, u, is derived by multiplying the correlator output by a nonlinear function of the predicted error e_p. This is sometimes referred to as actuation logic. The nonlinear function preserves sgn e_p while giving a gradual change in sign as e_p approaches zero—the switching line. This feed-forward sign information causes the control signal to reverse polarity quickly as the switching line is crossed. This path is needed because the delay in the assessment-correlation process is generally too long to provide the tight control needed in this region of the phase space. Thus, if the predicted error and the correlator are in agreement, the plant signal is positive, and, conversely, the plant signal is negative if these two signals do not agree.

The overall behavior of a self-organizing controller is as follows: Initially, there is no information concerning which polarity of control output produces the proper plant response. The noise signal then generates an experimental control signal which is evaluated by the controller, and if there is some correlation between the trial direction and system performance, this direction of control is continued. On the other hand, if there is no correlation, the system continues to search at random in each direction with equal probability until some correlation is found.

A particularly interesting application of self-organizing controllers is in multiple-input multiple-output control systems where the inputs and outputs are correlated in some unknown and/or time-varying manner. Control of these complex interactive systems is accomplished by searching each response assessment for correlations with each output element, as shown in Figure 6.12, where the correlator and actuation logic are combined as the actuation correlation logic and the sgn e_p feed-forward loops are not shown. Thus, all correlations which drive the system toward a multidimensional switching hyperplane are tested, and the system converges to the proper behavior.

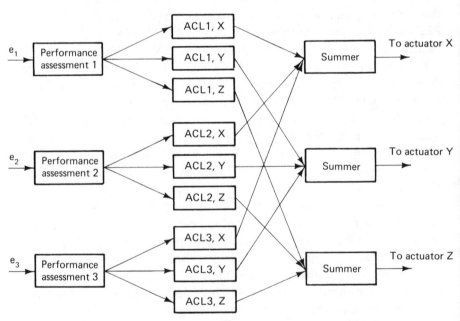

Figure 6.12. Multiple-input/multiple-output self-organizing controller. The sensors have been deleted for clarity.

6.6 HIERARCHAL MULTILEVEL SYSTEMS

The interaction of several actuators in a single goal control problem were considered in the previous section. Now, let us examine some interconnection schemes for several adaptive, learning, or self-organizing controllers where one or more controllers may influence the behavior of some other controller or controllers in a multiple-goal or -subgoal system.

Examples of the concept of hierarchal multilevel systems in both natural and man-made systems are easily found [11]. A most obvious example is the military command and control hierarchy from the president through the commanding generals to the individual private. The structure of management in most corporations is another example of a hierarchal multilevel system.

An example of a hierarchal system in nature is the common alley cat. The highest level is the animal's head, which contains the major overall sensors, ears and eyes; and the effectors, head motion, mouth and jaw; and the highest-level central control and decision device, the brain.

The next level in this system is the body, which serves as an "interface processor" between the highest level (head) and the lowest level, the extremities. There is, of course, the effector action of body motion at this level as well as the various touch, temperature, and kinesthetic sensors. However, the spinal cord, which relays and processes information which flows through the system, is the reason this part of the system is called an interface processor.

The extremities, legs and tail, are the lowest level of this system. The major function performed here is that of an effector. The main sensory action at this level is also associated with touch, temperature, and kinesthetics, while the amount of information processing at these levels is minimal.

The overall goal of the system is to perform the actions needed by coordinating and controlling each of the levels in some way. A model of a multilevel system which may be associated with the cat hierarchy is given in Figure 6.13. In this model, one may consider the first level to be a supremal unit which directs the actions of the lower levels.

Another type of multilevel system is one in which the control is distributed throughout the system. Such a system might operate in the following manner. The highest level of the system is provided with the overall objective by either internal or external means. This level then determines which portions of the task it can perform and how much will be relayed to lower levels. It then

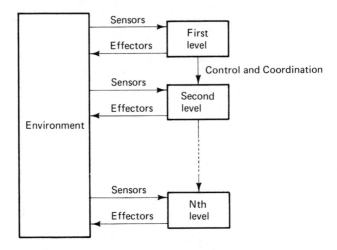

Figure 6.13. Model of hierarchal multilevel system.

sends the remaining tasks to the next lower level, which in turn computes a strategy and so forth until all levels of the system needed are oriented to this task.

The model given in Figure 6.14 illustrates these concepts, where an adaptive, learning, or self-organizing unit is located at each level of the system.

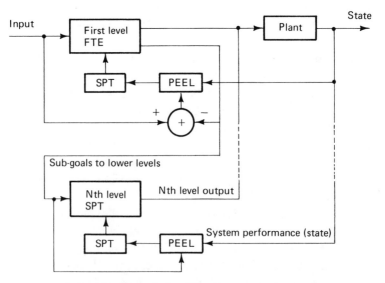

Figure 6.14. Hierarchal multilevel system of adaptive, learning, or self-organizing controllers.

The input to the whole system is presented to the first level, which does what it can and farms the remaining work to the next lower level, etc. The performance at each level is evaluated with respect to the work it "intends" to do—thus, the "summer" at the input to the performance evaluation element.

6.7 SUMMARY

Applications of the concepts of adaptation, learning, and self-organization developed previously in the area of control have been explored in this chapter.

The parameter adaptive control system, one of the simplest systems, has been defined, and the problems of performance assessment/identification have been described. The concepts of implicit and explicit identification and examples of these systems were presented.

The gradient search technique and its advantages and disadvantages in implicit identification systems were used as an example. The variation in gradient step size in response to a reward or punishment was used to introduce the concept of a learning control system.

A specific example of a self-organizing controller which has been applied to the control of high-performance aircraft was presented.

In the last section of this chapter we introduced the problems associated with large systems in which a hierarchy is implied.

6.8 EXERCISES

6.1. Given the accompanying *RC* circuit,
    (a) Find the state variable representation using the voltages across the capacitors as the state variables.
    (b) Find the eigenvalues of system matrix, A.

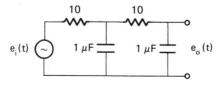

6.2. Describe the behavior of the parameter adaptive system shown here using frequency domain techniques for $A = -5$ and $B = 6$, and find the range of B for stable operation for $A = -5$, $+5$, and $+10$. Note: The system is stable if poles of its transfer function lie in the left half of the *s*-plane.

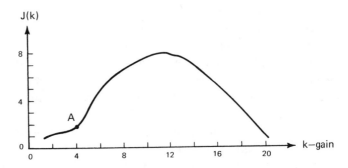

6.3. Describe the behavior of the gradient search technique for the maximum of the cost functional shown here for $\alpha = 10, 5$, and 2, where the system initially is at A.

6.4. Using the cost functional in Problem 6.3, describe the behavior of a learning control system where α can take on any one of the following values: 1, 2, 5, or 10.

6.5. The noise injected within the PSV encoder is one of the interesting features of the self-organizing controllers described in this chapter. Assuming that the soft limiter in the PSV encoder has a range of ± 10 volts, sketch the output of the summer and the PSV encoder for normally distributed noise of 1, 5, and 10 volts RMS (root mean squared) and inputs of 1, 3, and 7 volts. Describe qualitatively the effects of these values of noise on the search behavior of the self-organizing controller. (Hint: Use probability density and distribution functions to describe your results.)

6.6. Describe the behavior of a hierarchal multilevel system found in nature. Also, describe a man-made hierarchal multilevel system.

REFERENCES

1. DORF, RICHARD C., *Time Domain Analysis and Design of Control Systems*, Addison-Wesley, Reading, Mass., 1965.

2. PIPES, L. A., *Matrix Methods for Engineering*, Prentice-Hall, Englewood Cliffs, N.J., 1963.

3. PRICE, C. F., and W. B. KOENIGSBERG, "Adaptive Control and Guidance for Tactical Missles," *ONR, Code 461*, Vols. I and II, report under Contract No. N00014-69-C-0391, The Analytic Sciences Corporation, Reading, Mass., June 1970.

4. EHLERS, H. L., and R. K. SMYTH, "Survey of Adaptive Control Applications to Aerospace Vehicles," *Paper No. 68–970*, AIAA Guidance Control and Flight Dynamics Conference, Pasadena, Calif., Aug. 1968.

5. MENDEL, J. M., and K. S. FU, *Adaptive, Learning and Pattern Recognition Systems, Theory and Applications*, Academic Press, New York, 1970.

6. FU, K. S., "Learning Control Systems—Review and Outlook" IEEE Transactions on Automatic Control, Vol. AC-15, No. 2, pp. 210-221, April 1970.

7. FU, K. S., "Learning System Theory," in *System Theory*, L. A. ZADEH and E. POLAK, editors, McGraw-Hill, New York, 1969.

8. BARRON, ROGER, "Self-Organizing Controllers—Part I," *Control Engineering*, pp. 70–74, Feb. 1968.

9. BARRON, ROGER, "Self-Organizing Controllers—Part II," *Control Engineering*, pp. 69–74, March 1968.

10. *Analysis and Synthesis of Advanced Self-Organizing Control Systems*, Wright Patterson AFB, Ohio, final technical report, Contract AF 33(615)–3673, AFAL-TR-67-93, AF Avionics Laboratory, Adaptronics, Inc., April 1967.

11. MESAROVIC, M. D., D. MACKO, and Y. TAKAHARA, *Theory of Hierarchal Multilevel Systems*, Academic Press, New York, 1970.

7

CYBERNETIC TECHNIQUES IN COMMUNICATIONS SYSTEMS

INTRODUCTION

Cybernetic techniques as applied to communications is the subject of this chapter. These techniques have been particularly useful in systems such as radio transmission of data where fading, noise, and multipath distortion interfere with the communications. Similar problems also occur in wire/telephone-type communications systems where the paths and channels for communications between any two points are generally different each time communications are established. Thus, it is often necessary to learn the status of a channel in order to optimize the receiving system before information can be transmitted and later to adapt the receiver to changes in the channel characteristics.

Another problem which will be examined in this chapter is that of establishing paths between points in a communications network. Here, the paths between adjacent nodes in a network may be out of service or busy, and the routing system must learn the status of the net for proper operation.

7.1 COMMUNICATIONS SYSTEMS

We shall be concerned only with pulse transmission systems in this chapter, and, as most modern communication systems use these techniques, this is not too restrictive. Further, pulse systems are most amenable to the application of adaptive and learning techniques. The representation of a general pulse transmission system is given in Figure 7.1. Here, the information at the input to the system is encoded in some sense. For example, the coding may be simple analog-to-digital conversion, or, if the signal is already in digital form, a parity bit or error correction and/or detection coding may be imposed. This encoded signal drives the modulator, which maps the pulse sequence into an analog wave suitable for transmission over the channel. The channel is, of course, the source of all the problems of communications systems, as they have been known to introduce noise, nonlinearities, and phase and amplitude distortion and to drop out all together. At the receiving end, the demodulator maps the received analog waveform into a pulse sequence which is a "best guess" of the sequence transmitted. The decoder operates on the binary sequence to extract the information originally impressed on the encoder. The overall objective is to transfer the information from the input to the output within some a priori specified low error rate, where the error rate is the average number of disagreements per unit of time between the inputs and the outputs. The encoding and decoding processes require special techniques which are beyond the scope of this text. However, the modulator and especially the channel and demodulator are important here.

Figure 7.1. General pulse transmission system.

For simplicity, the modulation processes which we shall consider represent two kinds of pulse transmission techniques: pulse amplitude modulation (PAM) and pulse code modulation (PCM). These processes are illustrated for a sinusoidal information signal in Figure 7.2. In PAM, the pulse amplitude is a function of the amplitude of the input signal at some instant of time and, in PCM, the sequence of pulses (which may be present or not, 1 or 0) in some interval of time is a function of the amplitude of the input signal at some instant of time. A fundamental requirement in these systems is that the modulating signal be sampled, and the Nyquist criterion or sampling theorem states that a band-limited signal which is sampled at a rate equal to or greater

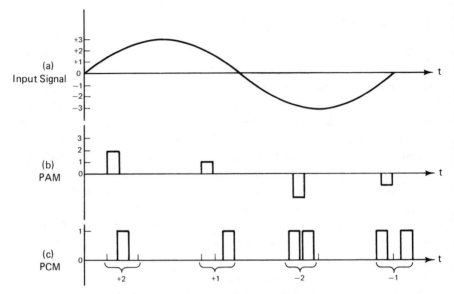

Figure 7.2. Pulse amplitude modulation and pulse code modulation.

than twice the upper band-limited frequency can be reconstructed exactly from these samples. Most information signals of consequence are band-limited, namely they are restricted to within some finite range of frequencies. For example, voice, video, and data signals are band-limited signals albeit to different bands: 300–4000 hertz, 0–5 megahertz, and approximately 0–10 megahertz, respectively.

Also, these modulation techniques require that the range of amplitudes of the input signal be quantized into a finite number of intervals. The range of the input signal in Figure 7.2(a) has been quantized into seven intervals. A PAM system transmits a pulse at each sample time whose amplitude is the quantized value at that time, as illustrated in Figure 7.2(b). In general, a PAM signal can be represented by the following series

$$x(t) = \sum_{k=-\infty}^{\infty} a_k s(t - KT) \tag{7.1}$$

where a_k is the quantized amplitude and $s(t)$ is the pulse shape which carries each element in the sampled sequence through the channel and T is the sample period.

PCM systems, on the other hand, transmit only binary pulses over the channel. The process of PCM carries the PAM technique one step further by coding each sampled quantized element into a sequence of binary digits where each group of N bits represents the quantized amplitude of the signal at that sample time. Thus, in Figure 7.2(c) each group of three bits carries the amplitude information for that sample. A representation of the PCM signal is

$$x(t) = \sum_{k=-\infty}^{\infty} \sum_{n=0}^{N-1} a_{kn} s\left[t - \left(k + \frac{n}{N} T \right) \right] \qquad (7.2)$$

where $a_{kn} = \{0, 1\}$, the binary alphabet, and $s(t)$ is as in Eq. (7.1). Equation (7.2) represents a series of sequences of N pulse intervals per sample period, T, where the pulse shape, $s(t)$, is sent in a pulse interval to represent a 1 and nothing is sent in a pulse interval to represent a 0.

7.2 THE CHANNEL

There are two distinct characteristics of the communications channel with which one must deal when using PAM and PCM. The first is gaussian noise, which is generally modeled as an additive term in a hypothetical noiseless channel. There are several sources of gaussian noise in a communications system, including thermal and shot noise in the transmitting and receiving equipment.

The second characteristic is often associated with multipath distortion wherein there exists more than one path from the transmitter to the receiver in a radio communications system. The effects of multipath distortion are dramatically illustrated when listening to FM stereo or watching color TV as an airplane passes between the transmitter and the receiver. Here either noise or distortion is heard from the FM receiver and the colors wash out on the TV set. A similar effect is observed on wire communications systems called linear distortion.

Linear distortion is generally specified as attenuation and envelope delay as a function of frequency [1]. The envelope delay, which is the derivative of the phase characteristic, is a measure of the relative time of arrival at the channel output of the various frequency components of the input signal. Now, it is a rare channel indeed whose attenuation and/or envelope delay is constant with frequency. Thus, the input signal is distorted as it passes through the channel. This distortion in pulse transmission systems causes an overlap in the arrival of the energy associated with successive symbols called intersymbol interference. If these channel characteristics are known, then it is generally possible to compensate at the receiver to remove the intersymbol interference. However, as suggested previously, the channel is not usually known exactly and has a tendency to vary with time. The range of different possible channel configurations even in a switched telephone network is so large that it is impractical to try to compensate each one. Thus, the problem of compensation (or equalization) of communications channels is one where adaptive techniques are necessary.

Finally, we can model the channel by a dispersion function $G(f)$ and additive noise, as shown in Figure 7.3. $G(f)$ is a transfer function which represents the characteristics of the channel without noise. The noise added to the output of $G(f)$ represents that added to the signal as it passes through the channel.

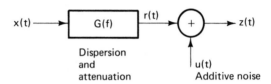

Figure 7.3. Model of the communications channel.

7.3 CHANNEL EQUALIZATION

Now that the problems introduced by the channel have been defined, let us investigate a method for equalizing these adverse effects. The signal transmitted is a series of pulses sent at discrete intervals of time. Therefore, the receiver filter $H(f)$ must be designed so that it can be sampled synchronously to produce an output sequence $\{b_k\}$ which is a best estimate of the input sequence $\{a_k\}$. To understand this problem in detail, it is useful to compare a typical waveform at the input to the receiver with an ideal waveform, as shown in Figure 7.4. The ideal waveform is maximum at the decision time for

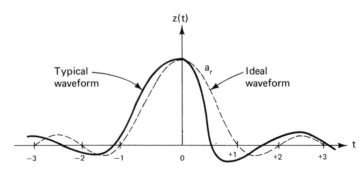

Figure 7.4. Typical received waveform and ideal waveform.

that interval and is zero for all other decision times, whereas the typical received waveform may have its maximum before or after the decision point and is not usually zero at the other decision points. The nonzero values of the received signal at other decision times thus interfere with the values of the other pulses at their decision times causing intersymbol interference. Equalization of the intersymbol interference then requires that the effects of a pulse at times other than its sample time be zero [2].

Let us designate the receiver response, $H(f)$, and sample its output periodically with period T, as shown in Figure 7.5. The output from the receiver can be compared to the transmitted symbol, and we can use a minimum mean-squared error criterion to design the receiver. This is one of several criteria which can be applied in the formulation of the receiver, another is, minimize intersymbol interference [1]. Let us consider the minimum mean squared error,

$$I = E[\{b_k - a_k\}^2] \tag{7.3}$$

Equation (7.3) can be minimized using techniques from the calculus of variations [3] to give

$$H(f) = S^*(f)G^*(f) \sum_{n=-\infty}^{\infty} d_n e^{-j2\pi nTf} \tag{7.4}$$

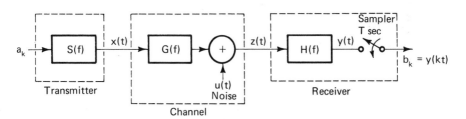

Figure 7.5. Transmitter, receiver, and channel.

where $S^*(f)G^*(f)$ defines a conjugate or matched filter which is optimum for additive white gaussian noise in the channel. The remainder of Eq. (7.4) defines a most interesting structure which consists of a series of delays, since the term $e^{-j2\pi nTf}$ in the frequency domain defines an nT-second delay and a weighted summing net. The last element, called a transversal equalizer, is illustrated in Figure 7.6. The purpose of the matched filter is to reduce the effects of noise while the equalizer reduces the intersymbol interference.

The impulse response of the transversal filter-equalizer is given by

$$e(t) = \sum_{n=-N}^{N} d_n \delta(t - nT) \tag{7.5}$$

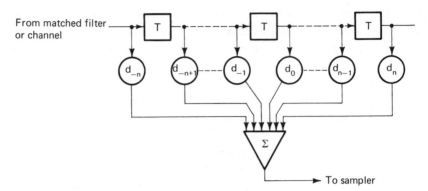

Figure 7.6. Transversal equalizer.

and, from before, the frequency domain response is

$$E(f) = \sum_{n=-N}^{N} d_n e^{-j2\pi n T f} \tag{7.6}$$

Consider an input $x(t)$ to the filter of Figure 7.6; then the output response, $x(t)*e(t)$ is

$$h(t) = \sum_{n=-N}^{N} d_n x(t - nT) \tag{7.7}$$

At the output of the sampler, however, we are concerned only with the value of Eq. (7.7) at the sampling times (kT):

$$h(kT) = \sum_{n=-N}^{N} d_n x[(k - n)T] \tag{7.8}$$

Thus, the output at each time kT is a function of the tap gains d_n and the equalizer input at times $(k - n)T$. Now, given a transmitted signal and a channel corrupted by white noise, we can compute the appropriate matched filter as well as the proper tap gains for the transversal filter. On the other hand, this information is not generally available, and we must incorporate techniques that do not require as much a priori knowledge for effective operation.

First, since we do not usually know $G(f)$ nor can we assume that the noise $u(t)$ is white and normally distributed, we are forced to sacrifice the matched-filter portion of the receiver and rely on the transversal equalizer to improve the detection process. Second, the intersymbol interference can generally be made arbitrarily small as the length of the transversal filter becomes large.

However, the number of delay elements $(2N + 1)$ is restricted, usually by cost, and must be chosen to accommodate the range of channels expected. Therefore, given a finite filter with $2N + 1$ "tap" gains d_n, the problem is reduced to determining these gains, and the method, of course, is adaptive.

There are several performance criteria which can be applied in order to derive the adaptation procedure; however, we shall restrict our attention to gradient techniques in this discussion. Thus, we form the function

$$d_n^{(k+1)} = d_n^{(k)} - \alpha \frac{\partial I}{\partial d_n} \qquad \forall\, k \qquad (7.9)$$

which moves the values of the gains in a direction such that the mean-squared error I is reduced. The term α is the step size factor and determines the relative magnitude of the incremental gain changes. The mean-squared error can be written by combining Eq. (7.3) and (7.8) as

$$I = E\left[\left\{\sum_{n=-N}^{N} d_n x(k - n)T - a_k\right\}^2\right] \qquad (7.10)$$

and

$$\frac{\partial I}{\partial d_n} = 2E[\{\phi(k)\}\{x(k - n)T\}] \qquad (7.11)$$

which is the correlation of the sample with the error before the nth gain element, d_n, where

$$\phi(k) = \sum_{n=-N}^{N} d_n x(k - n)T - a_k \qquad (7.12)$$

A block diagram of this adaptation algorithm for one of the $2N + 1$ gain elements is illustrated in Figure 7.7. Note that the decision element in Figure 7.7 maps the transversal filter output into a specific element from the set of input symbols. The reference signal a_r is the primary difficulty in implementing this system.

There are several techniques for supplying the reference signal to the adaptation mechanism [1]. One approach stores a known sequence of signals in the receiver, and, after a particular coded sequence is sent, these signals are transmitted through the channel. The received signals are then compared with the stored sequence to form the error signal. This condition is often referred to as the *training mode*. Since the known sequence is triggered by an external command, this system may be considered "learning with a teacher."

Another approach spreads the adaptation process over the operating time of the adaptive equalizer by sending pulses in a quasi-random pattern along

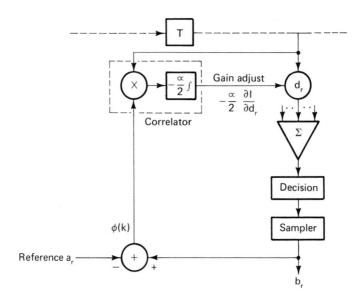

Figure 7.7. Adaptation of single gain element
using gradient technique.

with the data sequence. Another quasi-random generator located in the
receiver which is synchronized with the transmitter is used to form the error
signal.

Before the next adaptive approach is described, it is necessary to examine
the output of the equalizer described thus far. The output, at the sample
instants, is a signal which, if the intersymbol interference has been removed,
is a noisy version of the transmitted signal. Therefore, it is necessary to apply
a decision mechanism in order to determine the "best guess" of the transmitted signal. This decision mechanism takes the form of a single threshold
(clipper) for binary signals, two thresholds for three-level PAM, and $N - 1$
thresholds for N-level PAM. The determination of these thresholds is the
topic of the next section. Now, since specific output symbols are generated
from the receiver output, it is possible to use these decisions as estimates for
the reference input, as shown in Figure 7.8. Thus, if the error rate is relatively
low, a good estimate of the transmitted signal is obtained from the output,
and adaptation to relatively small changes in the channel can occur. However, if the channel changes rapidly or if the initial error rate is high, then
adaptation becomes difficult, if indeed possible at all. This final adaptation
technique, *decision-directed adaptation,* can be very effective when used in
conjunction with one of the other techniques, the training mode process, for

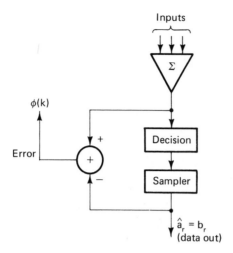

Figure 7.8. Decision-directed equalizer.

example. The training mode may be used upon establishing communications to initialize the tap gains, and the decision-directed process may be used to track changes in the channel characteristics while the communications are in process.

7.4 THE DECISION PROCESS

The final step before decoding in any pulse transmission system is the decision process, which classifies the signal at the sample times into one of the N levels being transmitted through the system. Thus, the signal after the sampler $y(nT)$ for each time n in a PCM system must be classified as 1 or 0. The problem is that the value of the samples at the output of the sampler are corrupted by noise, which complicates the decision process. If we assume that the noise is gaussian (normally) distributed, then we can represent the statistical properties of the sample $y(nT) = y_n$ for PCM as

$$p\left(\frac{y_n}{0}\right) = \frac{1}{\sqrt{2\pi}\sigma} \exp\left(\frac{-y_n^2}{2\sigma^2}\right) \tag{7.13}$$

$$p\left(\frac{y_n}{1}\right) = \frac{1}{\sqrt{2\pi}\sigma} \exp\left(\frac{-(y_n - \mu)^2}{2\sigma^2}\right) \tag{7.14}$$

where σ is the standard deviation of the noise and μ is the average received

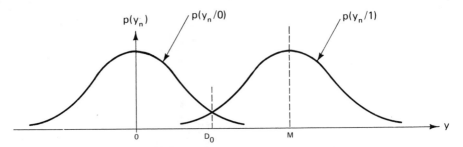

Figure 7.9. Conditional probability densities.

value when a 1 is transmitted. Thus, Eq. (7.13) is the conditional probability density of the received signal when a 0, no signal, is transmitted, and Eq. (7.14) is the conditional probability density of the received signal when a 1, signal, is transmitted. The measure of performance which is used to specify the received signal $y(nT)$ is the signal-to-noise ratio, which is μ/σ. The problem of determining whether a 0 or 1 is transmitted is illustrated in Figure 7.9, where one must specify a value in the signal voltage continuum above which we say a 1 was transmitted and below which we say a 0 was transmitted. An optimum decision strategy can be found using the likelihood ratio,

$$L(y_n) = \frac{p(y_n/1)}{p(y_n/0)} \tag{7.15}$$

where we compute the ratio for each y_n and compare its value with a threshold, D, and for

$$L(y_n) \geq D \qquad \text{we say 1 was transmitted}$$
$$L(y_n) < D \qquad \text{we say 0 was transmitted}$$

The value of D is given by

$$D = \frac{P_0 C_0}{P_1 C_1} \tag{7.16}$$

where P_0 and P_1 are the a priori probabilities that a 0 and a 1 are transmitted, respectively, and C_0 and C_1 are the "costs" associated with these decisions. The costs are generally assigned by the system designer and are based on the design constraints. Here we shall assume that the above costs are equal then the decision problem reduces to a comparison with respect to unity:

$$\frac{P_1 p(y_n/1)}{P_0 p(y_n/0)} = 1 \tag{7.17}$$

Thus, if the transmitted signal is such that the probability of 1 and 0 are equal, Eq. (7.17) reduces to

$$p\left(\frac{y_n}{1}\right) = p\left(\frac{y_n}{0}\right) \tag{7.18}$$

which means that the decision threshold is placed at the point where the two probability densities are equal: their intersection, shown as point D_0 in Figure 7.9.

Consider now the case where the a priori probabilities of the symbols being transmitted change with the data at the input or where the noise or signal plus noise probability densities change each time communications are established. Here we must resort to adaptive techniques for adjusting the decision thresholds. An embodiment of an adaptive decision system for binary signals is the threshold learning process (TLP), illustrated in Figure 7.10 [4]. The noisy-equalized samples are the input to the TLP in which the threshold T is subtracted from the input sample and then to an infinite clipper which forms the binary output.

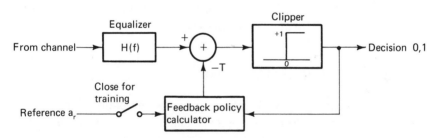

Figure 7.10. Threshold learning process for signal detection.

The feedback policy calculator in the TLP performs the functions of the performance evaluation element and system parameter transform of Chapter 5. The switch is used to place the system in either the operate or training mode. The operation of the system under training conditions is as follows. If the output is 1 when a 0 is transmitted, then we say that a "false alarm" has occurred and it is desirable to raise the threshold. Conversely, if the system responds 0 when a 1 is transmitted, then we say a "false dismissal" has occurred and it is desirable to lower the threshold. The training process for a discrete increment TLP is described completely in Figure 7.11. The discrete increment TLP allows D to vary over a range of values from, say, 0 to k in a finite number of discrete steps, say 1 unit each. Thus, if $y = 1$ and $u = 0$ and the threshold is at the upper limit, k, or if $y = 0$ and $u = 1$ and the

Channel input—u

		0	1
Decision y	0	Threshold unchanged	Move threshold down 1 step
	1	Move threshold up 1 step	Threshold unchanged

Figure 7.11. Feedback policy for discrete increment TLP.

threshold is at the lower limit, 0, then we cannot change the threshold, and it remains unchanged.

The TLP is generally trained initially, and then the switch is opened and the system operates for some period of time after which it may be retrained. The main problem with training a TLP is the same as that of the transversal equalizer, namely the reference a_r. However, the same techniques as used previously can also be applied here.

Although the TLP has been described here as applied to signal detection, applications of it in the area of control [5] as well as in models of human visual signal detection [9] have also been described.

7.5 COMMUNICATIONS NETWORKS

A communications network consists of nodes and branches, or links, as shown in Figure 7.12. The nodes represent communications switching centers, which may or may not have local users. For example, node 1 may represent the main telephone switching center in New York; node 2, Boston; node 3, Los Angeles; etc. A branch connecting two nodes indicates that some kind of bidirectional communications path exists between the respective nodes.

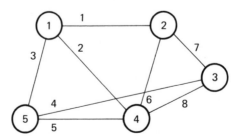

Figure 7.12. Model of a communications network.

Further, nodes connected directly are called *adjacent nodes.* Any link connecting two adjacent nodes i and j will have N_{ij} channels associated with it. The number of channels for different links varies and is chosen to meet the load requirements of the system. The particular characteristics of the channels will be disregarded here and may be teletype, telephone, video, data, etc. In general, however, the type of channel is important, as it specifies the channel's bandwidth. Now, given a communications network, the problem is to establish communications paths between pairs of nodes upon a request which originates from one of the nodes.

Conventional routing methods operate in one of several ways. A simple method designates two or more routes from each node to every other node a priori and assigns a priority to the sequence in which the alternate routes are utilized. These paths include the routes through each intermediate node; therefore, specification of two routes from node 1 to node 3 requires that, say, link sequences 1–7 and 2–8 be stored at node 1. There are, however, network conditions which occur that can create difficulties with this technique. For example, links 1 and 8 may be saturated (no channels available) or "temporarily" out of order, thus thwarting communications from node 1 to node 3 by either of these routes. Further, as the size of the network increases, the storage requirements at each node multiply rapidly.

One method used to change routing when the prespecified paths or intermediate nodes cannot be used is to communicate network status information to all nodes in the net as the network structure changes. The problem here is that the status information occupies useful communications channels and must also be routed through the system. Also, changes in the network which result from heavy use that saturate most of the channels must be communicated at critical heavy load periods, thus increasing the network loading even more. Other techniques have been proposed; however, a self-organizing technique appears to offer many advantages over the others [6] and is especially interesting here.

7.6 NETWORK SPECIFICATION

In general, the network has N nodes labeled $1, 2, \ldots, N$ and M_i, $i = 1, 2, \ldots, N$ links connected to the ith node. Thus, each node may be able to communicate directly with up to $N - 1$ other nodes.

All nodes in the network are identical, and each node will be given the same a priori information, namely the maximum number of nodes in the network, the name or code of the given node, and the name or code associated with every other node in the net. Also, the maximum number of links which can be associated with each node will be provided to that node.

Next, the signaling requirements for operation of the network must be defined. Each call propagated through the network will have associated with it the name of the calling node, the name of the called node, and a number called FAC, which indicates the number of facilities used for a given call. Thus, if a call has gone through four nodes, FAC $= 4$.

The selection of a link for processing a particular call is accomplished with a switching or connection matrix whose rows represent the $N - 1$ other nodes and whose columns represent the M_i links associated with the given node. The entries in the matrix are the probabilities or likelihoods $P_{jr}(i)$, which may represent the relative likelihood of reaching the jth node from the ith node via the rth link without the specification of any other links needed to complete the communications connection. Thus, the matrix associated with calls from node 1 in the network of Figure 7.11 is

$$
S_1 = \begin{matrix} & & & \multicolumn{3}{c}{Links} \\ & & & 1 & 2 & 3 \\ N & 2 & \begin{bmatrix} P_{21} & P_{22} & P_{23} \\ o & 3 & P_{31} & P_{32} & P_{33} \\ d & 4 & P_{41} & P_{42} & P_{43} \\ e & & & & \\ s & 5 & P_{51} & P_{52} & P_{53} \end{bmatrix} \end{matrix}
$$

Since the matrix entries may be probabilities, it is useful to apply the following constraints:

$$
\sum_{r=1}^{M_i} P_{jr}(i) = 1, \qquad j \neq i \tag{7.19}
$$

and

$$
0 \leq P_{jr}(i) \leq 1 \tag{7.20}
$$

The switching matrices are therefore called stochastic transition matrices where the individual entries cannot be unity or zero. The matrices can then be considered as a listing of alternate routes from the given node to all adjacent nodes. Here the link with the highest probability in each row is the first link tried for calls to the node associated with that row. This is one method for selecting at least the first part of the path for a given call. The node at the other end of the selected link then goes through a similar process, where the row associated with the called node is selected and the link with the highest probability is used and so forth through the other nodes until the call is completed. The question now arises as to what procedure is used if a link chosen is saturated or out of order? The answer is to choose the link with the next highest probability and so forth until either a free link is found or all links have been tried unsuccessfully in which case the call is blocked and cannot be processed.

The link selection technique determines the nature of the search process used to find the paths through the net. The above method is merely an ordered systematic search. However, the probabilities in the switching matrices can be used to implement a random search or random search with recalculation. To do this, the link to be used for an outgoing call is selected by a random sample from a distribution in which the link with highest probability has the highest probability of being selected. Thus, for one row of the matrix for node 1 of the net in Figure 7.11, one can toss a biased three-sided coin to select an outgoing link. The latter technique has been used successfully in several network studies [6, 7].

It should now be clear that the routing behavior of the system depends on the entries in the switching matrices, and, if we provide a mechanism for changing these values as a function of network performance, we have the necessary means for self-organization and learning. Thus, if a call is successfully routed through the network, it is desirable to increase the probability of using this route again. This is done by increasing the probability entries in each matrix associated with the call, and in a sense we "reward" the system. On the other hand, if the links selected are not successful in completing the call, the probability of using these links for this call again is decreased by reducing the probability entries in each matrix associated with the unsuccessful route, and the system is thus "punished."

It is now of interest to examine in some detail the method by which an alternate route is selected after the first choice has failed by being saturated or out of order:

1. The probability associated with the saturated link is reduced to some small value.
2. The resulting distribution is then normalized to meet the constraint given in Eq. (7.19).
3. A link is then selected based on the new distribution.
4. This process is continued until either a free link is found or there have been M_i unsuccessful attempts at finding a free link. If no free link is found, the call is blocked.

If the node where no free link was found is the originating node, the call is canceled and the row matrix $P_{jr}(i)$ is restored to its original condition. If the blocked node is not the originating node, the link or links connecting the originating node with the blocked node are punished.

A learning algorithm is required to reward and punish a given link within the constraints of the stochastic transition matrix. However, first consider the range of values which are allowed in the switching matrices. A zero associated with a link for a particular call indicates that there is no chance that this link will be used to process that call. This is undesirable since the number of alternative links available is reduced and some route may become desirable because of a change in network structure or traffic loading. Similarly, it is undesirable to allow a switching matrix entry to achieve a value of unity, as that link is the only one which will be chosen. Thus, expedient rather than optimum behavior is assured by limiting the upper and lower values of the matrix entries to MAX < 1 and BOT > 0, respectively.

Initially, if there is no a priori information concerning the structure or loading of the network, the probability entries in the matrix are assigned equal values:

$$P_{jr}(i) = \frac{1}{M_i} \qquad \forall\, j, r \qquad\qquad (7.21)$$

A specific learning algorithm will now be described which can be used to "train" the matrices under the constraints given above [8]. This algorithm can be used in any system which is defined by stochastic transition matrices and is not limited to applications in communications networks. First, to ensure the condition given in Eq. (7.21), let MAX $> 1/M_i$ and BOT $< 1/M_i$, and to preserve the probability measure

$$\text{MAX} = 1 - (M_i - 1)\text{BOT} \qquad\qquad (7.22)$$

This algorithm uses a multiplicative learning constant $\Delta \leq 1$, which, when multiplied by a probability to be rewarded, reveals the amount that term is to be increased.

The process of reward requires that the value of the rewarded entry be increased while the other terms in that row are decreased, and, conversely, the process of punishment requires that the value of the punished term be decreased while the other terms in that row are increased. The resulting row matrix after either of these processes must satisfy Eq. (7.19). We shall now examine the process of reward where $P_{jk}(i)$ is the present value of the term to be rewarded. Thus, if $P_{jk}(i) = \text{MAX}$, no further reward is possible and no changes are made; but if BOT $< P_{jk}(i) < \text{MAX}$, then find the reduced row matrix:

$$R_{jr}(i) = P_{jr}(i) - \text{BOT}, \qquad r = 1, 2, \ldots, M_i \qquad (7.23)$$

Thus, the column sum constraint of each term in the new row matrix is

$$S_j = \sum_{r=1}^{M_i} R_{jr}(i) = 1 - M_i(\text{BOT}) \qquad (7.24)$$

and must be satisfied both before and after any changes in the entries are made. The rewarded term in the new reduced matrix is given by

$$R'_{jk}(i) = (1 + \Delta)DR_{jk}(i) \qquad (7.25)$$

where D is a normalizing factor. And, to satisfy Eq. (7.24)

$$[R_{jk}(i)(1 + \Delta) + (S_j - R_{jk}(i))(1 - \Delta)]D = S_j \qquad (7.26)$$

Thus,

$$D = \frac{S_j}{S_j + \Delta(2R_{jk}(i) - S_j)} \qquad (7.27)$$

The new switching matrix can now be defined by

$$P'_{jr}(i) = (1 - \Delta)DR_{jr}(i) + \text{BOT} \qquad \forall \, r \neq k \qquad (7.28a)$$

and

$$P'_{jk}(i) = (1 + \Delta)DR_{jk}(i) + \text{BOT} \qquad (7.28b)$$

However, if $P_{jk}(i) = \text{BOT}$, this procedure will not work, and we define

$$R'_{jk}(i) = (1 + \Delta)\text{BOT} \qquad (7.29)$$

The column sum constraint gives

$$S_j D' + R'_{jk}(i) = S_j \qquad (7.30)$$

and

$$D' = \frac{S_j - R'_{jk}(i)}{S_j} \qquad (7.31)$$

The new switching matrix entries are

$$P'_{jr}(i) = R_{jr}(i)D' + \text{BOT} \qquad \forall \, r \neq k \qquad (7.32a)$$
$$P'_{jk}(i) = R'_{jk}(i) + \text{BOT} \qquad (7.32b)$$

The procedure for reducing the value of a particular entry is identical to the above except that the variables and constants are inverted as follows:

$$\text{MAX}' = 1 - \text{BOT} \tag{7.33a}$$

$$\text{BOT}' = 1 - \text{MAX} \tag{7.33b}$$

and

$$Q_{jr}(i) = 1 - P_{jr}(i) \qquad \forall\, r \tag{7.33c}$$

where these terms are used in Eq. (7.23), (7.24), (7.27), (7.28a), and (7.28b) or (7.29), (7.31), (7.32a), and (7.32b), and the new switching matrix entries are given by

$$P'_{jr}(i) = 1 - Q'_{jr}(i) \qquad \forall\, j \tag{7.34}$$

Now that a mechanism for reward and punishment has been established, the criteria which are applied to determine the direction in which the matrix modifications are made is of interest. These modifications are applied to force the system response to meet the constraint requirements imposed by the system design.

The first system requirement in a network routing problem is reliable communications. Therefore, all links associated with a successful call placed from any node i to any other node j are rewarded. On the other hand, links associated with a call which is blocked are punished as described previously.

A continual problem associated with any nondeterministic routing technique is the processing of a call in an endless loop of nodes called "ring around the rosey." Since this is an undesirable form of system behavior, it is necessary to provide a means for punishing this behavior. Recall that the network signaling requires that both the source and acceptor node signals or codes are sent with each call. Therefore, all links associated with a call that loops back to the source node will be punished when this so-called PATH LOOP constraint is applied. At this point, one will notice that loops or ring-arounds which do not come back to the originating node are not specifically punished by the PATH LOOP constraint. Adjustment of this behavior is embedded in the use of the third term of the network signals, namely FAC (the number of facilities utilized, to date, for a given call). If this number is exceeded by a specified amount while processing a particular call, then that call is terminated.

Two additional constraints called MAXFAC and MINIFAC, which are related to FAC, can be applied to the system's operation. MAXFAC is the maximum number of facilities which can be associated with any call. This may be a physical constraint which is a function of signal losses in the network, or it may merely be a system constraint. Thus, if $FAC \geq MAXFAC$, the call propagation is terminated, all associated links are punished, and the originating node processes the call again. If the MAXFAC constraint is exceeded on three successive trys with the same call, the call is canceled (it is blocked).

The other term, MINIFAC, is used for two reasons. The first is to place an adaptive constraint on the number of facilities used for any call, and the second is to provide a means for punishing ring-arounds which do not get back to the source node. Thus, an $N - 1$ word store is associated with each node which contains a running weighted average of the number of facilities used for the calls to every other node for the last g calls. Assume a value of $g = 3$, and the following expression is used to determine the new value of MINIFAC for a completed call,

$$MINIFAC = \tfrac{2}{3} MINIFAC' + \tfrac{1}{3} FAC \tag{7.35}$$

where MINIFAC' is the old value. Also, a multiplicative adaptive constant may be used with MINIFAC as follows. If

$$FAC \geq \gamma \times MINIFAC \tag{7.36}$$

the call propagation is terminated, the links are punished, and the call is placed again, etc., as above. The above two criteria limit the total number of facilities used for any calls. And, more specifically, the MINIFAC criterion, which becomes dominant as the network learns, tends to minimize the number of available paths and therefore the maximum number of facilities allowed for each communication. Note that, since MINIFAC is a running weighted average, the value of γ determines the rate at which the MINIFAC criterion can increase.

These four criteria, reliable communications, path loop MAXFAC, and MINIFAC, together with the reward and punishment procedures, have been shown [7] to provide all the basic means for self-organization and adaptation in a communications network.

The overall operation of even a small switching network with simultaneous and multiple demands from each node is a complex process indeed. However, the routing procedure described here can be thought of by considering that each node in the system is "doing *his* thing" without direct interest in any other node or links. Call requests entering a node from either a local user or another node are treated identically. Namely, the present node selects an outgoing link by a strategy generally based on the probability of success from past experience in using that link to process similar requests.

Therefore, the switching algorithm and matrices may be considered as the forward transfer elements; the constraints reliable communications, path loop, MAXFAC, and MINIFAC represent the performance evaluation element; and the learning algorithm performs as a system parameter transform element by converting "good" or "bad" behavior into changes in the matrix entries.

This routing technique can easily be related to other concepts presented in Chapters 4 and 5. First, the switching matrices are stochastic, and therefore an information measure can easily be applied. The entropy of a row of a switching matrix is

$$H_{ij} = \sum_{r=1}^{M} - P_{jr}(i) \log P_{jr}(i) \text{ bits} \tag{7.37}$$

Also, the information associated with the ith node is

$$H_i = \sum_{\text{all } j \neq 1} H_{ij} \text{ bits} \tag{7.38}$$

and the information associated with the whole network (system entropy) is

$$H = \sum_{i=1}^{N} H_i \text{ bits} \tag{7.39}$$

Further, the system is a stochastic automaton, as defined in Chapter 5.

The entropy measure is one indicator of system performance and can be related to the definition of a self-organizing system given in Chapter 5. However, other more conventional measures must also be applied to the evaluation of network behavior. One of these measures, called the grade of service, is the percentage of calls completed with respect to calls attempted over some time interval:

$$\text{G.S.} = \frac{\text{Calls completed}}{\text{Calls attempted}} \times 100\% \tag{7.40}$$

This measure is particularly important to the user, as it is his only sample of network routing performance. The other measure which is of value to the designer and operator of the system is the average path length needed to process calls through the net. Generally, lower costs are associated with shorter paths. The performance of a large (57 nodes, 88 links) network with respect to these measures entropy, grade of service, and average path length, where

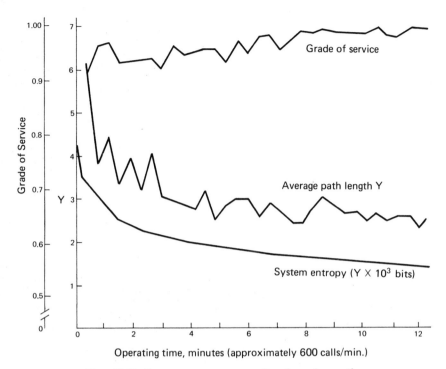

Operating time, minutes (approximately 600 calls/min.)

Figure 7.13. System parameters as a function of operating time for large communications network.

the switching matrices started with all entries equal, maximum entropy, is shown in Figure 7.13. As expected, the entropy decreases as the system organizes the routing, and similarly the MINIFAC constraint causes the average path length to decrease. The final result is that the grade of service increases as the network proceeds.

Finally, this system exhibits some self-repair capability since the performance evaluation is not a function of network status. Experiments with the large network where facilities carrying up to 30% of the traffic were disabled have given the following results. Immediately, the grade of service dropped from 99.5% to 84.5%, but 5 minutes later it was up to 90.2%. The effects of damaging a portion of a smaller network (9 nodes, 25 links) are also reflected in the entropy, as shown in Figure 7.14. Here, node 5 was destroyed after 1152 calls were processed by the network and the entropy jumped from 6 to 22 bits, but after some time the entropy dropped to 7 bits and service

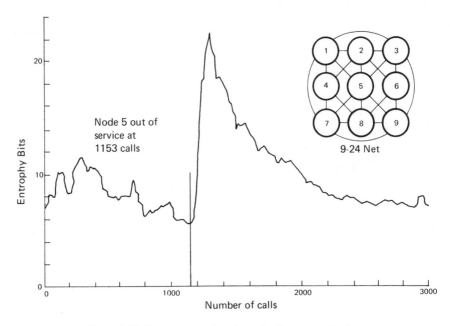

Figure 7.14. Entropy as a function of calls processed where node 5 was out of service from call 1153.

was restored to normal by incorporating previously unused or lightly used links. A network in which all facilities are fully used cannot exhibit these self-repair properties—self-repair here depends on the existence of redundant network facilities. The concepts of self-repair are examined further in Chapter 8.

7.7 SUMMARY

Three aspects of communications systems where self-organizing, adaptive, and learning techniques have been applied were presented in this chapter. Some of these techniques are presently in use in communications systems, while others are relatively new and may influence the design of new systems. In particular, the equalization and detection of binary signals sent over the telephone network have required extensive use of adaptive and learning techniques to increase the rate of reliable transmission of data to and from remote computers. The ever-increasing demand for digital data transmission capability will certainly spur development of new communications systems, which will undoubtedly incorporate adaptive, learning, and self-organizing techniques in their implementation.

7.8 EXERCISES

7.1. Find a 16-level PAM and PCM (4 bits) representation for the accompanying signal sampled once every 0.5 seconds. Does this give an accurate representation of the signal?

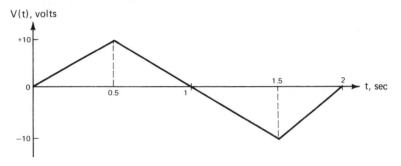

7.2. Given the accompanying transversal equalizer,
   (a) Write the time and frequency domain expressions for the filter for $T = 0.5$ seconds and $d_{-1} = 0.25$, $d_0 = 1.0$, and $d_{+1} = -0.50$.
   (b) Find the time domain response of the filter for the triangular input pulse.
   (c) Find values of the tap gains which will produce an output pulse as close as possible to the ideal response.

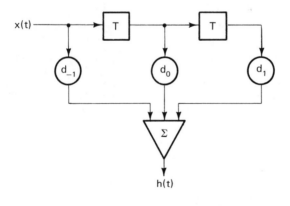

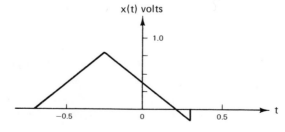

7.3. Given the accompanying three-node network (this problem is best solved via a computer simulation),

  (a) Set up the three switching matrices needed to route communications traffic where no a priori information is available.

  (b) Trace the network behavior for the following traffic schedule for $\Delta = 0.8$ using the learning algorithm given in this chapter. Calculate system entropy and grade of service for each interval. Also compute the average path length of all calls processed. Use ordered systematic search where a coin flip is used if entries are equal.

Time Called	From	To	Time Off
1	1	2	4
2	2	3	6
3	1	2	4
4	3	1	7
5	1	3	6
6	2	3	9
7	3	2	11
8	1	3	11
9	2	3	11
10	2	1	11

  (c) Has the best route to all nodes been found?

  (d) Remove link 2 and repeat parts (b) and (c).

7.4. Relate the law of requisite variety to the network routing problem described in Section 7.6. Where does the system obtain its order?

7.5. Consider the likelihood ratio for unequal costs $C_0 \neq C_1$ and unequal priori probabilities $P_0 \neq P_1$ and describe their effect on the decision threshold.

7.6. Develop a block diagram model of the transmitter, channel, and the adaptive equalizer and relate it to the general models given in Chapter 5.

REFERENCES

1. Lucky, R. W., J. Salz, and E. J. Weldon, Jr., *Principles of Data Communications*, McGraw-Hill, New York, 1968.

2. Rudin, H., Jr., "Automatic Equalization Using Transversal Filters," *IEEE Spectrum*, Vol. 4, No. 1, pp. 53–59, Jan. 1967.

3. Franks, L. E., *Signal Theory*, Prentice-Hall, Englewood Cliffs, N.J., 1969.

4. Sklansky, Jack, "Threshold Training of Two-Mode Signal Detection," *IEEE Transactions on Information Theory*, Vol. IT-11, No. 3, pp. 353–362, July 1965.

5. Sklansky, Jack, "Learning Systems for Automatic Control," *IEEE Transactions on Automatic Control*, Vol. AC-11, No. 1, pp. 6–19, Jan. 1966.

6. GLORIOSO, R. M., G. R. GRUENEICH, and J. C. DUNN, "Self-Organization and Adaptive Routing for Communication Networks," *IEEE Electronics and Aerospace Convention Record* (EASCON), Oct. 1969. IEEE Publication 69C31-AES Wash., D.C. pp. 243–250.

7. GLORIOSO, R. M., G. R. GRUENEICH, and D. McELROY, "Adaptive Routing in a Large Communications Network," *Proceedings of the 1970 IEEE Symposium on Adaptive Processes (9th), Decision and Control,* University of Texas, Austin, Dec. 1970. IEEE Publication 70C 58-AC, pp. xv. 5.1–vx. 5.4.

8. GLORIOSO, R. M., and G. R. GRUENEICH, "A Training Algorithm for Systems Described by Stochastic Transition Matrices," *IEEE Transactions on Systems, Man, and Cybernetics,* Vol. SMC-1, No. 1, Jan. 1971.

9. GLORIOSO, R. M., "A Stochastic Model of the Human Observer as a Detector of Signals Embedded in Noise," Ph.D. Dissertation, University of Connecticut, Storrs, Conn., 1967.

8

RELIABILITY AND REPAIR

INTRODUCTION

A general model and a definition of self-repair were given in Chapter 5. The routing technique presented in Chapter 7 responded to an out-of-service facility by adapting to the new network structure such that system performance was restored. The coding of the nervous system is also capable of successful operation in the face of momentary nerve failure as will be demonstrated in Chapter 9. The nervous system itself, of course, is prime example of a reliable system. It can tolerate removal or destruction of thousands of cells and continue to operate successfully. In fact, many brain cells die each day of our lives and are not replaced or repaired—an amazing system indeed.

Interest in the design of reliable systems originated with the first computer systems, which used a large number of components whose individual reliability was relatively high but, when used in a large system, resulted in a system with rather poor reliability. For example, the mean time between failures

(MTBF) of ENIAC, the first electronic digital computer, which was built in the early 1940s with 18,000 vacuum tubes was approximately 5 minutes.

The reasons the overall reliability of large systems can be poor and the methods for improving system reliability are the topics covered in this chapter. The orientation of this material is toward the digital computer because of the large number of components that are needed to create these machines. However, the principles of reliability underlying this work are applicable to other areas as well.

8.1 RELIABILITY OF SYSTEMS

The reliability of a complex system depends on the relationships among the elements of the system. The classic example is "A chain is only as strong as its weakest link." Here, the overall reliability depends on each element of the chain supporting the same load. If we denote the chain links $L_1, L_2, \ldots, L_n$ and a probability of reliable performance for each link, $p_1, p_2, \ldots, p_n$, then the reliability of the chain is

$$R = p_1 \times p_2 \times \ldots \times p_n \tag{8.1}$$

The probability that link i will fail is

$$q_i = 1 - p_i$$

and the probability that the chain will fail is

$$Q = 1 - R = 1 - (p_1 \times p_2 \times p_3 \times \ldots \times p_n) \tag{8.2}$$

This, of course, is consistent since the probability that the chain will fail plus the reliability (the probability that it will not fail) must be unity. For our chain, then, it is clear that it will fail if any link L_1 or L_2 or $L_3 \ldots L_n$ fails,

$$Q = P(F_1 \vee F_2 \vee F_3 \vee \ldots \vee F_n) \tag{8.3}$$

where F_i is the event "link i fails." A general schematic representation of this type of system where the failure of any one of n independent elements results in system failure is shown in Figure 8.1. Here the system flow, which

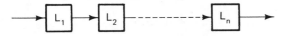

Figure 8.1. Series representation of a system.

may be force as in the chain, signals in a computer, or electric power distribution, is through a series of elements.

Consider the following: A controller for a computer consists of 100 different levels of logic where the probability of a failure of any level is 0.01. What is the reliability of the controller?

$$R = \prod_{i=1}^{n} p(\bar{F}_i) = \prod_{i=1}^{n} p_i$$

but $p_i = 1 - 0.01 = 0.99$ and $R = (0.99)^{100} \simeq 0.37$. This can be interpreted by saying that on the average only one of every three controllers built will not fail. This is very poor indeed.

Referring again to the weak link chain problem, it might appear reasonable to use more than one chain to hold the load. Then the system would fail only if all chains failed. The additional chains may not normally be needed, but the system would certainly be more reliable. The additional chains are called redundant elements of the system. A schematic representation of this parallel system is given in Figure 8.2.

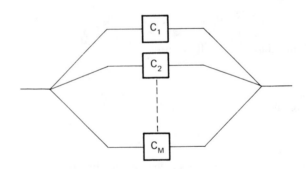

Figure 8.2. Parallel system for improving reliability.

The probability of failure of this parallel system with independent elements is

$$Q = P(F_1 \wedge F_2 \wedge \ldots \wedge F_n) \tag{8.4}$$

$$Q = q_1 \times q_2 \times q_3 \times \ldots \times q_n \tag{8.5}$$

and the reliability is

$$R = 1 - (q_1 \times q_2 \times \ldots \times q_n) \tag{8.6}$$

Note that the reliability can be stated by

$$R = P(\bar{F}_1 \vee F_2 F_1 \vee \bar{F}_3 F_1 F_2 \vee \ldots) \tag{8.7}$$

which in words is "The reliability of the system is the probability that element 1 does not fail, or that element 2 does not fail and element 1 does, or that element 3 does not fail and elements 1 and 2 do, etc." This can be written, for independent elements, as

$$R = p_1 + p_2 q_1 + p_3 q_1 q_2 + \ldots \qquad (8.8)$$

Suppose that a system is needed with a reliability of 0.99 and that the components available have a reliability of only 0.5. How many elements are needed to satisfy the design requirement?

First,

$$R \geq 0.99$$
$$Q \leq 1 - 0.99 = 0.01$$

Next,

$$Q = (q)^n = (0.5)^n$$

and

$$0.01 \geq (0.5)^n$$
$$\log 0.01 \geq n \log 0.5$$
$$-2 \geq -n \times 0.3$$
$$n \geq 6.6$$

It is possible to exceed the reliability requirement by using seven elements in parallel. Thus, a reliable system can be built from unreliable components [1]. Also, the construction of an ultrareliable system depends on the use of more components than would be necessary to build a less reliable system. This concept leads us to the conclusion that redundancy and reliability are directly related. This was, in fact, the case for the communications network routing described in Chapter 7. Reliability was achieved by having alternate, redundant paths through the network available to handle the traffic load.

The incorporation of redundancy in a computing system is not so simple as adding gates and flip-flops. Additional elements must be incorporated into the logical structure of the machine in a systematic way. Some of the methods for designing a reliable computing system are treated in the following sections.

It is also useful to analyze a system with respect to the expected time interval during which the system will operate reliably—the MTBF. Assume that the multiple components which make up a system fail independently of one another. Also, assume that the expected failure rate from each component is λ.

Thus, the probability, assuming the random occurrence of a failure, that all components survive to time t is

$$p(t) = e^{-\lambda t}$$

where $p(0) = 1$ which also can be stated "the first component fails after time t." Thus, if T is the random variable giving the time from 0 to the first failure, the reliability is

$$R[T > t] = e^{-\lambda t} \qquad (8.9)$$

which has a distribution function,

$$R[T \leq t] = 1 - e^{-\lambda t}$$

and probability density function is,

$$f(t) = \lambda e^{-\lambda t} \qquad (8.10)$$

which is the Poisson density function. The mean survival time (MTBF) for one component of our system is

$$S_1 = \int_0^\infty t f(t) \, dt = \int_0^\infty t \lambda e^{-\lambda t} \, dt = \frac{1}{\lambda} \qquad (8.11)$$

And, if there are m independent components in the system and the system fails if any component fails, then

$$R[T > t] = e^{-m\lambda t} \qquad (8.12)$$

and the probability density function for failures is,

$$f(t) = m\lambda e^{-m\lambda} \qquad (8.13)$$

which gives a MTBF of

$$S_m = \frac{1}{\lambda m} \qquad (8.14)$$

Now, suppose that the probability of failure of the components of a system is 0.001/hour (1 out of every 1000 of these components fails in any hour); then

$$S_1 = 1000 \text{ hours}$$

But, if there are 10,000 of these components in a system, then

$$S_{10000} = \frac{1,000}{10,000} \text{ hours} = 6 \text{ minutes}$$

Thus, a collection of components whose individual reliability appears quite good is not effective in a large system which depends on the reliable operation of each component. It should now be clear that the job of designing a sophisticated computer which will be highly reliable is no easy task. A spacecraft computer for a 2-year mission which operates continuously must have a MTBF greater than approximately 20,000 hours. There are three approaches one can take: (1) Increase the reliability of the individual components, (2) reduce the number of components needed, and (3) employ components which are not necessarily needed to do the job but improve reliability by being there—redundancy. The last approach is presented in the next section.

8.2 MODULAR REDUNDANCY

It has been made abundantly clear that a basic method for improving the reliability of a system is to incorporate redundant elements in the design. These additional elements are usually considered in large functional blocks or modules rather than as individual components. These modules are incorporated into a system in two basic ways: (1) They are in operation continuously and their output is considered in the total result, or (2) they exist as spares and are called upon only when needed. The first method was proposed in 1956 by John von Neumann [1] as a means for incorporating the features of a parallel system into a computational unit as well as a model of the reliability of the nervous system. Let us examine this approach [2].

If one has a computational (logical) module which may fail, then it is clear that if an identical module is supplied with the same input, a comparison of the two outputs gives an indication of the logical errors which may occur. If the units operate correctly when placed in service, then a disagreement in their outputs at a later time is an indication that one of the units has failed. A system such as this would detect errors in the computation except in the very unlikely event that both units fail simultaneously. However, a system which incorporates three or more identical units with the same input can be used to correct errors by choosing the output which a majority of the modules agree on. In the simplest case, three modules are needed where two of the modules are redundant. von Neumann also proposed that the proper output be chosen by a majority element or organ (as he called them), as discussed

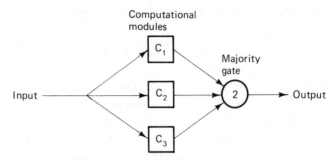

Figure 8.3. Triple modular redundancy to improve reliability.

in Chapter 9. This element has an output which agrees with the majority of inputs and this system, called triple modular redundancy (TMR), is illustrated in Figure 8.3. Although it appears intuitively that TMR can improve reliability, let us now examine the gain in reliability which is actually achieved. The system pictured in Figure 8.3 is only as reliable as the majority gate which makes the output decision. This is generally a simple device and often can be made much more reliable than the computational modules, Cs. Also, other configurations which use more than one majority gate can be defined. However, as a first approximation, let us naively assume that the majority gate cannot fail. The output then will be correct as long as two or more Cs have not failed. The reliability distribution is the probability that all three modules are functioning plus the probability that any two modules are functioning and the other is not,

$$R[T > t] = R^3 + 3R^2(1 - R) \tag{8.15}$$

where R is the reliability distribution of the individual modules as given above. Substituting for R in Eq. (8.15),

$$\begin{aligned}
R[T > t] &= e^{-3\lambda t} + 3e^{-2\lambda t}(1 - e^{-\lambda t}) \\
&= 3e^{-2\lambda t} - 2e^{-3\lambda t}
\end{aligned} \tag{8.16}$$

The MTBF can now be computed,

$$\text{MTBF(TMR)} = \frac{5}{6\lambda}$$

which is lower than the MTBF for a single element. However, computation of the reliability as a function of normalized time shows that for $\lambda t < 0.7$

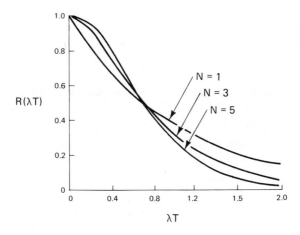

Figure 8.4. Reliability as a function of normalized time for modularly redundant systems of N elements.

the reliability of TMR is greater than for the single element, as illustrated in Figure 8.4 where $N = 3$.

A simple extension of the concept of TMR uses N units, where $N = 2n + 1$, feeding one majority gate; see Figure 8.5. The N module system, N Module Redundancy (NMR), will work properly if all Cs work properly, if all but one C function, and up to where all but n of the Cs function. If all failures are statistically independent, the distribution is

$$R[T > t] = \sum_{i=0}^{n} \binom{N}{i}(1 - R)^i R^{N-i} \qquad (8.17)$$

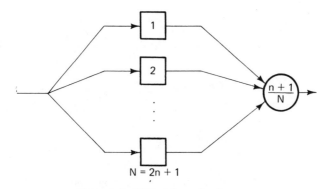

Figure 8.5. N Modular redundancy.

where

$$\binom{N}{i} = \frac{N!}{(N-i)!i!}$$

the binomial coefficient. The general distribution given in Eq. (10.17) can be used to compute the probability of failure as a function of normalized time, and some N module reliabilities are shown in Figure 8.4.

Now, let us consider the circumstance where a majority element that does not fail simply is not available. First, the system reliability must be modified by the reliability of the majority organ, R_m:

$$R[T > t] = R_m \sum_{i=0}^{n} \binom{N}{i}(1-R)^i R^{N-i} \tag{8.18}$$

Here, we have assumed that the system fails if the majority organ fails. Specifically for TMR, the survival probability is

$$R[T > t] = e^{-\lambda_m t}[3e^{-2\lambda t} - 2e^{-3\lambda t}] \tag{8.19}$$

Now, if $\lambda_m \geq \lambda$, the survival probability for a TMR system is less than that of a single computational element for all time. Thus, in a practical computational system using TMR or NMR, it is imperative that ultra reliability of the majority device be assured. If this is done, then the majority device will tend to restore the output of a system to its proper value. Hence, it has been called a restoring organ as well.

Another approach to the problem of majority organ reliability involves triplication of these units as well, as shown in Figure 8.6. Thus, a computer system which triplicates each subsection and replaces each module intercon-

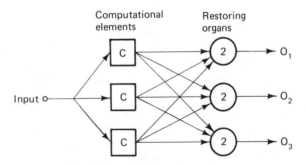

Figure 8.6. TMR as applied to both computational elements and majority (restoring) organs.

nection with three interconnections can provide reliable computation up to the point where a final single output must be decided. Here, either an external (perhaps human) observer or a very reliable restoring organ must make the decision. The responsibility placed on the restoring organs and especially this final element is great, and for this reason attempts have been made to distribute these decisions throughout a computational network. One approach to this in logical networks is described in the next section.

A simple extension of NMR has been described by Mathur and Avizienis [3]. Initially, assume that all modules are functioning normally. Later, if one or more modules fail, their outputs will differ from the outputs of the surviving modules. Thus, a simple comparator can be used to compare the outputs, and when a module fails, it can be replaced by switching in a new module. This scheme, of course, requires that some number of spares, S, be available. It is assumed that the $2n + 1$ active units have a failure rate of λ, while the spares, in the dormant mode, have a failure rate $\mu \leq \lambda$. The block diagram of Figure 8.7 illustrates the major elements of this system. There are $2n + 1 + S = N + S$ computational units, a switching unit, a disagreement detector, and a restoring organ in this system. The disagreement detector monitors the relative performance of the Cs, and if a failure

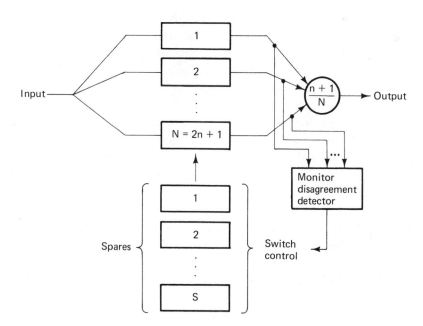

Figure 8.7. Hybrid (N, S) modular redundant system.

in one of the Cs occurs, it activates the switching unit, which in turn switches in a new C and turns off the old C. This approach has been called the hybrid (N, S) system with corresponding reliability $R(N, S)$. If we define a hybrid $(3, S)$ system, then we have a hybrid TMR system. The survival probability of this system can be defined as the probability that any two of the $S + 3$ units survive. If we now assume that $\mu = \lambda$, then the reliability is

$$R(3, S) = \sum_{i=0}^{n} \binom{S + 3}{i}(1 - R)^i R^{S+2-i}$$
$$= 1 - (1 - R)^{S+2}[1 + R(S + 2)] \tag{8.20}$$

Equation (8.20) must be modified by the probability that the disagreement detector, the switching unit, and the restoring organ survive given by R_{DSM}:

$$R(3, S) = R_{\text{DSM}}[1 - (1 - R)^{S+2}[1 + R(S + 2)]] \tag{8.21}$$

Equations (8.18), (8.19), and (8.21) indicate the critical section of any high-reliability system—the final decision and correction equipment.

8.3 QUADDED LOGIC [4, 5]

Quadded logic is a method of combinational logic design which embeds the restoring organ in the network by taking advantage of the corrective properties of AND and OR logic devices. The following discussion is centered on the application of these properties. However, first it is useful to define the kind of logical errors or faults which can occur.

Logical circuit elements have two output states, namely 1 or 0, and in modern high-gain circuits one of these outputs is achieved even if the input is not in either of these conditions. Thus, a loose connection or poor input gate will still cause the output of the following gate to be either 1 or 0. A failure in a logical network occurs when one or more outputs or inputs are always 0 or always 1 under all network conditions. Thus, a logical element which fails is said to be either stuck at zero (s-a-0) or stuck at one (s-a-1). The goal of the quadded logic configuration is to mask these faults.

The properties of AND and OR gates can be used to advantage to mask these faults. For example, consider the AND gate in Figure 8.8(a). A fault on the input which is s-a-1, say A, does not produce a faulty (stuck) output; however, an s-a-0 fault on either input does. Thus, s-a-1 faults can be restored by an AND gate. Similarly, s-a-0 faults can be restored by an OR gate. The only thing which must now be resolved is the way in which we assure that

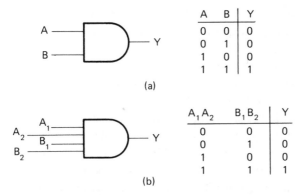

Figure 8.8. (a) AND gate. (b) Two-variable AND gate for quadded logic. The truth table is for a gate with no input faults.

s-a-1 faults are applied to AND gates and s-a-0 faults are applied to OR gates. To do this, one must be prepared to quadruple the logic and supply redundant inputs to the gates. Thus, the two-input AND gate becomes the four-input AND gate in Figure 8.8(b), where the redundant A and B inputs are the same logical functions derived from different parts of the network. Note that an s-a-1 fault on one of the logical input lines for each literal will not cause an output fault.

Next, let us examine the interconnection scheme necessary to correct faults using quadded logic gates. Given the network shown in Figure 8.9, one of the A inputs to the first AND gate is s-a-1 and one of the E inputs to the second AND gate is s-a-0. The s-a-1 fault on A_1 is restored by gate 1 since the correct logical value still is on A_2. The s-a-0 fault on E_1, however, propagates through gate 2, and D is also s-a-0. The OR gate restores the logic since D_2 is still correct. The general configuration for

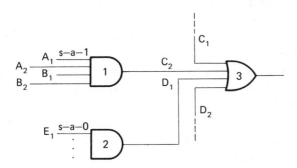

Figure 8.9. Logic configuration for quadded logic.

quadded logic then requires that redundant input AND and OR gates be staggered through the network. Thus, an s-a-1 fault on the input to an AND gate is corrected by that gate, and an s-a-0 fault is corrected by the following OR gate. Similarly, an s-a-0 fault on the input to an OR gate is corrected by that gate, while an s-a-1 fault is corrected by the following AND gate. It is important to note that this configuration can correct only single faults; double faults propagate through and are not corrected.

One additional logic function must be incorporated into the quadded logic configuration in order to realize any logic function, namely inversion. To be sure, inverters cannot be allowed to be part of the cascade, as no correction can take place there. Therefore, inverters are placed at the inputs to the AND and OR gates as shown in Figure 8.10, where they are eventually quadded. It is also possible to move the inversions forward to the outputs of the gates and quad the inverters there. The extension of these concepts to NAND and NOR logic should now be clear since a NAND gate is equivalent to a NOR gate with each input inverted.

Figure 8.10. Incorporating inversion in quadded logic.

Next, let us examine the specific interconnections necessary to implement a reliable logic network using quadded logic. To accomplish this, consider the simple logic network shown in Figure 8.11(a), which realizes the function $Y = (A + B)(C + D)$. Let us assume that this network is embedded in a larger network which will provide the proper number of redundant logic inputs for each input literal. Recall from Figure 8.8(b) that each input literal for each quadded logic gate has two inputs. Thus, since there will be four gates for each gate in the net of Figure 8.9, there are eight inputs associated with each literal. The specific interconnection of the quadded gates for the network of Figure 8.11(a) is shown in Figure 8.11(b). The complexity of the quadded logic net is clear in this figure; 4 logical inputs become 32 logical inputs, 2 two-input OR gates become 8 four-input OR gates, and 1 two-input AND gate becomes 4 four-input AND gates. Generally, however, quadded logic networks require eight times the hardware of the irredundant realization. The problem of generating the quadded network given the logic function is clearly quite formidable. However, algorithms which achieve this can certainly be formulated, thereby allowing automatic computer design.

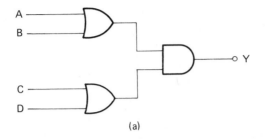

(a)

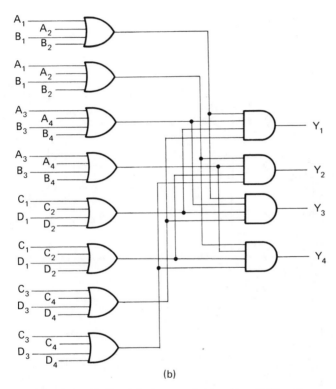

(b)

Figure 8.11. (a) Simple logic network. $Y = (A + B)(C + D)$.
(b) Quadded logic configuration for $Y = (A + B)(C + D)$.

The final output of a quadded network must still be resolved. A majority gate as used in NMR can be placed at the output of the last level to decide on the final output. This, of course, must be highly reliable if the full advantages of the quadded configuration are to be realized.

Finally, the realization of a computer must use storage elements as well as combinational logic circuits. Since the realization of flip-flops can be

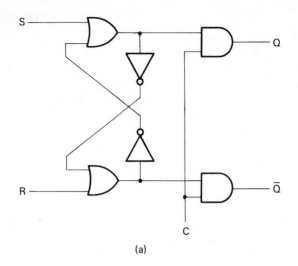

(a)

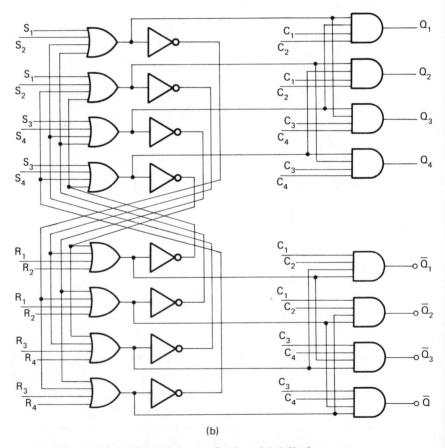

(b)

Figure 8.12. (a) Gate realization of *R-S* flip-flop.
(b) Quadded version of *R-S* flip-flop.

obtained using gates, these connections can also be quadded. A gate realization of an R-S flip-flop is shown in Figure 8.12(a). The quadded version of this device is given in Figure 8.12(b). Specific rules for quadding flip-flop circuits exactly are not known, and one must rely on cut-and-try methods. For example, one type of fault can exist in the flip-flop circuit but not get out of the feedback loop (see the Exercises). Another approach to repair in networks with memory is treated in the next section.

8.4 THE SEQUENTIAL PRIME IMPLICANT FORM [6, 7]

NMR techniques apply to any modular system, and quadded logic applies to combinational logic and to a certain extent to sequential networks. The sequential prime implicant form (SPIF) is a tool for testing the behavior of sequential networks. For example, it can be used to test elements for replacement in a hybrid modularly redundant system. The following treatment considers first the general nature of the SPIF and later its application to self-repairing systems.

First, let us consider the synchronous circuit given in Figure 8.13, where

$$Q_1 = \bar{Q}_2 C \vee Q_1 \bar{C}$$
$$Q_2 = Q_1 C \vee Q_2 \bar{C} \tag{8.22}$$

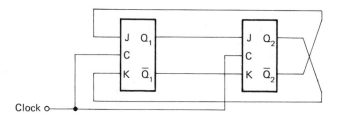

Figure 8.13. Synchronous sequential circuit.

describes the next state condition for each flip-flop. The overall behavior of a sequential network can be described by state transition diagrams—one for each possible input condition. The fact that there is only a single input, the clock, simplifies the problem. However, extension to other input configurations is straightforward. The state transition tables are given in Figure 8.14, where the diagram for $C = 0$ is trivial, as no changes take place under this condition. Note that the form of the state transition table resembles the maps used for minimization of combinational logic functions. Thus, another

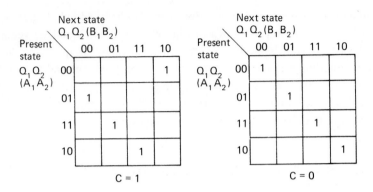

Figure 8.14. Transition tables for sequential circuit of Figure 8.13.

way of describing these state diagrams can be drawn from combinational logic. Relabel the present state A_1A_2 and the next state B_1B_2 and write the Boolean equations from the maps, as we would for combinational nets. Thus, for $C = 1$,

$$f(C = 1) = \bar{A}_1\bar{A}_2 B_1\bar{B}_2 C \vee \bar{A}_1 A_2\bar{B}_1\bar{B}_2 C \vee A_1 A_2\bar{B}_1 B_2\bar{C}$$
$$\vee\ A_1\bar{A}_2 B_1 B_2 C \tag{8.23}$$

and for $C = 0$,

$$f(C = 0) = \bar{A}_1\bar{A}_2\bar{B}_1\bar{B}_2\bar{C} \vee \bar{A}_1 A_2\bar{B}_1 B_2\bar{C} \vee A_1 A_2 B_1 B_2\bar{C}$$
$$\vee\ A_1\bar{A}_2 B_1\bar{B}_2\bar{C} \tag{8.24}$$

and

$$f = f(C = 0) \vee f(C = 1) \tag{8.25}$$

and we have the Boolean expression which describes the state behavior of the network. These Boolean expressions can now be manipulated as in any Boolean algebra [6]. The nature of the maps given above indicates that Eqs. (8.23) and (8.24) are the minimal forms for the network. Hence, they are called the sequential prime implicant form (SPIF). The SPIF, then, is a logical function which produces a logical one when proper transitions of the sequential network occur. Thus, $\overline{\text{SPIF}}$ indicates improper transitions and can be used to monitor failures in the sequential network. The use of $\overline{\text{SPIF}}$, however, requires that both the previous and present states for all memory elements be available. Since, for anything but the simplest of systems, the number of connections would be prohibitive, another way of generating the SPIF is needed.

To accomplish this, let us consider the case where only a restricted number of memory elements are monitored. The transition tables so generated are called projections of a SPIF. There are two types of projections; one can be found from the SPIF of the network and is called a complete projection, and the other is generated from observations of some of the memory elements and may or may not be complete. A projection which is not complete is called partial. For example, consider the network given in Figure 8.13, where the cycle of operation is

$$Q_1 \; Q_2$$

$$
\begin{array}{cc}
0 & 0 \\
1 & 0 \\
1 & 1 \\
0 & 1 \\
0 & 0 \\
\cdot & \cdot \\
\cdot & \cdot \\
\cdot & \cdot \\
\end{array}
$$

Now, if one tries to generate transition tables based on observation of only Q_1, then the accompanying tables will result. This projection is partial, and

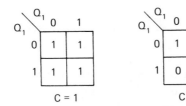

because there is more than one 1 per row, these tables are *contradictory*— the next state is not uniquely defined. Also, a table or SPIF where there is no 1 in one or more rows is called *unresolved*. The complete projection from Q_1 of this SPIF can be found from the original function by replacing terms associated with the other memory elements by 1s; here terms with a subscript of 2 are replaced by 1s:

$$f_1 = \bar{A}_1 B_1 C \vee \bar{A}_1 \bar{B}_1 C \vee A_1 \bar{B}_1 C \vee A_1 B_1 C \vee \bar{A}_1 \bar{B}_1 \bar{C}$$
$$\vee \; \bar{A}_1 \bar{B}_1 C \vee A_1 B_1 \bar{C} \vee A_1 B_1 \bar{C} \tag{8.26}$$

Equation (8.26) can be reduced by application of the Quine-McCluskey techniques to

$$f_1 = C \vee A_1 B_1 \vee \bar{A}_1 \bar{B}_1 \tag{8.27}$$

The transition tables for this projection are given in Figure 8.15. Another projection can be found for Q_2. The two projections can be combined by forming the product (AND) of the two projections to generate a new projec-

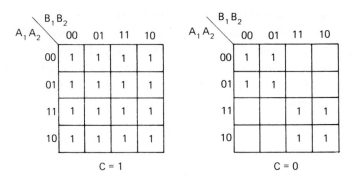

Figure 8.15. Transition tables for complete projection of the SPIF for Q_1.

tion. This projection will also be contradictory, indicating that another element must be monitored (the present and previous states of the other memory element in this case) to form the proper SPIF. For example, consider the projection formed by examining the previous state of both Q_1 and Q_2, the present state of Q_1, and the clock,

$$f_2 = C(\bar{A}_1\bar{A}_2\bar{B}_2 \vee \bar{A}_1A_2\bar{B}_2 \vee A_1A_2B_2 \vee A_1\bar{A}_2B_2) \vee \bar{C}(\bar{A}_1\bar{A}_2\bar{B}_2 \\ \vee \bar{A}_1A_2B_2 \vee A_1A_2B_2 \vee A_1\bar{A}_2\bar{B}_2) \tag{8.28}$$

The product of all projections of the SPIF will reveal the original SPIF of the net. In this example, the original SPIF, Eq. (8.25), is needed to describe all state transitions. However, the entire SPIF is not always needed to describe all allowable state transitions, and the problem reduces to finding a minimal set of projections with which one can differentiate proper from improper network operation. An ideal condition would be a minimal set of projections whose product forms the whole SPIF.

Next, once the projections are found, it is only necessary to build a logical network which indicates that an improper transition has occurred indicating a failure in the sequential network. This network can be designed based on the inverse SPIF, $\overline{\text{SPIF}}$. For our example, the inverse SPIF can be found from the maps of Figure 8.16, which are the complements of the maps in Figure 8.14. The function which indicates a failure in the network of Figure 8.13 is

$$f = C(\bar{A}_2\bar{B}_1 \vee A_1\bar{B}_2 \vee A_2B_1 \vee \bar{A}_1B_2) \vee \bar{C}(A_1\bar{B}_1 \vee \bar{A}_1B_1 \\ \vee \bar{A}_2B_2 \vee A_2\bar{B}_2) \tag{8.29}$$

A $\overline{\text{SPIF}}$-monitored sequential network can be incorporated into a system in several ways. First, two identical networks can be built into a system

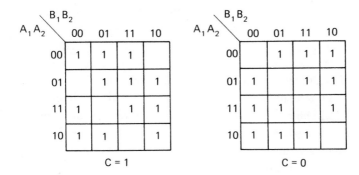

Figure 8.16. Maps for the inverse SPIF of example.

where one network is monitored. If the monitor indicates failure of this first network, the second network is automatically switched in. Another method uses two networks where each net is monitored. If the first net fails, the second net is switched in and an external alarm sounds. If the second net fails, the new network, which has hopefully been installed by the operator, is switched in. Another way to use this monitoring technique is in the hybrid modularly redundant system. The output of the $\overline{\text{SPIF}}$-designed monitor is used to initiate the switching in of a new module, as shown in Figure 8.7.

The techniques treated in this and the last section are concerned with specific logical approaches to the problem of masking faults that can occur in combinational and sequential switching circuits. These and other techniques must be integrated into a complete system in order to achieve computational reliability. The remainder of this chapter presents some approaches to the architecture of reliable computers.

8.5 ARCHITECTURE OF RELIABLE COMPUTERS
[8, 9, 10]

The interest in reliable computers began when a large number of components were first connected together and the resulting system reliability was unsatisfactory. Initial efforts were aimed at increasing the reliability of the individual components. Thus, the evolution from vacuum tubes to transistors, to integrated circuits, and to medium-scale and large-scale integrated circuits now enables us to design rather sophisticated computers with tolerable reliability. However, the reliability of computers which do not employ redundancy still cannot achieve the reliability needed in aerospace missions. For example, the required MTBF for short-mission computers is from 2000 to

5000 hours, and these computers typically employ triple modular redundancy in the arithmetic and control units [9]. The requirements for long space missions such as the Jupiter Fly-by place the extreme requirement of 10^5 hours on MTBF. Thus, a great deal of effort has been directed toward the design of computers which can achieve these specifications. The application of TMR to nonredundant computers typically yields a gain of only approximately 2 in MTBF. Thus, incorporation of TMR throughout present spacecraft computers would not significantly increase the MTBF. The architecture of a computer which attempts to achieve large MTBF is described in the remainder of this chapter.

The STAR (self-testing and repairing) computer was designed and built at the California Institute of Technology, Jet Propulsion Laboratory, as a vehicle for the development of high-reliability aerospace computers. The STAR was designed to cope with four major classes of faults: transient, permanent, random, and catastrophic. Transient faults may exist for only one machine cycle, whereas permanent faults are the s-a-0 or s-a-1 variety. Random faults are those that are not permanent and not fleeting or transient but occur at random intervals. Catastrophic failures occur when one failure causes faults which are distributed throughout the system.

The correction of faults in a computer system cannot be allocated solely to the hardware but must include the software as well. The imposition of additional work on the programmer, however, is, as in most other computer designs, something which is desirable to avoid. However, the backing up and restarting of a program after a fault is detected must be a software-hardware task. Certain error detection and correction tasks can be handled by either the hardware or the software, and, given this choice, most systems in STAR were implemented in hardware. For example, it is well known that noise which occurs on buses and in core memories can cause errors to occur in typically one bit of a parallel bit stream. Therefore, one redundant bit is often added to the system, which is 0 if there are an even number of 1s in the string and which is 1 if there are an odd number of 1s in the string. Thus, if the number of 1s is odd and this "parity" bit is 0, then one knows that an error in either the bit stream or the parity bit has occurred. If this occurs in reading a word from core memory, then one may merely read the same location again in which case the bit string and the parity bit probably agree. The rereading of a given location can be accomplished with either software or hardware. Additional redundant bits can be added to a bit string to detect and correct more than one fault [11, 12]; however, they will not be treated here. All machine words of STAR, both data and instructions, are encoded in error-detecting codes which act while a program is in execution.

The hardware of the STAR is organized around a module replacement system. Therefore, one or more spares and the associated switching hardware must be available to replace operating units when permanent faults are detected. Each of these modular units is self-contained and includes its own instruction decoder and sequence generator. This enables each unit to operate independently, thus isolating failures from other parts of the system. It is interesting to note that decentralization and distribution of control also allowed the communications network in Chapter 7 to achieve a high degree of reliability. All modules are permanently connected to the appropriate buses. Modules are designed to fail and power-down with their outputs in the zero state, thereby not disturbing the buses. This configuration also obviates the need for an input-output switching network for each module—the active module is the one which is powered. Since the remaining modules are not powered, their MTBF is generally greater than that for the powered modules.

The replacement of modules is controlled by a central processor called TARP (test and repair processor). The TARP contains the fault location logic and generates clock and control-sync signals, program recovery registers, and module power switching logic. It should be clear that the TARP must be extremely reliable since it controls the remainder of STAR. This high reliability was achieved by making the TARP a hybrid (3, 2) system. That is, it is TMR with two spares. Before we examine the details of the TARP, it is useful to examine the structure of the STAR, given in Figure 8.17. The TARP is connected via the control bus and the status lines to monitor each element of the system and controls the active modules via the power switch lines. The validity of every word sent on the two memory buses is checked with respect to the coding placed on the signals. Also, the status messages from the functional units are checked with respect to the predicted response. Faults or errors detected by the TARP interrupt normal operation, and the recovery mode is entered. In the recovery mode a *rollback point* address register points to the location where normal operation is to be resumed. Then either the TARP restarts the program at the rollback point or, if a module faults repeatedly, it is replaced and the program is restarted from the rollback point.

It is now of interest to examine the nature of the coding which is used in the STAR, as it is a simple but effective system. The STAR words are 32 bits wide divided into eight 4-bit "nibbles." Data are transmitted in a series-parallel manner on a four-line data bus, where one nibble is transmitted in parallel and the eight nibbles are transmitted in serial. The formats of the instruction and operand words are shown in Figure 8.18. Note that the seven

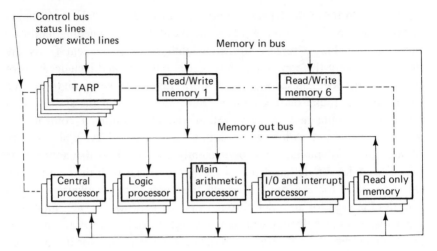

Figure 8.17. STAR architecture.

rightmost operand nibbles make up a b field and that the leftmost nibble makes up the c field. The 28-bit b field is the desired binary number, while the c field is the check nibble, which is computed from

$$c(b) = 15 - |b|_{15} \qquad (8.30)$$

where $|b|_{15}$ is the residue modulo 15 of the binary number b. If one considers $c(b)$ the lowest-order nibble, then the operand word is always a multiple of 15. The checking algorithm then merely computes a residue modulo 15 of the received word, and if it is nonzero, then an error has occurred. This same modulo 15 residue code is used on the address part of the instruction word, where

$$c(a) = 15 - |a|_{15} \qquad (8.31)$$

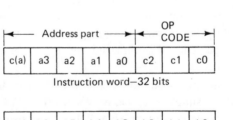

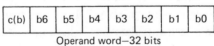

Figure 8.18. Instruction and operant word formats of STAR.

This code gives 4 bits of redundant error-detecting bits, one for each line of the data bus.

The op code is coded in a different way. Each of the three nibbles of the op code is encoded in a 2-out-of-4 code, where only 2 of the 4 bits can be 0 or 1 for valid codes. This leaves only 6 valid op codes per nibble and a total of 6^3 valid op code forms. The check circuit for op code errors then looks for nibbles where there are less than or more than two 1s or 0s.

The STAR computer is a very interesting design in that it employs several of the available techniques for repair and reliability in one computer, including TMR, hybrid (N, S) redundancy, module replacement, and error-detecting codes.

8.6 SUMMARY

An overview of the reliability and repair problem was presented in this chapter. The probability of failure, reliability, and MTBF analyses were introduced, and fundamental limitations were described.

Specific methods for designing reliable computational systems were offered. Each of these techniques—TMR, hybrid (N, S) modular redundancy, quadded logic, and SPIF analysis—offers solutions to some aspect of the problem. The description of the STAR computer provided an example of a specific design which incorporates several of these techniques.

8.7 EXERCISES

8.1. Calculate the reliability of the following networks:

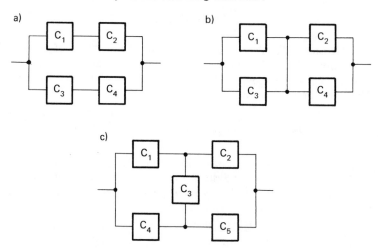

8.2. Given a component with an expected failure rate of 0.93/sec, find
(a) The MTBF of the component.
(b) The MTBF of a system with 10 of these components in series.
(c) The MTBF of a system with 100 of these components in series.

8.3. Compute the reliability of the complete TMR system shown in Figure 8.6, where the failure rate of the restoring organs is λ_r and of the Cs is λ.

8.4. Design a quadded network which realizes the function $Y = AB + CD$ using AND and OR gates.

8.5. Design a quadded network which realizes the logical function $Y = A(B + C)$ using NAND and NOR gates.

8.6. A system using 1000 components connected in series is to be constructed. The reliability of the system must equal or exceed 0.96. What is the required reliability of the individual components?

8.7. Show that the logical product of all projections of the SPIF of the network used as an example in Section 8.4 reveals the complete SPIF given in Eq. (8.25).

8.8. A counter which follows the sequence 00, 01, 11, 10 is to be part of a reliable system.
(a) Design the counter using J-K flip-flops.
(b) Find the SPIF of the entire network.
(c) Is there a minimal set of projections other than the complete SPIF which covers the network?
(d) Design an error-indicating network for this sequential circuit. Assume that flip-flop delays are twice the gate delays.

8.9. Find the fault which is propagated within the flip-flop of Figure 8.12(b) but does not get out.

REFERENCES

1. von Neumann, J., "Probabilistic Logics and the Synthesis of Reliable Organisms from Unreliable Components," Automata Studies, in *Annals of Mathematical Studies*, No. 34, C. E. Shannon and J. McCarthy, eds., Princeton University Press, Princeton, N.J., 1956.

2. Moore, E. F., and C. E. Shannon, "Reliable Circuits Using Less Reliable Relays," *Journal of the Franklin Institute*, Vol. 262, pp. 191–208 and 281–297, 1956.

3. Mathur, F., and A. Avizienis, "Reliability Analysis and Architecture of a Hybrid-Redundant Digital System: Generalized Triple Modular Redundancy with Self-Repair," *AFIPS Spring Joint Computer Conference Proceedings*, Vol. 36, pp. 375–383, 1970.

4. Tryon, J. G., "Quadded Logic," in *Redundancy Techniques for Computing Systems*, R. H. Wilcox and W. C. Mann, eds., Spartan, New York, 1962, pp. 205–228.

5. PIERCE, W. H., *Failure-Tolerant Computer Design*, Academic Press, New York, 1965.

6. BEIZER, B., "A New Theory for the Analysis, Synthesis, Cutting and Splicing of Sequential Switching Networks," Ph.D. Dissertation, University of Pennsylvania, Philadelphia, Pa., 1966.

7. ROBERTS, DAVID C., "A Processor for Implementing SPIF Techniques for Self-Repair, Part I—Theory and Application, Part II—Design Goals and Program Operation," *Computer Design*, Vol. 8, No. 12, pp. 59–64, and Vol. 9, No. 1, pp. 63–69, Dec. 1969 and Jan. 1970.

8. AVIZIENIS, A., G. C. GILLEY, F. P. MATHUR, D. A. RENNELS, J. A. ROHR, and D. K. RUBIN, "The STAR (Self-Testing and Repairing) Computer: An Investigation of the Theory and Practice of Fault-Tolerant Computer Design," *IEEE Transactions on Computers*, Vol. C-20, No. 11, pp. 1312–1321, Nov. 1971.

9. AVIZIENIS, A., "Design of Fault-Tolerant Computers," in *1967 Fall Joint Computer Conference, AFIPS Conference Proceedings*, Vol. 31, Washington, D.C., 1967, pp. 733–743.

10. AVIZIENIS, A., "An Experimental Self-Repairing Computer," in *Information Processing '68, Proceedings of the IFIP Congress*, Vol. 2, 1968, pp. 872–877.

11. ROTH, J. P., W. G. BOURICIUS, W. C. CARTER, and P. R. SCHNEIDER, "Phase II of an Architectural Study for a Self-Repairing Computer," *SAMSO-TR-67-106*, U.S. Air Force Space and Missile Systems Command, Los Angeles, Calif., Nov. 1967, AD 825460.

12. CARTER, W. C., and W. G. BOURICIUS, "A Survey of Fault-Tolerant Computer Architecture and Its Evaluation," *Computer (IEEE)*, Vol. 4, No. 1, pp. 9–16, Jan./Feb. 1971.

9

NEURONS
AND
NEURAL MODELS

INTRODUCTION

Thus far we have been concerned with specific physical systems in which the concepts of adaptation, learning, self-organization, and self-repair have been incorporated to advantage. As suggested in Chapter 5, however, these concepts also have significance in psychology and physiology. Certainly one can find examples of adaptation, learning, self-organization, and self-repair in nature and specifically the human nervous system and the brain. Ashby [1] described many of these processes in his specification of a *Design for a Brain*. Attempts to understand physiological systems and processes and to use this understanding in the creation of new designs have continued since that time. For example, this "bionic" approach was, in part, responsible for the development of the self-organizing controller described in Chapter 6 [2, 3]. This early interest in the use of physiological phenomena also led to the study of the basic processing element of nervous systems, the neuron.

Elementary neurophysiology is presented here as an introduction to some of the processing models of the neuron. Specific models describing detailed analog neuronal behavior will not be presented, however. These models have been applied to the design of adaptive, learning, self-repairing, and pattern recognition systems as well as the computer itself. They also provide a basis for the understanding of brain functioning.

9.1 PHYSIOLOGY OF THE NEURON

It should be emphasized that most of what is known about the neuron is based on experimental observation of sciatic (motor) neurons [4, 5]. These cells are relatively large and thereby lend themselves to external and internal probing. However, the behavior of all neurons is similar to these.

It would be foolish to entertain the supposition that the brain could be sufficiently characterized by studying only afferent neurons to the cortex of the brain, or sciatic nerve functioning. There are many phenomenologically obvious questions which preclude this reasoning: Where, for instance, is the memory located within the cerebellum and how is it organized, or where is the "screen" upon which consciousness is played? These questions have yet to be answered in even the anatomical sense.

Thus, although an attempt to model the brain in its entirety would prove to be an insurmountable task at this point in time, there is still much to be learned from the study of information processing in the nervous system. Recent work has indeed led to some very interesting models of portions of the brain which are both anatomically and phenomenologically sound. The main thrust of this work has been aimed at understanding portions of the brain which are highly stylized in their structure or in which it is known that certain behaviors are centered. Of note is the model of the reticular formation as developed by Kilmer et al. [6]. This part of the brain is analogous to a major state generator of a computer, as it is here that the overall state of the animal is determined, e.g., sleep, eat, groom, and mate. This model considers both the anatomical and behavioral aspects of this portion of the brain. Another portion of the brain, the cerebellum, has received a great deal of attention because of its uniform structure and the fact that the learning of many motor tasks centers in this structure. Marr [7, 8], Albus [9], and Mortimer [10] have developed theoretical and logical neural models of this most interesting region. A study of the behavioral and anatomical nature of perception and the eye-brain system has been undertaken by Didday [11] and Arbib [12]. Their work has attempted to understand the processing which takes place when an object is viewed and patterns in an animal's environment are recognized.

It is with these thoughts in mind that a physiological description of the neuron is included herein. The description is by no means to be considered anatomically or functionally exhaustive, but is rather intended to serve as a basis for the various attempts at modeling the logical behavior of this biological structure.

The neuron, shown in general form in Figure 9.1, consists of a nucleus and associated protoplasm (cytoplasm). This organism exists at a very high metabolic rate and is interconnected with numerous adjacent cells. An abundance of branches (dendrites) comprise the outer surface of the neuron; these units bring information into the cell body or soma.

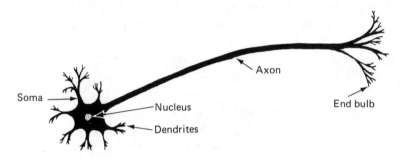

Figure 9.1. Neuron.

A long thin cylindrical fiber called the *axon* may be considered the output cable of the nerve cell. The axon is capable of electrochemically transmitting information concerning the state of the cell. Depending on the particular function of the neuron, the axon may vary in length from less than a millimeter up to a meter and in width from 0.1 micron to 1 millimeter. This substructure undergoes considerable arborization as it terminates in end bulbs near the dendrites of other neurons. These near-connections were termed "synapses" by Sir Charles Sherrington, who laid the basis of what is now known as synaptology [13]. An impulse traveling down the axon is terminated at the end bulbs and, if conditions permit, is regenerated by the next neuron in the chain. This retransmission was experimentally postulated by Sir Henry Dale and Otto Loewi some 40 years ago, the process being sometimes electrical and sometimes chemical. The speed of impulse propagation along the axonal fiber is given approximately by the following relationship:

velocity = frequency + diameter; this quantity may approach 100 meters per second in some of the intermuscular neurons.

A neuron will produce an output only when a sufficiently large number of impulses are presented to its dendritic area in a short period of time (the latent period of summation). In actual fact, some inputs hinder firing; thus, it would be correct to say that a neuron fires when the active excitatory inputs exceed the active inhibitory inputs by an amount equal to the "threshold value" of the cell. A portion of the soma called the *spike initiator loci* performs this summation and comparison, producing a pulsed output signal for the stated conditions of input.

To understand this process in greater anatomical detail, one must consider the previously mentioned work of Sir John Eccles [13]. Through the use of the electron microscope, it has been determined that the distance from the end bulbs or synaptic knobs to the synaptic membrane of the adjoining dendrite is a remarkably uniform 200 angstroms. This space has been termed the *synaptic cleft* and is shown in Figure 9.2. Throughout the structure of the end bulbs there are numerous tiny sacs (vesicles) which contain a transmitter substance for relaying the impulse to the attached neuron's dendrite. The transmitter substance triggers a neural reaction that is a function of the ionic composition of the cell and the axon.

The internal fluid of the cell is at a more negative potential (70 millivolts) than the surrounding solution of ions. This condition allows the concentration of chloride (Cl^-) ions to be about 14 times greater on the outside of the neuronic membrane. What is not fully explained, however, is the 30 to 1 concentration difference of the potassium (K^+) ions. This condition would require a potential difference of 90 millivolts, a disparity of some 20 millivolts

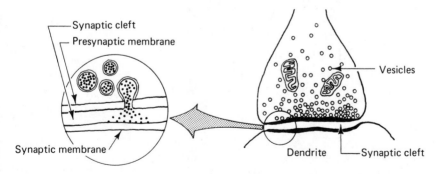

Figure 9.2. End bulb and the synaptic cleft.

from the existing conditions. Investigation also reveals that the concentration of sodium (Na⁺) ions outside the cell exceeds the internal concentration by a factor of 10. This is a truly remarkable state of affairs, since the sodium ions must be pumped against a potential of 130 millivolts (70 millivolts of internal potential plus 60 millivolts to allow for the concentration difference).

The biochemical status of the nerve cell is illustrated in Figure 9.3. Since the normal resting potential in the cell is −70 millivolts with respect to the outside of the cell, there must be a metabolic mechanism which maintains

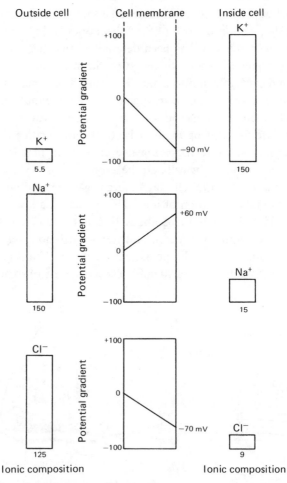

Figure 9.3. Relative densities of cellular ions and the potential gradient necessary to maintain these densities.

the unbalance of $-90 - (-70) + 60 = 40$ millivolts between the outside and inside of the cell. Thus, a metabolic sodium pumping mechanism has been hypothesized which maintains this difference.

The work of Hodgkin [14], Huxley [15], and Katz [16] has also shown that the propagation of the nerve impulse is accompanied by an abrupt change in the permeability of the cell membrane—sodium ions are allowed to enter the cell in an avalanche type of reaction which depolarizes the cell from 0.1 to 2 millimeters along its length. The fact that the axon now becomes positive constitutes the actual nerve impulse which is propagated along the axon. After the impulse has traveled the length of the axon, the membrane becomes impermeable to sodium, and an effective potassium gate opens. Thus, the resting potential of the cell is restored in about a millisecond.

The maximum rate at which pulses can be propagated down a nerve cell is approximately 500 pulses per second. The typical amplitude of a nerve pulse is approximately 100 millivolts; i.e., the pulse reaches $+30$ millivolts. The delay time between excitation of the nerve and pulse generation is from 0.1 to 1 millisecond.

With these facts in hand, one is now ready to consider the action at the synapse. The function of the excitatory synapse is to allow sodium ions to enter the cell body in a depolarizing action. When the cell has been depolarized to some threshold value, the nerve impulse is initiated. Each excitatory impulse is summed by actually changing the permeability of the cell to sodium ions in unit steps. This action allows the sodium ions to flow along their electrochemical potential gradient. The transmitter substance, acetylcholine, is the agent responsible for this change in permeability. This substance is injected across the synaptic cleft and attaches itself to the synaptic membrane within a few microseconds. The effect of the acetylcholine is diminished in about a millisecond by the enzyme cholinesterase. In the inhibitory synapse the transmitter substance acts to change the permeability of the cell membrane to allow either potassium ions to flow from or chlorine atoms to flow into the cell.

In summarizing, it should be noted that all the ions mentioned have diameters less than 2.9 angstroms; this dimension represents the resolvability limit of the best electron microscopes. Thus, it must be realized that much is still to be understood concerning neural functioning. Several gross manifestations of nervous activity have been examined along with the concepts of inhibition, summation, threshold values, and the chemical explanation of their functioning. The response of a neuron to its input has been termed "all or nothing." This is partially true in that a spike of voltage appears on the axon only if the algebraic sum of the inputs exceeds the threshold value of the cell. Further intensification of the inputs does not alter the characteristics of the output spike itself. On the other hand, the neuron does indicate the intensity of its inputs by its frequency of response, functioning in the manner of a voltage-controlled oscillator [17].

The frequency of neural activity of neurons in a physiological sensor system has been shown to be proportional to the logarithm of the intensity of the input stimulus. Thus, the majority of nervous information appears to be transmitted by the frequency of the nerve response. This is a significant fact from the standpoint of reliability. The failure of a single neuron to fire does not have the consequences it would have in an all-digital system; here the only effect is a blurring of the intensity function. The information train is not destroyed; the output is momentarily incorrect by a small value. This system is called integral pulse frequency modulation (IPFM) [18]. This fact has been overlooked in many all-digital approaches to neural modeling. Finally, the threshold value of a neural element is a function of time and is subject to various influences. For example, after once firing there is a "refractory period" during which the unit is incapable of *firing* again; repeated firings also raise the threshold value of the cell (the cell is said to fatigue).

9.2 INFORMATION CODING IN NERVE PULSES

Let us now consider the nature of the informational coding of nervous pulses in more detail. First, examine the plot of pulse frequency versus excitation as given in Figure 9.4. Here it is clear that the pulse frequency is directly proportional to the excitation. The information carried through the nervous system is contained in the *time between successive pulses*. For example, a high level of excitation generates a high-frequency pulse stream, whereas a low level of excitation generates a low-frequency pulse stream. Thus, for a particular amount of excitation, $s(t)$, the pulse sequence is

$$P_T = \sum_{n=1}^{\infty} \delta(\theta(t) - 2\pi n) \tag{9.1}$$

where an expression for $\theta(t)$ can be found from an analogy to frequency modulation:

$$\theta(t) = 2\pi K_0 \int_0^t s(t)\, dt + 2\pi\theta_0 + \omega_c t \tag{9.2}$$

Equation (9.2) represents the argument of the periodic carrier function of

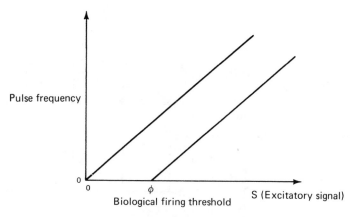

Figure 9.4. IPFM response characteristics.

frequency ω_c. Here, the carrier frequency ω_c and initial phase θ_0 are assumed to be zero. Therefore, the pulse generation criterion becomes

$$2\pi K_0 \int_0^t s(t)\, dt = 2\pi n \tag{9.3}$$

from Equation (9.1). Now, consider the interval after a pulse is generated where the instantaneous frequency is

$$\gamma_i = \frac{1}{t_i - t_{i-1}}$$

$$2\pi K_0 \int_{t_{i-1}}^{t_i} s(t)\, dt = 2\pi i, \qquad \text{where } i = n \tag{9.4}$$

The pulse generation criterion now becomes

$$\int_{t_{i-1}}^{t_i} s(t)\, dt = \frac{i}{K_0} \tag{9.5}$$

where $K_0 > 0$ and is a constant associated with characteristics of the cell. A simple model which generates IPFM pulses is illustrated in Figure 9.5. The current source charges the capacitor as a function of the stimulus e_s. When the voltage across the capacitor, $e(t)$, equals the firing threshold of the unijunction transistor, V_F, a pulse is generated at the output.

Now, consider the case where the input is a step function, $s(t) = S_0 u_{-1}(t)$:

$$K_0 \int_0^{t_i} S_0\, dt = i$$

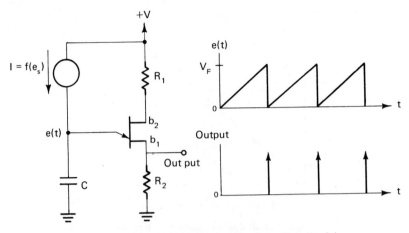

Figure 9.5. Model of IPFM generator where V_f is the firing potential of the unijunction transistor.

and

$$K_0 S_0 t_i = i$$

$$t_i = \frac{i}{K_0 S_0}$$

Also,

$$t_{i-1} = \frac{i - 1}{K_0 S_0}$$

Therefore, the pulse frequency is

$$\gamma_i = \frac{1}{(i/K_0 S_0) - [(i - 1)/K_0 S_0]} = K_0 S_0 \qquad (9.6)$$

which is a pulse train of constant frequency.

The nature of IPFM can now be summarized. The incremental amplitude of the input information is coded into a time interval where the longer the interval between pulses, the lower the value of the excitation and vice versa.

9.3 MODELS

In studying the numerous efforts in neural modeling, one can readily discern that several of the more significant attempts have stemmed from the original work of McCulloch and Pitts [19]. The McCulloch-Pitts model is not a complete physiological model of an actual nerve cell but rather a simple

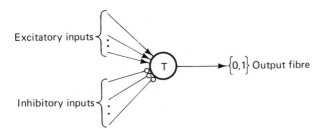

Figure 9.6. McCulloch-Pitts model.

two-state representation of the logical processing that occurs in nerve cells. The basic McCulloch-Pitts neural cell is shown in Figure 9.6. The output fiber of the cell relays information concerning the state of the neuron (firing or not firing) and eventually becomes an input to another cell (or the same cell). Any number of inputs is allowed, and they are divided into two classes. The excitatory input, represented by a line terminated in an arrowhead, tends to excite the cell in a unit increment toward firing. The excitatory lines carry a weight of 1 for the present discussion. The inhibitory input, represented by a line terminated in a small circle, is capable of totally inhibiting the cell from firing. Let T represent the numerical value of the firing threshold for the cell. The McCulloch-Pitts cell will fire when the sum of the excitatory inputs is equal to or greater than the threshold value, T, and no inhibitory input is activated, or, more formally,

Input Conditions	Output
$E \geq T, \quad I = 0$	Firing
$E \geq T, \quad I > 0$	Not firing
$E < T, \quad I = 0$	Not firing
$E < T, \quad I \leq 0$	Not firing

Thus, for the single cell the output at $t + \Delta T$ is not a function of the output at t.

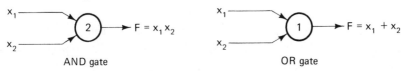

Ordinary Boolean logic functions can be readily implemented from this general configuration; examples of the logical AND and the logical OR are shown here. The numbers within the elements indicate the value of the thresh-

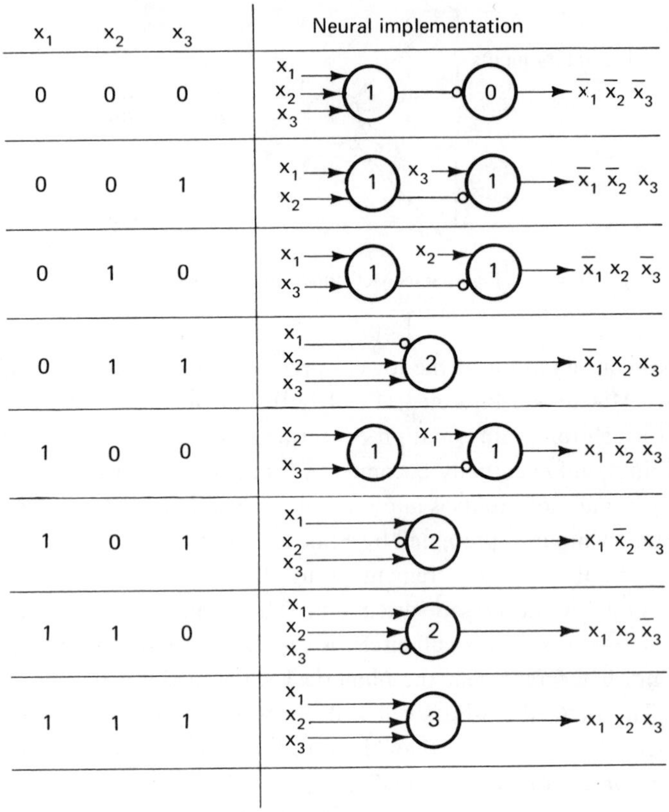

x_1	x_2	x_3	Neural implementation
0	0	0	$x_1, x_2, x_3 \rightarrow \boxed{1} \rightarrow \boxed{0} \rightarrow \overline{x}_1 \overline{x}_2 \overline{x}_3$
0	0	1	$x_1, x_2 \rightarrow \boxed{1} \xrightarrow{x_3} \boxed{1} \rightarrow \overline{x}_1 \overline{x}_2 x_3$
0	1	0	$x_1, x_3 \rightarrow \boxed{1} \xrightarrow{x_2} \boxed{1} \rightarrow \overline{x}_1 x_2 \overline{x}_3$
0	1	1	$x_1, x_2, x_3 \rightarrow \boxed{2} \rightarrow \overline{x}_1 x_2 x_3$
1	0	0	$x_2, x_3 \rightarrow \boxed{1} \xrightarrow{x_1} \boxed{1} \rightarrow x_1 \overline{x}_2 \overline{x}_3$
1	0	1	$x_1, x_2, x_3 \rightarrow \boxed{2} \rightarrow x_1 \overline{x}_2 x_3$
1	1	0	$x_1, x_2, x_3 \rightarrow \boxed{2} \rightarrow x_1 x_2 \overline{x}_3$
1	1	1	$x_1, x_2, x_3 \rightarrow \boxed{3} \rightarrow x_1 x_2 x_3$

Figure 9.7. Three-variable minterm realizations with neural elements.

old of the element. It is significant to note that the same cell was used in implementing these functions; the threshold value of the cell was merely changed. However, Figure 9.7 shows the basic implementation of all the minterms of three variables. It is significant to note that, in several cases, more than one cell is needed to form the minterm.

Another model of the logical behavior of the neuron is a variation on the basic McCulloch-Pitts cell. The linear weighted model (Figure 9.8) is a cell with basic characteristics which are similar to those already mentioned with the important difference that the inhibitory inputs now have a weight of -1. Thus, an inhibitory line carries no more importance than the excitatory input. The cell fires when the difference between the sum of the active excitatory inputs and the sum of the active inhibitory inputs is equal to or

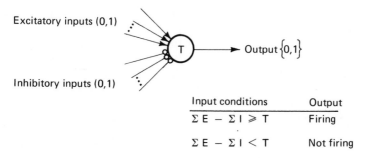

Figure 9.8. Linear weighted cell model.

greater than the threshold value of the cell. An example of how logic may be performed with this element is shown in the accompanying network, which provides an output if one, two, or three but not four of the inputs are true. One may readily see that the type of logic involved is essentially the same as the McCulloch-Pitts neuron, the only difference being in the specific implementation.

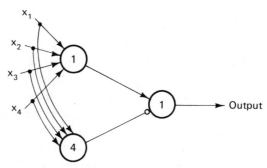

A final model is the majority organ used in Chapter 8. Here the output fires if a majority of the inputs are excitatory.

It is also useful to hypothesize methods whereby memory may be implemented within a neural array. A simple neural memory model incorporates the fact that there is an inherent delay in the propagation of signals through a neuron. Thus, it is reasonable to consider the *unit delay organ* shown in Figure 9.9(a). Here, an input at some time t appears at the output at time $t + \Delta T$. A memory element which uses the delay in a feedback arrangement is shown in Figure 9.9(b). A single pulse entering the write line when the inhibit is zero propagates through the cell continuously until the inhibit line is activated, causing the pulse to be "forgotten."

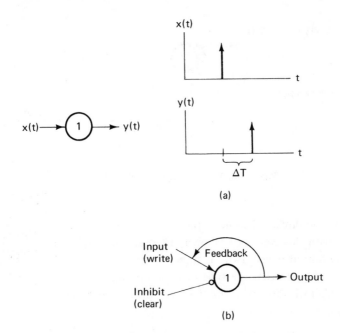

(a)

Input (write)
Feedback

Inhibit (clear)

1

Output

(b)

Figure 9.9. Unit delay organ and its use as a memory element.

Another model for neural memory has been hypothesized from clinical data. Medical case histories have indicated [20] that the perception of an event must be stored in a man's brain for a period of time before he will have recall of that event. A man who receives a serious injury affecting brain functioning will not be able to recall events for some 20 to 30 minutes prior to the injury. It would then seem that one may speak of a short-term memory which reinforces itself in time, thus becoming a long-term memory. Physiologically, it has been postulated that the end bulbs increase in size with repeated use or that specific proteins are formed, changing the threshold of the cell. The exact nature of this process is unknown, however, a neural cell can be used to implement this function by lowering the threshold of the cells involved in repeated use. Thus, consider the cell shown in Figure 9.10(a) whose behavior

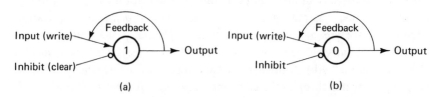

(a)

(b)

Figure 9.10. Short-term and permanent memory configuration with neural elements.

is identical to the memory cell shown in Figure 9.9(b). After repeated firings, the cell threshold becomes lower and eventually looks like the cell in Figure 9.10(b), where the threshold has been reduced to zero and, since the inhibition in this state has no effect, the cell will continue firing indefinitely, thereby implementing permanent memory.

9.4 THRESHOLD LOGIC

The logical behavior of neurons as represented by the models given in this chapter has led to the specification of a logical element which has been used to implement computer elements as well as certain types of pattern recognition systems. Thus, it is useful both practically and pedagogically to investigate this so-called threshold logic element.

A general single-level threshold logic element is shown in Figure 9.11. This device has N binary inputs and a binary output function F. Each input line X_i has a weighting factor W_i operating on the binary input. W_i is allowed to take on both positive and negative values. The transmission function (F true or equal to 1) is present when the sum of each input multiplied by its respective weighting value is equal to or exceeds the threshold T. This is expressed as,

$$F = 1 \text{ if, } \quad \sum_{K=1}^{N} X_k W_k \geq T$$

Conversely, the negation (F false or equal to 0) is present when the weighted sum is less than the threshold. This condition is written,

$$F = 0 \text{ if, } \quad \sum_{K=1}^{N} W_k X_k < T$$

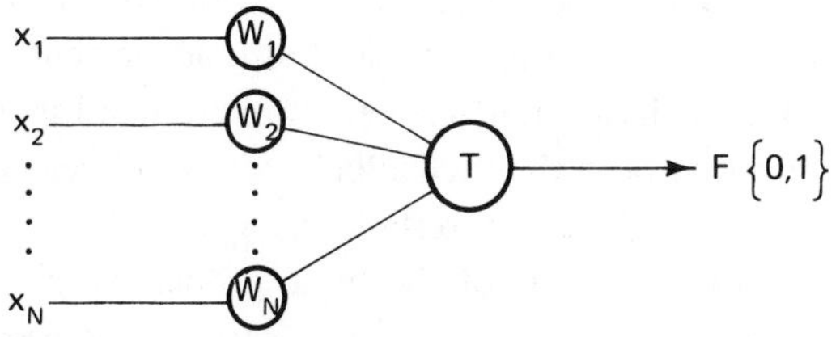

$$F = 0 \text{ if } \sum_{K=1}^{N} W_k X_k < T$$

$$F = 1 \text{ if } \sum_{K=1}^{N} W_k X_k \geq T$$

Figure 9.11. General single-level threshold logic element.

Basically the threshold element renders a single yes or no decision as to whether or not a given set or class of inputs is present. This dichotomy may be viewed geometrically. As in logic design, any Boolean function may be written in disjunctive normal form. This form involves the OR function on the standard product terms (minterms). These minterms may be mapped into an N-dimensional cube in a Euclidean hyperspace. Functions of three variables may be mapped onto the cube as shown in Figure 9.12.

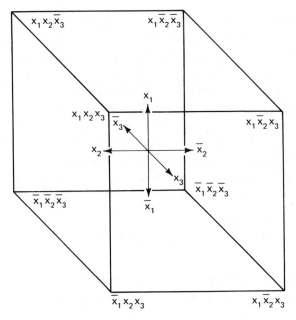

Figure 9.12. Three-variable hyperspace.

If the vertices representing the minterms of F can be separated from those of $\bar{F}$ by a single hyperplane, then the function is said to be linearly separable and can be realized by a single threshold element. Several examples of logic realization with threshold elements are given in Figure 9.13. It should now be apparent that both the McCulloch-Pitts and linear weighted neurons are special cases of single-level threshold elements.

First, let us consider some of the basic properties of linearly separable functions [21]. Some definitions are necessary for consideration of these properties:

1. A *switching function F* is any Boolean function of binary variables X_1, $\ldots$, X_n. A $+$ in a switching function will indicate logical union and the

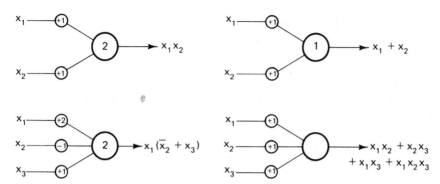

Figure 9.13. Examples of threshold logic.

juxtaposition of two or more variables such as, X_1X_2, will indicate intersection.

2. A *plane function P* is defined as being any function of the form

$$\sum_{K=1}^{N} W_k X_k$$

where the W_k are real constants.

These definitions plus the previous discussion on linearly separable functions lead to the first property of threshold logic elements.

Property 1: Any linearly separable switching function can be realized by a single threshold element.

The consequences of this property are immediately obvious. Any hypercube, such as is shown in Figure 9.12, can be separated into two distinct regions by a plane function P. Additionally, the plane function P, which has as its basic element $W_i X_i$, is the weighted sum of binary inputs. Any plane function can be realized with a single threshold element.

Property 2: If a linearly separable function is expressed in nonredundant disjunctive form,† no variable can appear both complemented and uncomplemented.

A function which has this property is called a *unate* function. Note that the unateness of a function is a necessary but not sufficient condition for

---

†Here non-redundant disjunctive form means that the function has been reduced and is written in a sum of products form.

linear separability. For example, consider the exclusive OR in two variables:

$$F = \bar{X}_1 X_2 + X_1 \bar{X}_2$$

This function is easily represented as the two solid points in the hyperspace for two variables in Figure 9.14 (in this case the hyperspace is merely a plane).

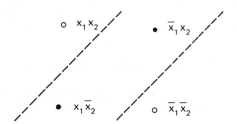

Figure 9.14. Hyperspace representation of two binary variables.

It is clear that no single linear hyperplane (in this case a straight line), which separates the two desired points from all the others, can be drawn. The function can be separated only by two linear hyperplanes, as illustrated by the dotted lines. Thus, the exclusive OR function, which is not unate, is not linearly separable. A plane function P which separates a space is called a separating plane (S.P.) function.

Property 3: If a variable appears uncomplemented in the nonredundant disjunctive expression of a linearly separable function, its coefficient in the S.P. function is positive; conversely, if the variable appears complemented, its coefficient is negative.

This property is necessary in order to maintain the algebraic consistency of the definition of the threshold element. Thus, a complemented term tends to inhibit the generation of an output from the element when that form is true by decreasing the value of the function with respect to the threshold,

$$-W_k X_k + P' = T \tag{9.7}$$

and an uncomplemented term tends to facilitate the generation of an output from the element when that term is true by increasing the value of the function with respect to the threshold,

$$W_k X_k + P' = T \tag{9.8}$$

Property 4: A unate function is linearly separable if and only if the function obtained from the reduced minterm form by uncomplementing all the complemented variables is itself linearly separable. In addition, the separating plane equations of the two functions are related as follows: If a complemented variable is uncomplemented, the sign of its coefficient is changed from negative to positive, and the magnitude of that coefficient is added to the threshold. And, if an uncomplemented variable is complemented, the sign of its coefficient is changed from positive to negative, and the magnitude of that coefficient is subtracted from the threshold.

This property is clear if one considers that the physical realization is independent of the sense of any of the literals, whereas the function realized is dependent on the sense of the literals. For example,

$$F(X_1, X_2, \ldots, X_M = 1, \ldots, X_N) = F(X_1, X_2, \ldots, \bar{X}_M = 1, \ldots, X_N)$$

and conversely

$$F(X_1, X_2, \ldots, X_m = 0, \ldots, X_N) = F(X_1, X_2, \ldots, \bar{X}_M = 0, \ldots, X_N)$$
$$(9.9)$$

Thus, the sense of the literal does not affect the linear separability of the function, although the functions realized are different. Consider the realization of the function

$$Y = X_1 \lor X_2$$

with the S.P. equation

$$X_1 + X_2 = 1$$

as shown below.

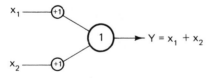

If one changes the sense of the literal X_2 to $\bar{X}_2$, the new function

$$Y = X_1 + \bar{X}_2$$

is still linearly separable. Its realization is shown below.

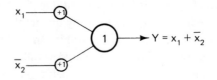

Consider the binary relationship

$$-\bar{X} = X - 1 \tag{9.10}$$

Similarly, the weighted variables satisfy the relation

$$-W_k\bar{X}_k = W_kX_k - W_k \tag{9.11}$$

Now it is possible to convert a complemented literal to an uncomplemented literal and vice versa by direct substitution of Eq. (9.10). For example, the S.P. equation for the function $Y = X_1 + \bar{X}_2$,

$$X_1 + \bar{X}_2 = 1$$

can be changed to one with uncomplemented literals by substituting

$$\bar{X}_2 = 1 - X_2$$

which gives a new S.P. equation,

$$X_1 + 1 - X_2 = 1$$

and

$$X_1 - X_2 = 0$$

which is the S.P. equation for the function

$$Y = X_1 + \bar{X}_2$$

Property 5: If F is linearly separable with the S.P. equation

$$\sum_{K=1}^{N} + W_kX_k = T \tag{9.12}$$

then the complement of F is linearly separable with the S.P. equation

$$\sum_{K=1}^{N} - W_kX_k = -T \tag{9.13}$$

For example, the realization of the function

$$Y = X_1 + X_2 X_3$$

is possible with the S.P. equation

$$2X_1 + X_2 + X_3 = 1.5$$

The complement of the function is

$$\bar{Y} = \overline{X_1 + X_2 X_3}$$

and

$$\bar{Y} = \bar{X}_1 \bar{X}_2 + \bar{X}_1 \bar{X}_3 \tag{9.14}$$

and the S.P. equation is

$$-2X_1 - X_2 - X_3 = -1.5$$

The gate which realizes $\bar{Y}$ in Eq. (9.14) is illustrated in Figure 9.15. It is clear that the gate in Figure 9.15 does realize $\bar{Y}$ as given.

$X_1\ X_2\ X_3$	$\sum W_k X_k$	$\bar{Y}$	
0 0 0	0	1	
0 0 1	−1	1	$T = -1.5$
0 1 0	−1	1	
0 1 1	−2	0	
1 0 0	−2	0	
1 0 1	−3	0	
1 1 0	−3	0	
1 1 1	−4	0	

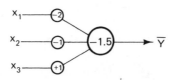

Figure 9.15. Threshold realization of $\bar{Y} = \bar{X}_1 \bar{X}_2 + \bar{X}_1 \bar{X}_3$.

Property 6: If F is linearly separable with the S.P. equation

$$\sum_{K=1}^{N} W_k X_k = T$$

then the complement of F is realizable with the S.P. equation

$$\sum_{K=1}^{N} W_k \bar{X}_k = \sigma - |T|$$

where

$$\sigma = \sum_{K=1}^{N} |W_k|$$

Thus, the complement of the function used in the illustration of Property 5 can also be realized with the S.P. equation

$$2\bar{X}_1 + \bar{X}_2 + \bar{X}_3 = 2.5$$

$X_1\ X_2\ X_3$	$\bar{X}_1\ \bar{X}_2\ \bar{X}_3$	$\sum W_k \bar{X}_k$	Y	
0 0 0	1 1 1	4	1	
0 0 1	1 1 0	3	1	
0 1 0	1 0 1	3	1	$T = 2.5$
0 1 1	1 0 0	2	0	
1 0 0	0 1 1	2	0	
1 0 1	0 1 0	1	0	
1 1 0	0 0 1	1	0	
1 1 1	0 0 0	0	0	

Property 7: If F is linearly separable with the S.P. equation

$$\sum_{K=1}^{N} W_k X_k = T$$

then the dual of F is realizable with the S.P. equation

$$\sum_{K=1}^{N} W_k X_k = \sigma - T$$

where the dual of $Y = F(X_1, X_2, \ldots, X_n)$ is

$$Y^d = \bar{F}(\bar{X}_1, \bar{X}_2, \ldots, \bar{X}_n)$$

The dual of

$$Y = X_1 + X_2 X_3$$

is

$$Y^d = X_1 \cdot (X_2 + X_3)$$

which is accomplished by complementing the function and then complementing each literal in the resulting expression. The S.P. equation of the dual above is

$$2X_1 + X_2 + X_3 = 4 - 1.5 = 2.5$$

$X_1\ X_2\ X_3$	$\sum X_k W_k$	Y^d	
0 0 0	0	0	
0 0 1	1	0	
0 1 0	1	0	
0 1 1	2	0	$T = 2.5$
1 0 0	2	0	
1 0 1	3	1	
1 1 0	3	1	
1 1 1	4	1	

The properties given above illustrate some of the characteristics which are useful in the analysis and synthesis of threshold logic networks. These properties are by no means exhaustive but are fundamental and serve as a basis for understanding this device.

9.5 SUMMARY

The brief physiological description of the neuron has served to introduce some of the detail associated with processing in "natural" systems. A serious student of engineering cybernetics must continually be aware of new discoveries in neurophysiology and brain functioning as a source of new design approaches. Certainly, the brain and nervous system represent a rather unique system which has functioned, evolved, and survived over the ages and merits the attention of engineers and computer scientists.

The processing and communications processes which take place in nervous systems were also introduced in this chapter. The all-or-nothing pulse generation associated with nerve elements was illustrated by means of IPFM. IPFM has also had certain impact in the area of automatic control because of its inherent noise rejection properties—another example of the bionic approach [22].

Some logical processing models of nervous behavior were also considered in this chapter. These models led directly to the threshold logic element as a processing device. The properties introduced here will serve as a basis for threshold logic synthesis in Chapter 10.

9.6 EXERCISES

9.1. Write the truth table for the neuron circuit shown here. With respect to conventional AND, OR, and NOT logic, what function does the second neuron perform?

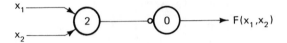

9.2. Consider the neuron-effector circuit shown below. The neuron is under steplike excitation $i(t)$ and is generating the pulse train $e(t)$. The effector is responding directly to the instantaneous pulse rate as follows:

$$R(t) = \frac{1}{t_{i+1} - t_i} \qquad \text{for } t_{i+2} > t \geq t_{i+1}$$

where t_i is the time of occurrence of the ith pulse.
(a) Plot the effector response, $R(t)$.
(b) Plot the effector response, $R(t)$, for the case where the neuron fails to fire at pulse time 4.

9.3. Draw a circuit using neural models with total inhibition which realizes the exclusive OR

$$F = A\bar{B} + \bar{A}B$$

9.4. Find a circuit using neural models with total inhibition which is equivalent to the majority organ with three inputs used in Capter 8.

9.5. An element in a memory network in which the threshold varies as a function of the number of times the element fires is given below. The initial threshold is unity.
(a) Write an expression and plot the value of the threshold as a function of the firings, N, if the threshold decreases by 0.1 with each firing. How many firings are required for the memory to become permanent?
(b) Write an expression and plot the value of the threshold as a function of firing if the threshold decreases by 0.1 with the first firing and decreases by twice the previous increment thereafter. How many firings are required for the memory to become permanent?
(c) Write an expression and plot the value of the threshold as a function of firing if the threshold decreases by 0.4 with the first firing and decreases by

one-half the previous increment on subsequent firing. What is the value of the threshold as N approaches infinity?

9.6. Write an expression for the pulse frequency output of an IPFM generator under the following excitation conditions:
(a) Ramp input, $s(t) = ts_0$, $t \geq 0$.
(b) Square law input, $s(t) = t^2 s_0$, $t \geq 0$.

9.7. Write the separating plane function and draw a schematic for a threshold logic realization for

$$Y = X_1 \bar{X}_2 + \bar{X}_2 X_3 + X_1 X_3$$

9.8. Which of the following functions are realizable with a single threshold element?
(a) $Y = X_1 X_2 + \bar{X}_1 \bar{X}_2$.
(b) $Y = X_1 \bar{X}_2 \bar{X}_3 + X_1 X_2 \bar{X}_3 + X_1 X_2 X_3 + X_1 \bar{X}_2 X_3$.
(c) $Y = X_1 \bar{X}_2 \bar{X}_3 + \bar{X}_1 X_2 \bar{X}_3 + X_1 X_2 X_3 + \bar{X}_1 \bar{X}_2 X_3$.
(d) $Y = \bar{X}_1 \bar{X}_2 \bar{X}_3 + \bar{X}_1 X_2 \bar{X}_3$.
(e) $Y = X_1 X_2 + \bar{X}_1 X_2 + X_1 \bar{X}_2 + \bar{X}_1 \bar{X}_2$.
(f) $Y = \bar{X}_1 X_2 \bar{X}_3 \bar{X}_4 + X_1 \bar{X}_2 \bar{X}_3 \bar{X}_4 + \bar{X}_1 X_2 \bar{X}_3 X_4 + X_1 \bar{X}_2 \bar{X}_3 X_4$
$\qquad + X_1 X_2 \bar{X}_3 X_4$.

REFERENCES

1. Ashby, W. R., *Design for a Brain*, Science Paperbacks, Chapman & Hall, London, 1966.

2. Lee, R. J., "Letter to the Editor," *Astounding Science Fiction*, July 1953.

3. Centner, R. M., J. M. Idelsohn et al., "Bionics Self-Adaption Capability," *Technical Report AFAL-TR-67-35*, Bendix Research Laboratories for Air Force Avionics Laboratory, Wright Patterson Air Force Base, Dayton, Ohio, April 1967.

4. Eccles, J. C., *The Physiology of Nerve Cells*, The Johns Hopkins Press, Baltimore, 1957.

5. Katz, B., *Nerve, Muscle and Synapse*, McGraw-Hill, New York, 1966.

6. Kilmer, W. L., W. S. McCulloch, and J. Blum, "A Model of the Vertebrate Central Command System," *International Journal of Man-Machine Studies*, Vol. 1, pp. 279–309, 1969.

7. Marr, D., "A Theory for Cerebral Neocortex," *Proceedings of the Royal Society, London, B.*, Vol. 176, pp. IGI–234, 1970.

8. MARR, D., "Simple Memory: A Theory for Archicortex," *Philosophical Transactions of the Royal Society, London, B.*, Vol. 262, No. 841, pp. 23–81, 1971.

9. ALBUS, JAMES S., "A Theory of Cerebellar Function," *Mathematical Biosciences*, Vol. 10, No. 1, Feb. 1971.

10. MORTIMER, J. A., "A Cellular Model for Mammalian Cerebellar Cortex," *Technical Report*, Computer and Communication Sciences Department, University of Michigan.

11. DIDDAY, RICHARD L., "The Simulation and Modeling of Distributed Information Processing in the Frog Visual System," Ph.D. Thesis, Stanford University, Stanford, Calif., 1970.

12. ARBIB, M. A., "How We Know Universals: Retrospect and Prospect," *Mathematical Biosciences*, Vol. 11, pp. 95–107, 1971.

13. ECCLES, J. C., "The Synapse," *Scientific American*, Vol. 212, No. 1, pp. 56–66, Jan. 1965.

14. HODGKIN, A. L., "The Ionic Basis of Nervous Conduction," *Science*, Vol. 145, pp. 1148–1153, Sept. 1964.

15. HUXLEY, A. F., "Excitation and Conduction in Nerve: Quantitative Analysis," *Science*, Vol. 145, pp. 1154–1159, Sept. 1964.

16. KATZ, B., "Nature of the Nerve Impulse," in *Biophysical Science, A Study Program*, J. L. Oncley et al., eds., Wiley, New York, 1959, Chapter 50.

17. JONES, R. W., et al., "Pulse Modulation in Physiological Systems, Phenomenological Aspects," *IRE Transactions on Bio-Medical Electronics*, Vol. BME-8, No. 1, Jan. 1961.

18. LI, C. C., "Integral Pulse Frequency Modulated Control Systems," Ph.D. Dissertation, Northwestern University, Evanston, Ill., 1961.

19. McCULLOCH, W. S., and W. PITTS, "A Logical Calculus of the Ideas Immanent in Nervous Activity," *Bulletin of Mathematical Biophysics*, Vol. 5, 1943.

20. WOOLDRIDGE, D. E., *Machinery of the Brain*, McGraw-Hill, New York, 1963.

21. LEWIS, P. M., and C. L. COATES, *Threshold Logic*, Wiley, New York, 1967.

22. PAVLIDIS, T., and E. I. JURY, "Analysis of a New Class of Pulse-Frequency-Modulated Feedback Systems," *IEEE Transactions on Automatic Control*, Vol. AC-10, No. 1, pp. 35–43, Jan. 1965.

10

THRESHOLD LOGIC

INTRODUCTION

The use of the threshold logic element both as a logical device and as an element in an adaptive system is considered in this chapter. Presently, the apparent advantages of threshold devices as elements in computer systems have not been realized, and their eventual application appears limited. On the other hand, threshold element arrays have been used in cybernetic systems especially for pattern recognition. The study of threshold logic includes many of the concepts which will be useful in our examination of pattern recognition in Chapter 11 as well as in placing the logical behavior of the neural models presented in Chapter 9 in perspective.

10.1 NUMBER OF LINEARLY SEPARABLE FUNCTIONS

It is clear from the previous discussion that all functions of N variables cannot be realized by a single threshold element. The question then arises, How many of the 2^{2^N} functions of N variables can be realized by a single threshold element? It is most difficult to enumerate all linearly separable functions of N variables. However, one may readily establish an upper bound [1]. The threshold function given in Chapter 9,

$$\sum_{K=1}^{N} W_k X_k = T \tag{10.1}$$

where we now let $T = W_0$, can be considered as a function of W rather than X and can be written as

$$\sum_{K=1}^{N} W_k X_k - W_0 = 0 \tag{10.2}$$

Consider that an equation such as (10.2) exists for each of the 2^N combinations of the X_k in a $(N + 1)$-dimensional W space. Each combination therefore defines a plane which divides W space into two regions. For the case of a single literal, X_1, each region defines the values of the weighting variables W_1 and W_2 for which a particular function is realized. For example, for a single binary variable, the equations of the $2^N = 2$ planes are

$$W_1(1) - W_0 = 0$$
$$W_1 = W_0$$

and

$$W_1(0) - W_0 = 0$$
$$W_0 = 0$$

These planes, the W_1 axis and a 45° line passing through the first and third quadrants, define regions in W space for which values of W_1 and W_0 will realize each of the Boolean functions indicated below:

X	F_0	F_1	F_2	F_3
0	0	1	0	1
1	0	0	1	1

Figure 10.1 illustrates this in the two-dimensional W space. Any point in a given region in W space defines the values of the variables W_0 and W_1 which will realize the function associated with that region. Thus, the point ($W_1 = 2$, $W_0 = 1$) will realize the function $F_2 = X$ with the plane equation, $2X - 1 = 0$. There are four regions in the above two-dimensional W space and thus four linearly separable functions of one variable. The number of regions into which the 2^N planes divide W space is equal to the number of linearly sepa-

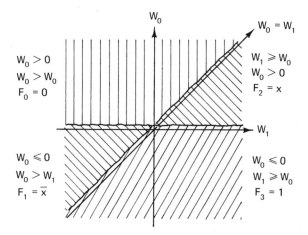

Figure 10.1. Distinct regions in W space.

rable functions of N variables. It is important to note that some of the 2^N planes, for $N > 1$, do not define any different regions in the W space. Therefore, the example of one variable is unique, and in general it is difficult to calculate the exact number of distinct regions whose boundaries are defined by the plane equations. However, the maximum number of regions which *any* P planes, not necessarily defined by plane equations, divide an S space can be calculated. First, let $R(P, S)$ be the maximum number of regions that P, $(S - 1)$-dimensional hyperplanes divide S space. In the limit,

$$R(P, 1) = 2 \qquad \text{for } P \geq 1$$
$$R(1, S) = 2 \qquad \text{for } S \geq 1$$

and $R(P, S)$ can be evaluated by applying a recursion equation which reduces the resultant expression to one of the forms above. If one considers only $P - 1$ hyperplanes in S space, then there are $R(P - 1, S)$ regions. The Pth hyperplane can be divided into at most $R(P - 1, S - 1)$ regions by the original $P - 1$ planes. Thus, a new region is added only if the new plane is intersected by one of the $P - 1$ planes, and the desired recursion relation is

$$R(P, S) = R(P - 1, S) + R(P - 1, S - 1) \qquad (10.3)$$

Performing one recursion on the right-hand side of (9.3) gives

$$R(P, S) = R(P - 2, S) + 2R(P - 2, S - 1) + R(P - 2, S - 2)$$

Another recursion gives

$$R(P, S) = R(P - 3, S) + 3R(P - 3, S - 1) + 3R(P - 3, S - 2)$$
$$+ R(P - 3, S - 3)$$

Continuing this process $R - 1$ times,

$$R(P, S) = \binom{P-1}{0}R(1, S) + \binom{P-1}{1}R(1, S - 1) + \binom{P-1}{2}R(1, S - 2)$$
$$+ \cdots + \binom{P-1}{P-1}R(1, S - P + 1) \tag{10.4}$$
$$= \sum_{i=0}^{P-1} \binom{P-1}{i}R(1, S - i) \tag{10.5}$$

But $R(1, S - i) = 2$. Therefore (10.2) becomes

$$R(P, S) = 2\sum_{i=0}^{P-1} \binom{P-1}{i}$$

Note that in (10.4) if P is greater than or equal to S, the resultant terms are degenerate, as

$$R(1, Q) = 0 \qquad \text{for } Q \leq 1$$

Therefore,

$$R(P, S) = 2\sum_{i=0}^{S-1} \binom{P-1}{i} \tag{10.6}$$

The upper limit on the number of linearly separable functions of N variables in $(N + 1)$-dimensional W space is

$$U(N) = 2\sum_{i=0}^{N} \binom{2^N - 1}{i} \tag{10.7}$$

It is possible to obtain a solution of (10.7) in closed form by noting that for N large,

$$2\sum_{i=0}^{N-1} \binom{2^N - 1}{i} \ll 2\binom{2^N - 1}{N} \tag{10.8}$$

Therefore,

$$U(N) \simeq \frac{2(2^N - 1)!}{N!(2^N - 1 - N)!} \tag{10.9}$$

Since the numerator contains N more terms in the $2^N - 1$ factorial expression than the $2^N - 1 - N$ factorial expression of the denominator, a further approximation is

$$U(N) \simeq \frac{2(2^N)^N}{N!} \tag{10.10}$$

Stirling's approximation is a closed-form approximation for $N!$, where N is large:

$$N! \simeq \sqrt{2}\,(\pi N)\left(\frac{N}{e}\right)^N \tag{10.11}$$

Finally, Eq. (10.10) can be rewritten as

$$U(N) \simeq \frac{\sqrt{2}}{\pi N}\left(\frac{e2^N}{N}\right)^N \tag{10.12}$$

The actual number of realizable threshold functions $E(N)$ has been calculated by others using enumeration and linear programming techniques [1,2,3] for up to seven variables. Table 10.1 lists the number of functions $F(N) = 2^{2^N}$; the upper limit of the number of threshold functions of N variables, $U(N)$; and the number of realizable threshold functions, $E(N)$, as a function of N. It is interesting to note that $F(N)$ increases at a much higher rate than does $E(N)$ or $U(N)$, indicating that single-level threshold logic becomes less powerful as N increases.

Table 10.1. Number of Functions, Number of Realizable Threshold Functions of N Variables, and Maximum Number of Realizable Threshold Functions as a Function of N

N	$F(N)$	$E(N)$	$U(N)$
1	4	4	4
2	16	14	14
3	256	104	128
4	65,536	1882	3882
5	$4,295 \times 10^9$	94,572	412,736
6	$18,4480 \times 10^{16}$	15,028,134	151,223,522
7	$\simeq 3.4 \times 10^{38}$	8,378,070,864	189,581,406,208

The design of a practical threshold element, however, requires some additional consideration. The concept of a gap describes the requirements on the region in which a decision can be made for a particular function. For example, consider the three-input AND gate shown in Figure 10.2. If the threshold is made $T = 3$, then the appropriate decision such that the three-input AND is realized can be made. Note, however, that if the threshold is

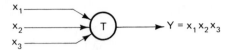

Figure 10.2. Threshold AND gate for $T = 3$.

made slightly greater than 2, the decision can also be made. Thus, the threshold can be such that

$$2 < T \leq 3$$

and in general the notation is

$$l < T \leq U$$

and the separating plane equation is

$$Y = (X_1 + X_2 + X_3) \; 3:2$$

and in general the separating plane equation is written as

$$Y = (W_1 X_1 + W_2 X_2 + W_3 X_3 + \ldots + W_n X_n) \; U:l$$

Also, the concept of a gap comes into play when one is dealing with real systems where tolerance, temperature, noise, and other parameters come into play and the ideal input output relationship given in Figure 10.3(a)

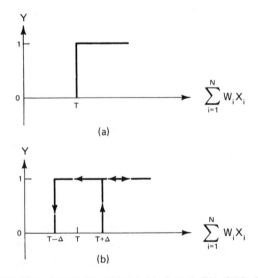

Figure 10.3. Comparison of (a) ideal and (b) physically realizable threshold functions.

cannot be realized. Instead, the threshold transfer function may exhibit hysteresis, as shown in Figure 10.3(b).

Thus, the wider the gap one can obtain in the theoretical realization of a particular function, the wider the tolerance on the components used in the physical realization of the device to perform the operation.

10.2 RELATIVE COEFFICIENT VALUES OF SINGLE LOGICAL ELEMENTS

At this point, it is of interest to consider the relative magnitude of the weights of the coefficients of the variables in the S.P. equation. The assignment of these weights must be related to the relative influence of a particular variable on the truth or falsehood of the function being realized. For example, consider the function

$$Y = X_1 + X_2 X_3$$

The fact that the variable X_1 alone can control the value of the function Y indicates that it must have this influence in the S.P. equation. Also, since the combination by logical AND of the variables X_2 and X_3 can influence the value of the function Y, the total weight of these two variables must equal that of X_1. However, individually the variables X_2 and X_3 must have weights less than that of X_1. Thus, the relative weights of the three variables are

$$W_1 > W_2 = W_3$$

which is consistent with its S.P. equation:

$$2X_1 + X_2 + X_3 = 2$$

Another way of looking at the relative weights of the variables is to examine the relative number of minterms which are included in the expressions associated with a given variable. Thus, consider the function where a variable, X_1, appears as a single term in the irredundant disjunctive form and no other variable appears alone:

$$F(X_1 X_2 \ldots X_N) = X_1 + F'(X_1, X_2, X_3, \ldots, X_N)$$

Thus, the number of minterms associated with the variable X_1, $N(X_1) = 2^{N-1}$, is greater than the number of minterms associated with any other variable, and the weight of X_1 in the S.P. equation must also be greater than the weight of any other variable. If two or more variables appear alone in the irredundant disjunctive form, then all these variables have equal weight which is greater than the weights associated with any other variables.

Next, consider terms in the irredundant disjunctive form which contain two variables, say

$$F(X_1, X_2, \ldots, X_N) = X_2X_4 + X_2X_3 + F''(X_1, X_2, \ldots, X_N)$$

The variables associated with more two-variable terms than the other variables not already ordered (here the only time that variables are considered ordered is when a greater-than relationship has been established) must have more minterms associated with them than any of the remaining variables but less than the number of minterms associated with a variable which appears alone. Variables which appear alone can influence the value of the function, as the truth of the function can be totally affected by the value of one of these single-variable terms. Thus, minterms included by a single-variable term and also associated with a higher-order term or terms cannot be considered when weighting variables associated with higher-order terms.

For the example above, the relative weight magnitudes when the two-variable terms are considered are

$$W_1 > W_2 > W_3 = W_4$$

Thus, the set of variables associated with the largest number of minterms must have greater weight than all the remaining variables and so forth but less weight than any single-term variable.

The process of relative weight assignment is continued until either all the variables have been considered or until all the terms in the irredundant disjunctive form have been examined.

This process can be seen more clearly by examining the following example. Given the function

$$Y = X_1 + X_2X_3 + X_3X_4$$

one can easily generate a Karnough map. However, here the map is generated such that the minterms associated with single-variable terms are considered first and are indicated by the subscript of the associated variables, two-variable terms are considered next, and minterms not associated with the single-variable terms are indicated by the subscript of the associated variables. The entries in the map, i, indicate minterms affected by that literal, X_i. It is clear in the accompanying map that X_1 has more influence on the value of

X_3X_4 \ X_1X_2	00	01	11	10
00			1	1
01			1	1
11	3-4	2-3-4	1-2-3-4	1-3-4
10		2-3	1-2-3	1

the function than any other variable, etc.; the relative coefficient order is then as follows:

$$W_1 > W_3 > W_2 = W_4$$

From the above, the procedure for establishing the weight magnitude hierarchy is as follows:

1. Consider all single-variable terms in the irredundant disjunctive form with complemented variables uncomplemented; these variables have greater weight than any other variables. If there are no single-term variables, proceed to order the two-variable terms as given in step 2.
2. Examine all the next higher-order terms; the variables in the lower-order set, other than single variable terms, which have not been ordered can now be ordered by weighting variables which appear in more of these terms greater than any other variables in that set. Variables which first appear in this order set can now be ordered in a similar manner. Variables associated with more of these terms have greater weight, etc. Variables in the first sets which have not been ordered may be ordered when the next higher-order terms are considered.
3. Examine the next higher-order terms and weight the variables as above.
4. Continue the ordering procedure until all variables have been ordered or all terms have been examined. At this point, it is possible that some variables have not been ordered and have weights which are equal to the weights of one or more other variables.

For example, order the relative magnitude of the weights of the variables in the function

$$Y = X_2 + \bar{X}_1 X_3 + X_3 \bar{X}_4 + X_3 X_5 X_6 + \bar{X}_1 X_5 X_6$$

First, the function is unate; hence, it may be linearly separable, and one can then uncomplement all complemented variables:

$$Y = X_2 + X_1 X_3 + X_3 X_4 + X_3 X_5 X_6 + X_1 X_5 X_6$$

Now examine all single-variable terms. Here X_2 is the only single-variable term; therefore, the magnitude of W_2 is greater than the weights of any other variables. Next, examine the set of two-variable terms,

$$X_1X_3$$
$$X_3X_4$$

and note that X_3 appears in two terms and that X_1 and X_4 each appear once. Thus,

$$W_3 > W_4 = W_1$$

and including the single-term element, X_2, the ordering now is

$$W_2 > W_3 > W_4 = W_1$$

Next, the three-variable terms are examined:

$$X_3X_5X_6$$
$$X_1X_5X_6$$

Here, only the variables X_1, X_5, and X_6 need be considered, as X_3 has already been ordered. X_1 appears in one term; therefore, its weight is greater than that of X_4. Both X_5 and X_6 appear twice in the three-variable terms, and there they must have equal weights. The final order of weight magnitudes is

$$W_2 > W_3 > W_1 > W_4 > W_5 = W_6$$

Thus, it is possible to find the order of the relative magnitudes of single threshold realizations of unate switching functions. The difficulty here is that only functions of three variables or less are necessarily linearly separable if they are unate. Therefore, one cannot be assured that the relative order is significant with respect to a realization unless the function has three or fewer variables.

10.3 SYNTHESIS OF SINGLE-LEVEL THRESHOLD LOGIC ELEMENTS

The ordering procedure given in the previous section suggests a synthesis procedure for single-element threshold functions. The procedure outlined here does not guarantee a realization for functions of more than three variables, nor does it necessarily give minimum realizations; its treatment here is to give the reader an insight into threshold logic element realizations.

The following procedure is based on the fact that a relative coefficient order has been found for a unate function in an irredundant disjunctive form where all complemented variables have been uncomplemented. For example, given a function where the maximum number of variables in any term in the irredundant disjunctive form is M and the minimum number of variables in any term is m. Since the relative effect of each term of the function must have equal influence on the value of the function, the sum of the weights of the variables in terms with the minimum number of variables must equal or exceed the threshold, and the sum of the weights of the variables in terms with the maximum number of variables also must equal or exceed the threshold and also the sum of the variables in the other terms. Consider the following function of three variables:

$$Y = X_1 X_2 + \bar{X}_3$$

Since the function is unate, we can say it is also linearly separable and uncomplement the complemented variables:

$$Y = X_1 X_2 + X_3$$

The realization can be changed to account for the complement by using Property 4 (Chapter 9). The coefficient magnitude order is

$$W_3 > W_2 = W_1$$

and

$$M = 2$$
$$m = 1$$

Also, since the weight of the two-variable and the single-variable terms must equal or exceed the threshold,

$$W_3 = 2$$
$$W_1 = W_2 = 1$$
$$T = 2$$

and the S.P. equation is

$$X_1 + X_2 + 2X_3 = 2$$

and if one considers the threshold gap, the S.P. equation is

$$Y = (X_1 + X_2 + 2X_3)\ 2:1$$

The process of assigning weights and threshold values here is one of considering the relative weights of the variables and assigning values such that the inequality is satisfied. This procedure is easily accomplished by inspection for functions of three or fewer variables; in fact, it is possible to enumerate all realizations of functions of three or fewer variables, which is done in the next section, but it becomes increasingly difficult to obtain realizations by inspection for greater than three variables. The generalization of this procedure, however, leads to another way of defining the requirements for a single threshold realization of a given function, namely simultaneous inequalities.

A function is linearly separable and therefore single threshold element realizable if there exists a set of real numbers $(W_1, W_2, \ldots, W_N, U, l)$ such that the following inequalities hold,

$$\left.\begin{array}{ll} \sum_{i=1}^{N} W_i X_i^P > U & \text{for } F(P) = 1 \\[2ex] \sum_{i=1}^{N} W_i X_i^P < l & \text{for } F(P) = 0 \end{array}\right\} \quad U > l$$

where $F(P)$ is a function of the exponents P which have values of 0 or 1. $F(P) = 1$ defines the set of exponent values such that the function Y is true, and $F(P) = 0$ defines the set of exponent values such that the function Y is false. There are $n + 2$ unknowns, and there are 2^n inequalities. These inequalities can be solved simultaneously by eliminating one variable at a time, as is done with simultaneous equalities, or the equations can be solved using the methods of linear programming in which the gap may be maximized. A simple example of the procedure used to find a threshold realization by simultaneous inequalities follows. Given the AND function

$$Y = X_1 X_2$$

the requirements for its realization can be tabulated:

X_1	X_2	Y	$\sum W_k X_k$
0	0	0	$0 < l$
0	1	0	$W_2 < l$
1	0	0	$W_1 < l$
1	1	1	$W_1 + W_2 > U$

Thus, one can examine the acceptable region in the W_1-W_2 plane, where the inequalities above are satisfied. Note, however, that if one wished to maximize the gap, $U - l$, that $U = 2l$ will do this.

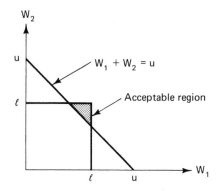

Table 10.2. All One-, Two-, and Three-Variable Threshold Functions

Switching Function	Realization	
$Y = X_1$	$Y = (X_1)$	$1:0$
$Y = X_1 + X_2$	$Y = (X_1 + X_2)$	$1:0$
$Y = X_1 X_2$	$Y = (X_1 + X_2)$	$2:1$
$Y = X_1 + X_2 + X_3$	$Y = (X_1 + X_2 + X_3)$	$1:0$
$Y = X_1 X_2 + X_2 X_3 + X_1 X_3$	$Y = (X_1 + X_2 + X_3)$	$2:1$
$Y = X_1 X_2 X_3$	$Y = (X_1 + X_2 + X_3)$	$3:2$
$Y = X_1 + X_2 X_3$	$Y = (2X_1 + X_2 + X_3)$	$2:1$
$Y = X_1(X_2 + X_3)$	$Y = (2X_1 + X_2 + X_3)$	$3:2$

It is now possible to tabulate all single threshold realizable functions of up to three variables, as shown in Table 10.2 [4]. Note that Table 10.2 can be used when some or all of the variables are complemented by making use of Property 4 (Chapter 9). For example, the procedure for realizing

$$Y = X_1 X_2 + X_1 \bar{X}_3 \tag{10.13}$$

is as follows:

1. Note that

$$Y = X_1(X_2 + X_3) \tag{10.14}$$

is realizable from Table 9.2 by

$$Y = (2X_1 + X_2 + X_3)\, 3:2 \tag{10.15}$$

2. By changing the sense of the variable X_3, Eq. (9.13) can be realized by

$$Y = (2X_1 + X_2 + \bar{X}_3)\, 3:2 \tag{10.16}$$

The complemented variable, $\bar{X}_3$, in (10.16) can be changed to an uncomplemented variable by using Property 4 (Chapter 9). Since $X_3 + \bar{X}_3 = 1$, Eq. (10.16) becomes

$$Y = (2X_1 + X_2 - X_3)\,2:1 \tag{10.17}$$

It should now be apparent that efficient synthesis of threshold circuits of more than three variables is a difficult process. Although synthesis methods for these devices exist [1], they are beyond the scope of this text.

10.4 SYNTHESIS OF NONLINEARLY SEPARABLE FUNCTIONS

Thus far, we have been concerned with synthesis using single-level devices which realize linearly separable functions. The realization of nonlinearly separable functions requires more than one threshold logic device.

Since conventional logic is merely a special case of the general threshold logic, nonlinearly separable functions can easily be realized by defining an AND, OR, and NOT with threshold devices and using standard synthesis techniques. However, the remainder of this section will be devoted to a synthesis technique which was developed to describe some of the methods whereby logical functions can be synthesized using a neural model with presynaptic inhibition.

There are several other, perhaps better, methods for synthesizing nonlinearly separable functions with threshold elements. The method presented here was chosen first because it is interesting and effective and second because it has historical significance in the development of networks of neural models. Presynaptic inhibition, when activated, eliminates the effects of the excitatory input to which it is attached. This, in effect, provides a second level of logic by performing the logical equivalent of a conventional AND with an inverting input before the threshold is applied. As shown in Figure 10.4, multiple

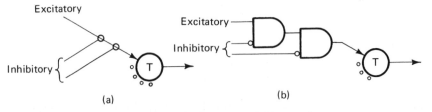

(a)   (b)

Figure 10.4. Presynaptic inhibition and its conventional equivalent.

inhibit inputs can be associated with any excitatory input. The synthesis procedure which evolved from the work of McCulloch [5] and was formalized by Blum [6], which allows synthesis of all functions of N variables, will now be considered. A simple example is the Blum implementation of the exclusive OR in two variables:

$$F(X_1, X_2) = X_1\bar{X}_2 + \bar{X}_1X_2 \qquad (10.18)$$

The synthesis of (10.17) is immediately obvious from the definitions above and is illustrated in Figure 10.5.

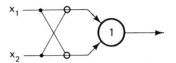

Figure 10.5. Blum realization of the two-variable parity function.

The initial step in the procedure is to obtain the function in disjunctive normal form and to map it into a primary Venn diagram. For example, consider the function

$$F(X_1X_2X_3) = X_1X_2X_3 \qquad (10.19)$$

for which the Venn diagram is

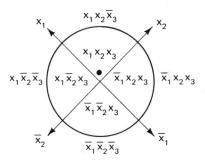

The desired term is indicated by a jot in the appropriate space, here $X_1X_2X_3$. It is clear from the above that each minterm is represented by a distinct region in the Venn diagram. A weight is now assigned to each minterm region in the diagram such that the weights of the minterms of the desired function are greater than those which are not part of the function. This ensures that the function on which the threshold element operates is linearly separable. The only restriction on the weight assignment is that the weight of the null minterm $(\bar{X}_1\bar{X}_2 \ldots \bar{X}_N)$ must always be zero. These weights are the maximum threshold values of the second-level element which will realize the corresponding minterms. Thus, by assigning different weights to the minterms, it is possible to change the function which is realized by changing only the threshold of the threshold gate. However, it is possible to realize any desired function by assigning weights of only 1 and 0. For functions in which the null minterm does not appear, a weight of $+1$ is assigned to the desired terms and 0 to the others. Conversely, for functions in which the null minterm does appear, a weight of 0 is assigned to the desired terms and a weight of -1 is assigned to the remaining terms. Therefore, for the function given by Eq. (10.18) the weight assignment is

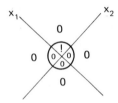

It is now possible to write a set of equations associated with the weight assignment, as shown in Table 10.3. The underlining under Associated Equations is read "inhibited by." Equation 1 indicates that the algebraic sum of the excitations and inhibitions when $X_1\bar{X}_2\bar{X}_3$ is true equals zero. Also, equation 4 indicates that the algebraic sum of excitations and inhibitions when $X_1X_2\bar{X}_3$ is true or when X_1 is not inhibited by X_2, $X_1\underline{X_2}$, and X_2 is not inhibited by X_1, $X_2\underline{X_1}$ is zero. The other equations can be described in a similar manner. The order of the equations in Table 10.3 treats minterms with the most complemented terms first, etc. The remainder of the synthesis procedure is based on assigning weights to $(N-1)$-dimensional Venn diagrams that satisfy the equations in Table 10.3.

Table 10.3. Equations Associated with Minterms

Minterms	Associated Equations
1. $X_1\bar{X}_2\bar{X}_3$	$X_1 = X_1\underline{X_2}\underline{X_3} = 0$
2. $\bar{X}_1X_2\bar{X}_3$	$X_2 = X_2\underline{X_1}\underline{X_3} = 0$
3. $\bar{X}_1\bar{X}_2X_3$	$X_3 = X_3\underline{X_1}\underline{X_2} = 0$
4. $X_1X_2\bar{X}_3$	$X_1X_2 = X_1\underline{X_2} + X_2\underline{X_1} = 0$
5. $X_1\bar{X}_2X_3$	$X_1X_3 = X_1\underline{X_3} + X_3\underline{X_1} = 0$
6. $\bar{X}_1X_2X_3$	$X_2X_3 = X_2\underline{X_3} + X_3\underline{X_2} = 0$
7. $X_1X_2X_3$	$X_1X_2X_3 = X_1\underline{X_2}\underline{X_3} + X_2\underline{X_1}\underline{X_3} + X_3\underline{X_1}\underline{X_2} = 1$

If one assumes in order that each of the uncomplemented variables X_i are true in each minterm, then it is possible to represent the left-hand side of each of the equations in Table 10.3 by three $(N-1)$-dimensional Venn diagrams with jots in the appropriate regions. For example, the first term on the right-hand side of equation 7 is represented by

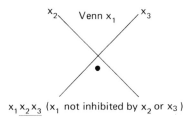

where the four spaces represent the following:

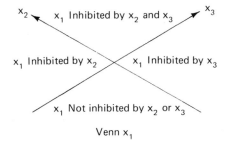

Thus, the space to the left of the line labeled X_3 represents inhibition by X_2, and the space to the right of the line labeled X_2 represents inhibition by X_3. Values can now be assigned to the spaces indicated by jots such that equation 7 is satisfied:

$$X_1\underline{X_2}X_3 + \underline{X_1}X_2\underline{X_3} + X_1X_2X_3 = 1$$

$1 + 0 + 0 = 1$

$$x_1\underline{x_2}x_3 + \underline{x_1}x_2\underline{x_3} + x_1x_2x_3 = 1$$

Note that the weight assignment above is not the only one for which equation 7 is satisfied. For instance, the following weight assignments and others will also satisfy equation 7:

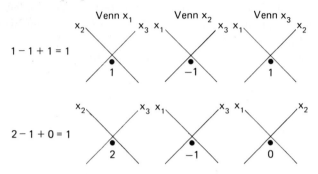

One can now represent each of the equations in Table 10.3 successively from equations 7 to 1, and by carrying the assigned weights from equations 7 to 6 and so forth, all equations can be satisfied simultaneously. The jots are inserted for each equation as it is considered, whereas the weights assigned are carried to successive equations. Each equation must be satisfied with respect to the regions where jots are entered. Thus, for the example given by Eq. (10.19), the complete assignment is

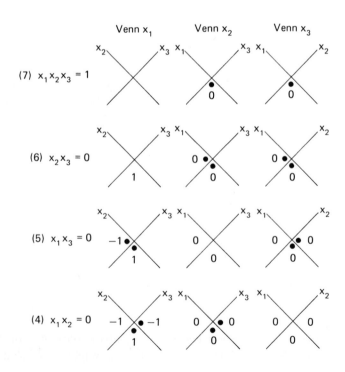

Note that up to this point the sum of the weights associated with the jots for each equation satisfy the corresponding equation. Also, note that the weights carried from the previous equations are used to satisfy the new equation only if a jot appears in that region.

The last three equations can now be satisfied by assigning weights to the remaining region in each of the Venn diagrams such that the respective equations are satisfied:

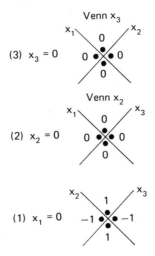

These three Venn diagrams define the structure of the network, where a positive weight indicates an excitatory input and a negative weight indicates an inhibitory input for the variable associated with that Venn. Thus, the variables X_2 and X_3 have no inputs to the final threshold element. On the other hand, X_1 has two excitatory and two inhibitory inputs to the final threshold element. The final network is shown in Figure 10.6. The interpreta-

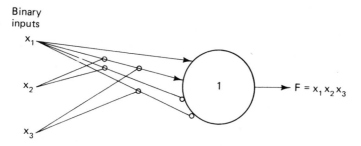

Figure 10.6. Realization of the function $F = X_1 X_2 X_3$.

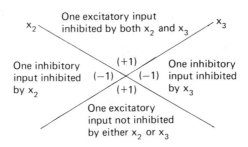

Figure 10.7. Interpretation of Venn X_1.

tion of the regions and the associated weights in Venn X_1 are illustrated in Figure 10.7. A summary of this procedure is given below:

1. Put the function to be synthesized in disjunctive normal form.
2. Map the function into the primary Venn diagram, placing jots in the regions for which the function is true.
3. Assign weights to the regions of the primary Venn diagram such that the weights assigned to the desired function's minterms are greater than the other minterms. The weight of the null minterm is always zero.
4. Write the equations associated with the minterms using the primary Venn diagram.
5. Fill the $(N - 1)$-dimensional Venn diagrams such that the above equations are satisfied, starting with the tautology $(X_1 X_2 \ldots X_N)$ and working to the terms with a single uncomplemented variable.
6. Synthesize the network from the final set of N Venn diagrams, where a positive number denotes excitatory inputs and a negative number denotes inhibitory inputs.
7. Choose the threshold of the second-level element such that it is no greater than the smallest weight of the minterms of the desired function.

The ability to synthesize neural networks that are functionally complete certainly satisfies one reasonable requirement for an element: to operate in a complex computational system such as the brain. This alone, however, does not explain any process of adaptation or learning in networks of these devices.

10.5 ADAPTIVE ELEMENTS AND NETWORKS

Many of the early attempts to create systems which exhibit adaptive, learning, or pattern recognition behavior started with the basic neural model, or the threshold logic unit, and made parts of them variable so that their behavior might be dynamically modified. These elements then served as forward transfer elements from which these various systems could be built.

One of the early and fundamental modifications of the basic neural element is the Adaline (adaptive linear element) proposed by Widrow [7]. The Adaline shown in Figure 10.8 has provisions for independent adjustment of each of the weights on the input to the threshold section. Thus, based on the assessment of the network's performance, these parameters can be adjusted. It is known, however, that this single threshold configuration is not functionally complete, and therefore we must consider multilevel configurations. A multiple adaptive linear element or Madaline for two levels is shown in Figure 10.9. The adjustments in the Madaline are only on the weights of the first-level inputs. These weights may be adjusted either continuously or incrementally over some finite range of both positive and negative values. Thus, the Madaline is a functionally complete realization of an adaptive logic system.

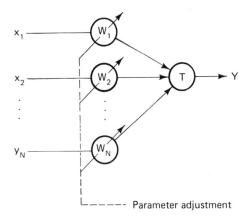

Figure 10.8. Adaline (adaptive linear element): weights are adjusted as a function of performance assessment.

Another class of networks of threshold devices is the Perceptron, which was first described by Rosenblatt [8] and later developed by Minsky and Papert [9]. The initial formulation of the Perceptron structure was based on observations of the brain and brain cell organization. The richness of inter-neuronal connections in the brain appear to have little order, and thus one might say that initially these connections are random and, as the individual learns, that the weighting of the interconnections are varied. Thus, the simple Perceptron illustrated in Figure 10.10 consists of three basic elements: the S (sensory) units, the A (association) units, and the R (response) units, where

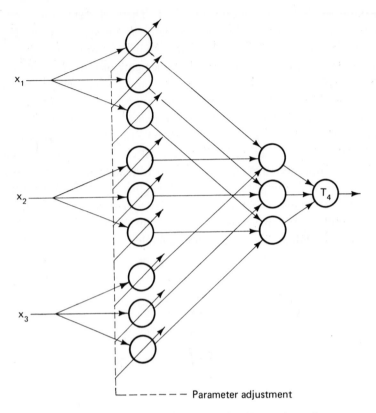

Figure 10.9. Madaline (multiple adaptive linear element): a two-level net with adjustable input weighting.

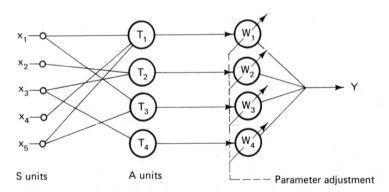

Figure 10.10. A simple Perceptron.

the connections between *S* and *A* units are selected in a random manner and the weights between the *A* units and the *R* unit are varied as a function of network training. The *S*, *A*, and *R* units are each threshold devices where the S_ith unit responds to a stimulus by emitting a signal if the *i*th signal exceeds the *i*th threshold. It should be clear from our previous study of threshold devices that proper interconnections between the *S* and *A* units will allow realization of all functions of *n* variables. A good deal of research on the convergence characteristics of Perceptrons with various random interconnection schemes has been developed by Rosenblatt [8]. Further, the *S* units have been built into matrices of photo sensors, as shown in Figure 10.11, and the network has been trained to recognize certain patterns presented to this artificial retina. This type of processing will be explored more fully in Chapter 11.

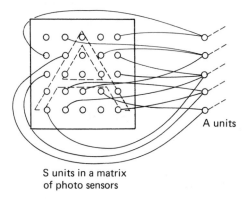

S units in a matrix
of photo sensors

Figure 10.11. Retina used for pattern recognition with Perceptron.

10.6 SUMMARY

The limits on the number of functions realizable with a single threshold device were considered in the first part of this chapter. From this it is clear that configurations of multilevel threshold devices are required to realize all functions of *n* variables. The Blum procedure provides a means for the synthesis of all functions of *n* variables with multilevel threshold devices where the first-level gate structure is fixed. It is important to note again that conventional AND, OR, and NOT logic is merely a special case of generalized threshold logic. Finally, adaptive elements of threshold-type devices have been considered. The ability to vary a set of parameters associated with the forward transfer characteristics of these elements makes them a natural for incorporation in cybernetic systems.

10.7 EXERCISES

10.1. Order the relative weight magnitudes of the following function:

$$Y = \bar{X}_1 X_2 + \bar{X}_1 X_3 + \bar{X}_1 X_4 X_6 + \bar{X}_1 X_5 X_6 + X_2 X_3 X_4 + X_2 X_3 X_5 + X_2 X_4 X_5 + X_3 X_4 X_5 X_6$$

10.2. Develop a single-element realization and write the separating plane equation for

$$Y = \bar{X}_1 X_2 X_3 + X_4 \bar{X}_1$$

10.3. Write the separating plane equation, draw a threshold logic realization, and design a conventional AND, OR, and NOT realization for

$$Y = X_1(\bar{X}_2 + \bar{X}_3)$$

10.4. Given the coincidence function

$$Y = X_1 X_2 + \bar{X}_1 \bar{X}_2$$

(a) Synthesize Y using the Blum technique.
(b) Synthesize Y using individual threshold gates which realize AND, OR, and NOT.
(c) Compare the above two realizations.

10.5. Given the accompanying neural network,
(a) Find the function realized.
(b) What functions are realized if each threshold is increased by 1? Decreased by 1?

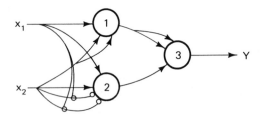

REFERENCES

1. LEWIS, P. M., and C. L. COATES, *Threshold Logic*, Wiley, New York, 1967.

2. WINDER, R. O., "Enumeration of Seven Argument Threshold Functions," *IEEE Transactions on Electronic Computers*, Vol. EC-14, No. 1, pp. 315–325, June 1965.

3. MUROGA, S., T. TSUBOI, and C. R. BANGH, "Enumeration of Threshold Functions of Eight Variables," *IEEE Transactions on Computers*, Vol. C-19, No. 9, pp. 818–825, Sept.1970.

4. LEWIS, P. M., and C. L. COATES, "Realization of Logical Functions by a Network of Threshold Components with Specified Sensitivity," *IRE Trans. Electronic Computers*, Vol. EC-12, No. 5, pp. 443–453, Oct. 1963.

5. McCULLOCH, W. S., "Agatha Tyche: Of Nervous Nets—The Lucky Reckoners," in *Mechanization of Thought Processes*, proceedings of a symposium held at the National Physiological Laboratory, Nov. 24–27, 1958, No. 1C, Vol. II, Her Majesty's Stationery Office, London, 1958, pp. 611–634.

6. BLUM, MANUEL, "Properties of a Neuron with Many Inputs," in *Principles of Self-Organization*, H. Von Foerster and G. W. Zopf, Jr., eds., Macmillan, New York, 1962.

7. WIDROW, B., "Generalization and Information Storage in Networks of Adaline Neurons," in *Self-Organizing Systems—1962*, M. C. Yovitts, G. T. Jacobs, and G. D. Goldstein, eds., Spartan, New York, 1962.

8. ROSENBLATT, F., *Principles of Neurodynamics*, Spartan, New York, 1962.

9. MINSKY, M., and S. PAPERT, *Perceptrons*, M.I.T. Press, Cambridge, Mass., 1969.

11

PATTERN RECOGNITION

Although some facets of the pattern recognition problem have been presented in previous chapters, we shall now consider it in more detail and attempt to identify its critical aspects. The recognition process is often applied to reading machines which operate on data which are obtained by optical means or to signals which may be associated with acoustic processes such as speech. The operations on these data or signals which allow one to use a machine to perform tasks such as reading typed or handwritten text or to recognize the spoken word can be broken down into five major areas: the input systems, feature extraction, discrimination, response selection, and the output systems. Before these areas are examined, it is useful to consider the general pattern recognition problem.

11.1 WHAT IS PATTERN RECOGNITION?

The term and process of pattern recognition is applied to all manner of information structures and signals. What, then, is the difference between a pattern and a signal? If one has no convenient mathematical description of the information structures or signals, then they are generally referred to as patterns. Also, patterns often take on a multidimensional nature and are expressed as *n*-dimensional vectors.

The elements of the *n*-dimensional vectors are related in some way to the pattern to be recognized. For example, the vital life signs and symptoms may make up the vector when an automatic medical diagnosis by pattern recognition techniques is to be made. These elements are sometimes called features of the pattern. A critical aspect of pattern recognition, then, is the selection of the proper features; a medical diagnosis of an infection is difficult if body temperature, a good indicator of the presence of infection, is not included in the pattern vector.

Now, once the features have been specified, it is necessary to discriminate between these features which make up the patterns to be recognized. Thus, for medical diagnoses, for example, it is necessary to be able to discriminate between a common cold, bronchitis, and pneumonia. This part of the pattern recognition problem, discrimination, is relatively well defined and therefore has been the object of a good deal of effort [1, 2].

A general model of a pattern recognition system is given in Figure 11.1. The input element converts the pattern from an abstract form such as a drawing, photo, voice, or a series of medical observations and measurements to specific physical quantities such as a voltage waveform or an optical pattern. The second element, the preprocessor, may not exist independently; however, its function, the extraction of the proper features from the input signal, is a necessary element of a pattern recognition system. The discriminator then operates on the features such that the different patterns to be recognized each generate as unique an output as possible, which can then be categorized by the response selector. The final element is the output system, which converts the result to the form desired by the user. Examples of output systems are printers, the setting of news type, Braille feelers (for reading machines for the blind), and magnetic tape formatted properly for subsequent processing (as used in automatic bill paying and accounting systems).

The input system and feature extraction processes will be examined first, and the discriminator and response selector will be studied later.

Figure 11.1. General model of a pattern recognition system.

11.2 INPUT SYSTEMS

As stated above, the purpose of the input system is to convert an abstract form into a set of physical properties which can be operated on by the remainder of the pattern recognition system. Input systems can be as simple as keyboards and push-button arrays or complex, high-speed scanners which automatically read hundreds of documents per minute. A keyboard input is useful in systems where there is a great deal of alphanumeric information and where speed is not critical. Another method for handling alphanumeric as well as pictorial and graphic inputs is the flying spot scanner described below.

The flying spot scanner is a simple, inexpensive, and versatile device for converting images on reflecting or transparent surfaces into electrical signals. Typically, the spot is provided by a cathode-ray tube (CRT), which is focused onto the reflecting surface by a lens, as illustrated in Figure 11.2. The position of the spot on the CRT and hence on the reflecting surface is controlled by the voltages on the horizontal and vertical plates of the CRT. In this manner a spot of light can be positioned to any place on the object surface. The amount of light reflected from the spot is indicated by the output of the light sensors, which are positioned around the object being scanned. The sensors may be photomultipliers, photo diodes, or phototransistors. The output from the sensors is quantized into from 2 to N levels depending on the problem. For example, 2 levels are generally used for reading alphanumeric symbols, whereas 8 or more levels may be needed for photographic recognition problems.

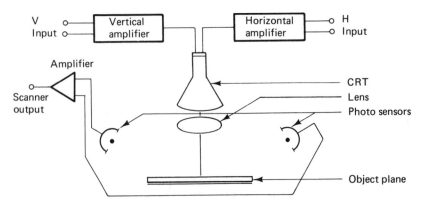

Figure 11.2. General configuration of a flying spot scanner.

There are several ways in which the spot can be positioned. The simplest is the raster scan, as used for television, in which the spot is moved from left to right and from the top down, as shown in Figure 11.3. Generally, the spot is moved in increments, thereby describing blocks or resolution elements on the object space. The extraction of features from a raster scan is usually more difficult than the curve-tracing method described later.

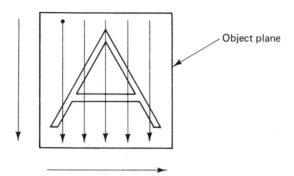

Figure 11.3. Scan directions for conventional raster scan.

Let us now examine some input systems for sound and speech recognition [3, 4]. The electrical input is provided by a microphone, and the processing beyond that point may be either digital or analog. This processing may be considered as the feature extraction process of the system. Most acoustic systems attempt to analyze the spectral-time response (sound spectrogram) of the speech waveform, an example of which is given in Figure 11.4. The spectrograms for different words spoken by the same speaker are sufficiently different to use them as a basis for word recognition. The nature of speech is not understood well enough to provide high-accuracy interspeaker word recognition using the spectrogram—or any other method for that matter.

A block diagram which is representative of many of the speech recognition systems built to date is shown in Figure 11.5. The microphone output drives a number (up to 22) of $\frac{1}{3}$-octave filters spread over the speech spectrum. Each of the outputs of the filters is usually processed in some often nonlinear way. For example, peak detection or logarithmic amplification or both may be applied. These outputs are then multiplexed and applied to an analog-digital converter for subsequent processing by a digital computer or system. The output of this system is sampled by the processor in fixed intervals from 10 to 100 milliseconds depending on the specifics of the system in question.

Thus, if there are 20 filters and a sampling rate of 50 milliseconds, then for utterances of 1-second duration, a vector of 400 elements is generated for

Figure 11.4. Sound spectrogram of the two-syllable word *ago*.

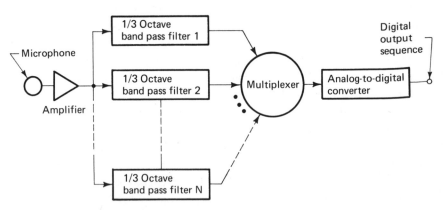

Figure 11.5. Typical input/feature extraction system for speech recognition.

processing by the remainder of the system. The object of the subsequent processing is to reduce these data to a single result—the word which was spoken. The methodology for making this decision is discussed later. Let us now study some feature extraction schemes for reading machines.

11.3 FEATURE EXTRACTION

The goal of the feature extraction process is to generate an *n*-dimensional vector from the input system which captures the "essence" of the pattern to be recognized. It is this elusive "essence" which makes feature extraction the least understood and hence the most difficult part of a pattern recognition system to design.

Feature extraction techniques cover the gamut from ad hoc intuitive schemes through biological and behavioral analogs to sophisticated analytical techniques. In this section we shall describe examples of the first two of these approaches.

First, consider the effects of a quantized raster scan for feature extraction. Here, we shall assume that the character size is known a priori and that the character has been properly positioned in the center of the scan. These two problems, character size and position, are not insignificant in practical pattern recognition problems [5]. The quantized raster scan can be visualized as a matrix of resolution elements, as illustrated in Figure 11.6. For alphanumeric characters, it is useful to quantize each resolution element into two values, 0 and 1, to represent the absence or presence, respectively, of a mark in that element, as illustrated in Figure 11.6(b). The input to the remainder of the system is the 30-bit word derived by taking each resolution value as that element is scanned. For example, the word resulting from the scan of Figure 11.6(b) is 001110111111101001111111000000.

The reorientation of the character in the raster scan results in a completely different binary sequence. This can be overcome to some extent by scanning

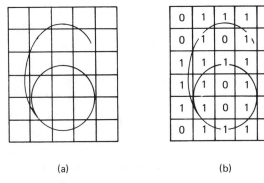

(a)   (b)

Figure 11.6. (a) Representation of raster scan by resolution elements. (b) Quantized representation of (a).

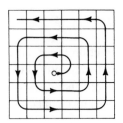

Figure 11.7. Spiral scan to reduce the effects of rotation of
the character on the scan output.

in a spiral, as shown in Figure 11.7. Here, if the number of resolution elements
is sufficiently large, the binary sequence generated will be shifted only by
an amount proportional to the rotation of the character. However, the spiral
scan is very sensitive to translation.

As the number of symbols to be recognized increases, the number of
resolution elements needed also increases up to where 60×100 matrices
may be needed. Thus, 6000 points must be scanned, formatted, stored, and
processed in the recognition process. One way to reduce the amount of data
taken, handle a large number of characters and fonts (kinds of print), and
provide a good feature set for the recognition of handwritten characters
called contour tracing has been developed [5, 6]. The square trace is the simplest contour-tracing algorithm. Here, if the last point in a black-on-white
field was black, then make a 90° turn left to determine the next resolution
element to be tested. On the other hand, if the last point was white, then make
a 90° turn right to find the next resolution element to be tested. The square
trace algorithm is illustrated in Figure 11.8. It is possible, however, to become
locked into a rectangular scan of four successive black or four successive
white resolution elements, as shown in Figure 11.9(a). This can be overcome
in most cases by making a 45° move after three elements of the same kind
have been encountered. If the edges of the character contour are not sharply
defined, it is possible to trap into a six-element sequence of one-color points,
shown in Figure 11.9(b). This condition is a trace error, these points are
ignored, and the next point to be tested is chosen at random around the trap
points. The locations of the white-to-black transitions are the only points
stored as features of the character being scanned. Typically, a 50×100
matrix requires approximately 600 tests and storage of 300 points for contour
tracing rather than 5000 points tested and stored for raster and spiral scans of
the same array.

The next class of feature extraction systems to be considered is that

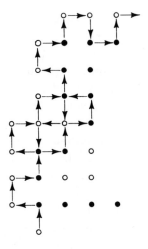

Figure 11.8. Operation of the square trace algorithm for contour tracing.

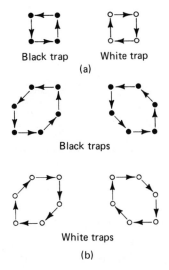

Black trap   White trap

(a)

Black traps

White traps

(b)

Figure 11.9. (a) Trace traps for square trace algorithm. (b) Trace traps for modified square trace algorithm.

derived from biological and behavioral studies of both animal and human visual systems.

For example, justification of contour tracing as a feature extraction technique can be found in both biological and behavioral experiments. A neurophysiological study of the optic nerve complex of the frog [7] indicated that the processing of visual information includes a mechanism for detecting the edge (contour) of a pattern. Other features in the frog's eye such as concavity and convexity detectors have also been used in feature extraction systems. Another study by Hartline and Ratliff [8] of the eye of Limulus (horseshoe crab) has also found that edge enhancement is an important feature for this creature as well. Studies of the human visual system from a behavioral point of view [9, 10] indicate that edge enhancement and contours are important for human perception as well. The importance of the contrast of edges can easily be illustrated by looking at the line drawing in Figure 11.10 where a complete image is conveyed by edges only. This fact is also used to advantage in color television processing where some edge enhancement is provided before the picture is transmitted. Here, images appear sharper and the effects of noise on the TV signal are not as pronounced as they would be without edge enhancement.

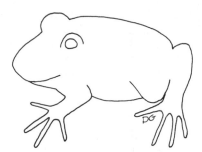

Figure 11.10. Line drawing which illustrates the effects of edges on perception. Note that only edges are needed to convey the "essence" of the image.

These various features have been incorporated in the Minos pattern recognition machine developed at Stanford Research Institute for the U.S. Army Electronics Command [11]. Here many normalized images of the pattern to be recognized are projected in parallel through masks with the various features etched upon them. Thus, edges, concavity and vertical, horizontal, and diagonal lines, etc., can all be detected by photosensors placed behind the mask. The outputs of the photosensors are then passed through threshold devices. The outputs from these units then make up the n-dimensional vector which is the input to the pattern discriminator. An example of the edge detection feature mask used in Minos is given in Figure 11.11(a), where the white areas are opaque. Edges in several discrete

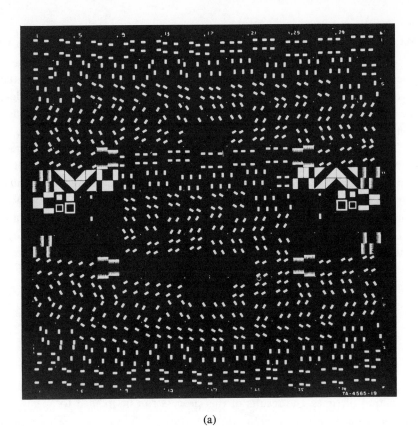

(a)

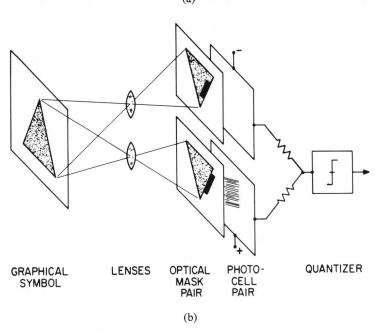

GRAPHICAL   LENSES   OPTICAL   PHOTO-   QUANTIZER
SYMBOL   MASK   CELL
                      PAIR   PAIR

(b)

Figure 11.11. (a) Mask plate for Minos for edge detection. (b) Processing system for Minos mask plates.

orientations are detected by photocell pairs placed behind images of the object, as shown in Figure 11.11(b). Thus, if an edge pair indeed is on an edge, the differential output of the quantizer will indicate the light-to-dark transition of the input symbol.

There are, of course, other features and methods for incorporating these features found in biological systems into a pattern recognition system. It is important for the designer to be aware of them in the development of these systems. However, the selection of the proper features for the problem at hand is indeed difficult and may even be classified as "art." There are some systematic methods for selecting features [12, 13] which are beyond the scope of this text. However, the uses of transforms in the feature extraction process are of interest.

11.4 TRANSFORMATIONS IN FEATURE EXTRACTION

Recall the input system for speech recognition discussed in Section 11.2 where the input signal is passed through banks of filters and analyzed as a function of time. The results of this process can be likened to an instantaneous Fourier analysis of the input waveform. Since there is a delay in propagation through each of the filters, one may apply the Fourier transform over each of the delay intervals to create the feature set of spectral density as a function of time. The advent of the fast Fourier transform algorithm [14] and the ability to perform Fourier analysis on a digital computer make this a useful tool of pattern recognition.

If the input waveform is denoted by $f(t)$, then the Fourier transform is given by

$$F(\omega) = \mathfrak{F}[f(t)] = \int_{-\infty}^{\infty} f(t)e^{-j\omega t}\, dt \qquad (11.1)$$

Thus, the frequency domain becomes the feature space in which the discriminator must operate. This space is generally large, and one must narrow its focus to regions in which there is a "significant" correlation between features which can be used to discriminate between input patterns. For example, it is well known that little speech information is present above 3 kilohertz or below 300 hertz. Therefore, the feature space between 300 hertz and 3 kilohertz is probably all that is needed to perform speech recognition. However, if one considers that speech recognition apparatus must include temporal analysis of the spectral density, then it is reasonable to define the feature space as the product of the spectral density space and the utterance duration time space, typically less than 1 second. Thus, the feature space for speech recognition is indeed large and must be reduced further [15].

One might also incorporate the Fourier transform in image recognition by applying it, for example, to each vertical scan or part thereof, creating a spectral density for each line of the image. However, since an image exists in two dimensions, it has been found useful to apply the Fourier transform in two dimensions. The two-dimensional Fourier transform is especially important in recognizing two-dimensional images because it can easily be realized using optical techniques. Let us now examine the two-dimensional Fourier transform.

An image can be represented by an intensity function in two dimensions, $f(x, y)$. The Fourier transform in two dimensions is

$$F(u, v) = \int_{-\infty}^{\infty} \int_{-\infty}^{\infty} f(x, y)e^{-j(ux+vy)} \, dx \, dy \tag{11.2}$$

and $f(x, y)$ is given by the inverse Fourier transform

$$f(x, y) = \frac{1}{(2\pi)^2} \int_{-\infty}^{\infty} \int_{-\infty}^{\infty} F(u, v)e^{j(ux+vy)} \, du \, dv \tag{11.3}$$

The Fourier transform can also be represented in discrete form for computer implementation, where

$$F(u, v) = \frac{1}{N} \sum_{x=0}^{N-1} \sum_{y=0}^{N-1} f(x, y)e^{(-j2\pi/N)(ux+vy)} \tag{11.4}$$

is the forward transform and

$$f(x, y) = \frac{1}{N} \sum_{u=0}^{N-1} \sum_{v=0}^{N-1} F(u, v)e^{(j2\pi/N)(ux+vy)} \tag{11.5}$$

is the inverse transformation. $F(u, v)$ is also a two-dimensional intensity function but in the u, v plane, where intensity transitions in the x direction of the x-y plane generate spectral components in the v direction along the u axis of the u-v plane while intensity transitions in the y direction of the x-y plane generate spectral components in the u direction along the v axis of the u-v plane. These intensity variations in the x and y directions are described in the u, v plane as spatial frequencies. Thus, it is possible to filter out specific frequencies by applying a spatial filter, $H(u, v)$ to $F(u, v)$:

$$G(u, v) = H(u, v)F(u, v) \tag{11.6}$$

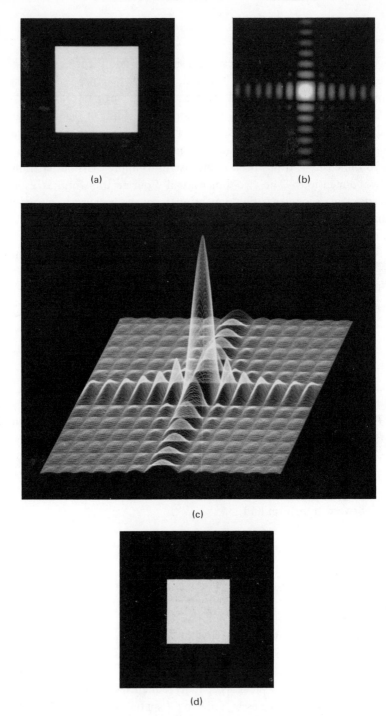

Figure 11.12. Two-dimensional images, Fourier transforms, and spatial filtering.

The function given in Eq. (11.5) may represent the features of a particular pattern to be recognized. One distinct advantage of spatial filtering for feature extraction is that it can easily be accomplished with optical techniques [16]. Another advantage of this approach is that all elements of the two-dimensional image are processed in parallel. A square image, its two-dimensional Fourier transform image, and a three-dimensional representation of the transform are shown in Figure 11.12. A spatial filter which passes the first two harmonics of the image is a transparent circle whose radius is just greater than the distance to the second harmonic, shown in Figure 11.12(d). The effects of spatial filtering on the letter *E* are shown in Figure 11.13, where the inverse Fourier transform of the filtered images has been applied. It is interesting to note that some of the "essence" of the letter is still present even if only the direct-current component and first harmonic are passed through the filter. Thus, features for the letter *E* might reasonably be direct current and the first through the third harmonics. The perceptual aspects of spatial filtering with respect to what stimulus cues the human visual system responds has been treated by Ginsburg [17].

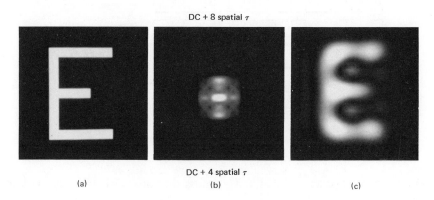

Figure 11.13. The effects of spatial filtering on an image.

Another transformation which particularly lends itself to computer implementation is the Walsh-Hadamard transformation [18, 19]. This transformation is unique in that its basis is not sines and cosines but orthogonal rectangular waves called Walsh functions whose values alternate between -1 and $+1$. Thus, they may be considered as sequences of binary numbers, and the number of $+1$ to -1 and -1 to $+1$ transitions per fundamental time interval is called the *sequency*. These orthogonal functions are illustrated in Figure 11.14. One can also represent these functions by defining the smallest

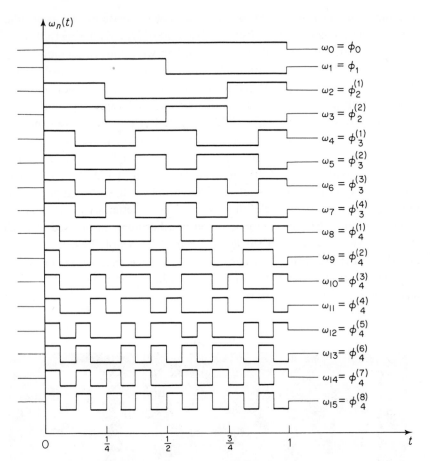

Figure 11.14. Walsh functions indexed by the number of sign changes in the interval $0 < t < 1$.

interval of interest as -1 or $+1$. Therefore, the sequence is given by a vector whose elements are $+1$ or -1.

Now, if one is concerned with a specific number of time intervals, then the Walsh sequences can be represented in matrix form as follows. If there are two intervals as in a 2 by 2 array of resolution elements, then the functions in order of increasing sequency are

$$H_2 = \begin{bmatrix} 1 & 1 \\ 1 & -1 \end{bmatrix} \tag{11.7}$$

Equation (11.7) is also known as the lowest-order Hadamard matrix, where a Hadamard matrix is a square matrix of $+1$s and -1s whose rows and columns are orthogonal to one another. The orthogonality property indicates that

$$[H][H]^T = N[I] \tag{11.8}$$

where I is the identity matrix and the normalized Hadamard matrix $(1/\sqrt{N})[H]$ is an orthonormal matrix. Hadamard matrices of an order $2N$ can be constructed from matrices of order N by the following:

$$H_{2N} = \begin{bmatrix} H_N & H_N \\ H_N & -H_N \end{bmatrix} \tag{11.9}$$

Hadamard matrices of order higher than 2 must be a multiple of 4.

The discrete Walsh-Hadamard transformation for a one-dimensional function $f(x)$ is similar to the Fourier transformation except that the basis involves $+1$ and -1 and not powers of e,

$$F(\mu) = \frac{1}{\sqrt{N}} \sum_{x=0}^{N-1} f(x)(-1)^{p(x,\mu)} \tag{11.10}$$

where

$$p(x, \mu) = \sum_{i=0}^{N-1} (\mu_i x_i) = \sum_{i=0}^{N-1} (\mu_i \wedge x_i) \tag{11.11}$$

The terms μ_i and x_i are the ith bits of the binary representation of the decimal numbers μ and x, respectively. Note that the summation in Eq. (11.11) is to the base 10. It is interesting to note that $(-1)^{p(x,u)}$ for successive values of x and u defines a Walsh sequence or a Hadamard matrix (see the Exercises). Similarly, the discrete two-dimensional Walsh-Hadamard transformation is given by

$$F(u, v) = \frac{1}{N} \sum_{x=0}^{N-1} \sum_{y=0}^{N-1} f(x, y)(-1)^{p(x,y,u,v)} \tag{11.12}$$

where

$$p(x, y, u, v) = \sum_{i=0}^{N-1} (u_i x_i + v_i y_i) \tag{11.13}$$

and the u_i, x_i, v_i, and y_i are as given above.

The Walsh-Hadamard transformation can easily be carried out using a digital computer since it can be computed using only logical operations and adds. This transformation can easily be used on $N \times N$ arrays of resolution elements by direct application of equations (11.12) and (11.13). The resulting intensity function in the u, v plane can be then used to generate the feature vector for the discrimination/response selection portion of the pattern recognizer.

11.5 THE DISCRIMINATION AND RESPONSE SELECTION PROBLEMS (CLASSIFICATION) [20]

Thus far, we have been concerned with generating a set of measurements of some input which contain the "essence" of the patterns which we wish to recognize. In general, we can represent the output of a feature extraction system as an n-tuple, $x_1, x_2, x_3, \ldots, x_n$, where this set of numbers is sometimes called the pattern and the elements are called components or features of the pattern. Thus, the discrimination problem is to classify the n measurements as being a member of one of r different responses of the output set Z, as illustrated in Figure 11.15.

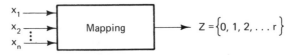

Figure 11.15. Model of pattern classifier.

The n inputs can each be associated with a single dimension of an n-dimensional Euclidean space, and each set of measurements X define a point in space. The task of the classifier is to map the points in the n-dimensional Euclidean space into the r members of the output set. A simple approach to this is to divide up the Euclidean space into r decision regions where each region is associated with one of the possible input patterns. The surfaces in the space of X which separate one pattern from all other patterns are called decision surfaces. This is identical to the separation of functions in threshold logic by separating planes treated in Chapters 9 and 10.

11.6 DECISION SURFACES AND DISCRIMINANT FUNCTIONS [1, 21, 22]

The decision surfaces in the X space are defined by the intersection of planes described by discriminant functions. Discriminant functions are chosen such that for all points in X associated with response, i, $g_i(X) > g_j(X)$ for $i, j = 1, \ldots, r$, $i \neq j$. Therefore, the ith discriminant function has the

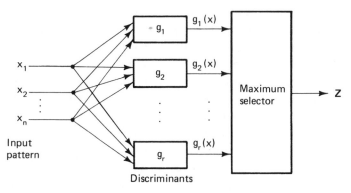

Figure 11.16. Model of pattern classifier.

largest scalar magnitude when the ith pattern is present at the input. This model of a pattern classifier is given in Figure 11.16. The operation of the classifier is as follows: The input pattern X is presented, the discriminants are formed, the maximum selector determines the discriminant, l, with the largest value, and the input is then classified as the lth pattern.

One of the most important problems in pattern recognition is the selection of the discriminant functions to be used. There are several ways in which one may select discriminant functions, and each depends on the type and complexity of the pattern recognition task. For example, in the simple process of dichotomization as in the simple detection problem using TLPs described in Chapter 7, the process may be completely described by the nature of the problem. For TLPs the discriminant functions can be described exactly. Other problems may require that certain approximations be applied in the development of the discriminant functions. Finally, one may have very little information to form a basis from which one can design the appropriate discriminant functions. In the latter two cases the final discriminant functions must depend to some extent on adjustments made on the operation of the system. Thus, it may be necessary to apply learning techniques to the design of discriminant functions. This leads one to the concept of a trainable pattern classifier and the associated training techniques.

There are two techniques for training pattern classifier systems: parametric and nonparametric methods. Parametric methods are used when each of the possible input categories is known a priori to be representable by a set of parameters, where some of the parameter values are unknown. The case where all the parameters are known a priori is more easily solved than the case where only one or more parameter value is unknown. In the first case, the proper discriminants would easily be designed such that the input patterns are recognized. The latter case requires that certain measurements of the unknown parameter values be made, and a discriminant function based on these measurements can then be set up.

A simple parametric method for one unknown parameter value might require that a series of measurements of that parameter be taken and the mean value of these samples be used as an estimate of the value of that parameter.

Consider the case where two parameter values are unknown. Here one may estimate the mean values of each of the parameters in the hyperspace of X as X_1 and X_2. A reasonable choice for the discriminant function is the perpendicular bisector of the points X_1 and X_2. The following discriminant function will perform as that kind of discriminant and is illustrated in Figure 11.17:

$$g(X) = (X_1 - X_2) \cdot X + \tfrac{1}{2}|X_2|^2 - \tfrac{1}{2}|X_1|^2 \qquad (11.14)$$

A most difficult case of pattern recognition discriminant function generation is where the parameters to be used are not known a priori. In these nonparametric cases one may assume a functional form for the discriminant functions, and the coefficients of these functions may be found by training methods. Some of the forms which may be assumed are linear, quadric, piecewise linear, or Gilstrap's multinomial, for example. Other methods utilize cascaded linear and nonlinear functions or matrix representations of the input vector X and eigenvectors of the matrix as discriminants of the system.

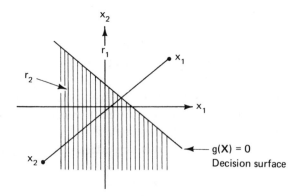

Figure 11.17. Perpendicular bisector of means as a discriminant function.

A common functional form which is often assumed is the linear discriminant function

$$g(X) = w_1 x_1 + w_2 x_2 + \cdots + w_n x_n - w_0$$

Note that this is identical to the realization of the threshold logic element described earlier. A pattern recognition learning system which uses linear discriminant functions is called a linear machine. A linear machine is illustrated in Figure 11.18. Here r linear discriminant functions are described where each function is associated with one of the r possible pattern classes. The w_{i0} represent the weights or thresholds of each of the linear functions.

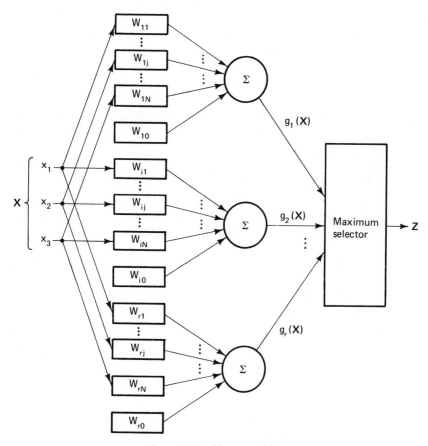

Figure 11.18. Linear machine.

Another technique for classification of patterns is called the minimum-distance classifier. Here each of the r_i possible pattern classes are associated with a point P_i in E^d (d-dimensional Euclidean space). Thus, the pattern into which a particular input X is classified is associated with the point to which the input is closest. Here the Euclidean distance is given by

$$|X - P_i| = \sqrt{(X - P_i) \cdot (X - P_i)} \qquad (11.15)$$

Note that since X and P_i are vectors that $(X - P_i) \cdot (X - P_i)$ represents the dot product and $(X - P_i)(X - P_i)^T$ the matrix product. Thus, one calculates the magnitude above for all i and then selects the pattern for which the magnitude is minimum. The points $P_1, P_2, \ldots, P_r$ are called prototype points, as they are generally associated with "idealized," noiseless, versions of each of the input patterns.

Next, note that the use of $|X - P_i|^2$ is equivalent to the above; however, squaring both sides of Eq. (11.15) gives

$$|X - P_i|^2 = (X - P_i) \cdot (X - P_i) = X \cdot X - 2X \cdot P_i + P_i \cdot P_i \qquad (11.16)$$

Now it is clear from Eq. (11.16) that the comparison of X and P_i is only a function of the last two terms, and a comparison of the following terms is equivalent to Eq. (11.16):

$$\max(X \cdot P_i - \tfrac{1}{2} P_i \cdot P_i) \qquad \text{for } i = 1, \ldots, r \qquad (11.17)$$

Thus, the minimum-distance classifier selects the largest of the r terms computed by Eq. (11.17), and the discriminant functions are

$$g_i(x) = X \cdot P_i - \tfrac{1}{2} P_i \cdot P_i \qquad \text{for } i = 1, \ldots, r \qquad (11.18)$$

Equation (11.18) is linear and therefore the weights associated with each of the x_d points in the r equations are

$$w_{ij} = p_{ij} \qquad \begin{matrix} i = 1, \ldots, r \\ j = 1, \ldots, r \end{matrix} \qquad (11.19a)$$

and the thresholds are

$$w_{i0} = -\tfrac{1}{2} P_i \cdot P_i \qquad i = 1, \ldots, r \qquad (11.19b)$$

The dot product $X \cdot P_i$ is also known as template matching, correlation detection, and matched filtering.

The template-matching process can be thought of as follows. Assume that the problem at hand is to recognize the numbers 0 through 9 as printed by an IBM executive typewriter. First, one must make templates of these characters, for example, transparencies of the characters whose densities are such that the light passing through each transparency under the same illumination is equal. The process of pattern recognition then requires that transparencies of the input patterns be compared with the templates by projecting through the two transparencies and selecting as the response the pattern associated the template which passes the largest amount of light.

Another technique for template matching is to divide a given optical pattern into regions, which can be done with a photocell matrix, as illustrated in Figure 11.19(a). To each photocell, a binary storage register is connected. This register is connected to a set of 10 logical AND gates, where each gate

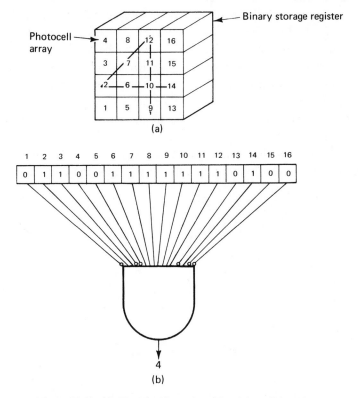

Figure 11.19. (a) Template match with photocell matrix. (b) Shift register with 4 stored in it and template for 4 given by logical AND gate.

is associated with one of the input symbols. The inputs to each gate correspond to the inputs associated with each template, as is illustrated in Figure 11.19(b) for the number 4.

The limitations on the pattern recognition capabilities of the linear machine and the minimum-distance classifier are the same as the limitations placed on single-level threshold realizations of Boolean functions treated in Chapter 10. That is, the functions $g_i(X)$ must be linearly separable,

11.7 NONLINEAR DISCRIMINANTS

The separation of regions in a hyperspace which are not linearly separable can often be accomplished with surfaces which are nonlinear. For example, the realization of binary parity functions cannot be accomplished with the linear hyperplanes associated with single-level threshold logic. However, it is entirely possible to realize parity functions with more than one level of logic as shown by the Blum realization in Chapter 10. The hyperplanes associated with multilevel threshold functions therefore must be nonlinear. For example, the hyperplanes for two-variable parity appear as in Figure 11.20. It is clear from Figure 11.20 that the hyperplanes are not linear over the entire space but that they are linear over some of the space. Thus, these hyperplanes are called piecewise linear, and the resulting implementation is called a piecewise linear machine.

Assume that one has r finite point sets $\mathcal{P}_1, \mathcal{P}_2, \ldots, \mathcal{P}_r$, where each of the ith point sets consists of L_i points. Now, define the Euclidean distance

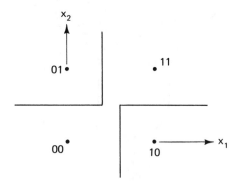

Figure 11.20. Nonlinear hyperplane realization for two-variable parity.

$E(X, \mathcal{P}_i)$ from the arbitrary point X to the point set $\mathcal{P}_i$ by

$$E(X, \mathcal{P}_i) = \min_{j=1,\ldots,L} |X - P_i^{(j)}| \tag{11.20}$$

the minimum distance between X and each point in $\mathcal{P}_i$. Now, define a minimum-distance classifier with respect to the point sets $\mathcal{P}_i, \mathcal{P}_2, \ldots, \mathcal{P}_r$ which classifies a given pattern X into the category associated with the closest point set. Here, the $P_i^{(j)}$ are the points in $\mathcal{P}_i$.

Therefore, as before, define for each $i = 1, \ldots, r$ the function

$$g_i(X) = \max_{j=1,\ldots,L_i} \{P_i^{(j)} \cdot X - \tfrac{1}{2}P_i^{(i)} \cdot P_i^{(j)}\} \tag{11.21}$$

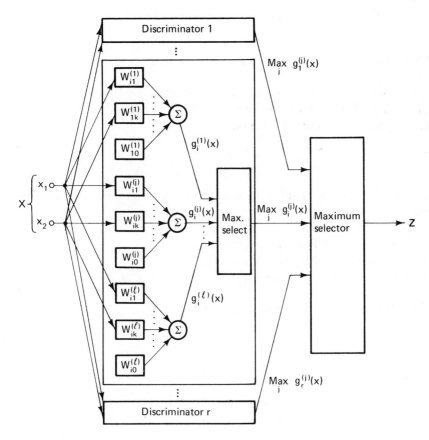

Figure 11.21. Piecewise linear pattern recognition system.

Thus, we have defined a minimum-distance classifier with respect to L_i different prototypes in each pattern class. This suggests a different notation for the general form for the discriminant functions,

$$g_i(X) = \max_{j=1,\ldots,L_i} \{g_i^{(j)}(X)\} \qquad i = 1,\ldots,r \qquad (11.22)$$

where each $g_i^{(j)}(X)$, the subsidiary discriminant functions, are given by

$$g_i^{(j)}(X) = w_{i1}^{(j)}x_1 + w_{12}^{(j)}x_2 + \ldots + w_{id}^{(j)}x_d + w_{i0}^{(j)} \qquad (11.23)$$

The function $g_i(X)$ is dependent on the subsidiary discriminant functions, and the final discriminant functions are then piecewise linear functions. A model of this type of discrimination system is shown in Figure 11.21. The piecewise linear machine is a general machine for dealing with nonlinearly separable functions, and the minimum-distance classifier is just a special case.

11.8 QUADRIC DISCRIMINANT FUNCTIONS

Another method for realizing nonlinearly separable functions makes use of nonlinear discriminant functions. A special kind of nonlinear discriminant is the quadric discriminant function:

$$g_i(X) = \sum_{i=1}^{N} w_{ii}x_i^2 + \sum_{j=1}^{N-1}\sum_{k=j+1}^{N} w_{jk}x_jx_k + \sum_{j=1}^{N} w_jx_j + w_0 \qquad (11.24)$$

The parameters associated with quadric discriminant functions are summarized as follows:

1. N weights as coefficients of x_i^2 terms ... w_{ij}.
2. N weights as coefficients of x_j terms ... w_j.
3. $N(N-1)/2$ weights as coefficients of x_ix_j terms, $k \neq j$ ... w_{ik}.

Note that the w_{jk} terms can be described as follows:

$$\left.\begin{array}{ccc}
& & w_{(N-1)N} \\
& & \cdot \\
& & \cdot \\
& & \cdot \\
w_{45} & \cdots & w_{3N} \\
w_{23} & \cdots & w_{2N} \\
w_{12} & \cdots & w_{1N}
\end{array}\right\} N-1$$

$$\underbrace{\hspace{5cm}}_{N}$$

and that there are $N(N-1)/2$ terms in the above representation. Since the discriminant function here is complex, it is desirable to represent $g_i(X)$ in matrix form. Let matrix A have components given by

$$a_{jj} = w_{jj} \qquad j = 1, \ldots, N$$
$$a_{jk} = \tfrac{1}{2} w_{jk} \qquad j, k = 1, \ldots, N, j \neq k$$

Also, let

$$B = \begin{pmatrix} b_1 \\ \cdot \\ \cdot \\ \cdot \\ b_N \end{pmatrix}$$

where

$$b_j = w_j, \qquad j = 1, \ldots, N$$

and let $C = w_0$.

Now,

$$g(X) = X^t A X + X^t B + C \tag{11.25}$$

The term $X^t A X$ is called the quadratic form.

The decision surfaces of this type of machine are sections of second-degree surfaces called quadric surfaces.

The physical implementation of quadric discriminants is not much more complicated than that for linear discriminant functions; however, it is certainly more expensive.

A model for a quadric discriminator is given in Figure 11.22. It is clear that the quadric processor requires several multipliers, which makes the

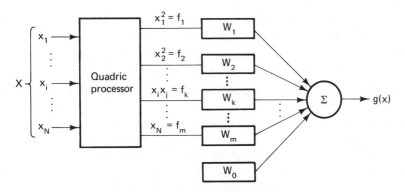

Figure 11.22. Quadric discriminator.

quadric processor considerably more expensive than a linear machine. There are N components of x_i^2 terms, $N(N-i)/2$ components of x_ix_1 terms, and N components of the x_i terms. Thus, there are $N/2(1+N)$ multipliers for N input dimensions.

Now, examine another form for a quadric discriminator:

$$g(X) = w_1f_1 + w_2f_2 + \ldots + w_mf_m + w_0 \qquad (11.26)$$

where each of the f_1 are quadric functions.

It is interesting to observe that the above representation is a linear discriminant function on the outputs of the nonlinear processors.

11.9 SUMMARY

We have examined several aspects of pattern recognition from input system through discrimination. The output system has not been discussed because its form depends more critically than the other parts of the system on the particular application. Generally, the output from the discriminator is in a form which can easily be interfaced to digital or analog hardware such as printers, displays, loudspeakers, and computers.

The sophisticated reader may lament the fact that his "pet" technique of pattern recognition has been left out of this chapter. However, it is hoped that this introduction will give the reader a relatively broad brush of this fascinating area and encourage him to refer to the references for additional reading.

11.10 EXERCISES

11.1. Discuss the relative differences in scanning with horizontal versus vertical lines, especially with respect to image size and position.

11.2. Explain why it is difficult to use a spiral scan with systems that have a small number of resolution elements. Use examples in your answer.

11.3. Devise an algorithm for contour tracing which eliminates as many "traps" as possible.

11.4. Find the Fourier transform of the letters O, A, and T centered in a 5×8 array. Note features which are different between characters. (It is recommended that a digital computer be used to solve this problem.)

11.5. Find the Walsh-Hadamard transform of the letters O, A, and T centered in an 8×8 array. Note features which are different between characters. (It is recommended that a digital computer be used to solve this problem.)

11.6. Show that $g(X)$ in Eq. (11.14) is the perpendicular bisector of the line between X_1 and X_2.

11.7. Show that $(-1)^{p(x,\mu)}$, where $p(x, \mu) = \sum_{i=1}^{N-1} \mu_i x_i$, generates Walsh sequences for x and μ integers, and for increasing integer values of x and μ, generates Hadamard matrices. Note that N must be odd for Walsh sequences and a multiple of 4 for Hadamard matrices of order higher than 2.

11.8. Draw a block diagram for the quadric machine described by Eq. (11.26).

REFERENCES

1. PATRICK, E. A., *Fundamentals of Pattern Recognition*, Prentice-Hall, Englewood Cliffs, N.J., 1972.

2. SEBEYSTIAN, G. S., *Decision Making Process in Pattern Recognition*, Macmillan, New York, 1962.

3. POLS, LEWIS C. W., "Real-Time Recognition of Spoken Words," *IEEE Transactions on Computers*, Vol. C-20, No. 9, pp. 972–978, Sept. 1971.

4. GLENN, JAMES W., and MYRON H. HITCHCOCK, "With a Speech Pattern Classifier, Computer Listens to Its Master's Voice," *Electronics*, Vol. 44, No. 10, May 10, 1971.

5. TROXEL, D. E., F. F. LEE, and S. J. MASON, "A Reading Machine for the Blind," *Digest of the 7th International Conference on Medical and Biological Engineering, 1967.*

6. KOLERS, PAUL A., and MURRAY EDEN, eds., *Recognizing Patterns; Studies in Living and Automatic Systems*, M.I.T. Press, Cambridge, Mass., 1968.

7. LETTVIN, J. Y., H. R. MATURANA, W. S. MCCULLOCH, and W. H. PITTS, "What the Frog's Eye Tells the Frog's Brain," *Proceedings of the IRE*, Vol. 47, pp. 1940–1951, 1959.

8. HARTLINE, H. K., and F. RATLIFF, "Inhibitory Interaction of Receptor Units in the Eye of Limulus," *Journal of General Physiology*, Vol. 39, pp. 357–376, 1957.

9. HALL, E. L., R. P. KRUGER, S. J. DWYER, III, D. L. HALL, R. W. MCLOREN, and G. S. LODWICK, "A Survey of Preprocessing and Feature Extraction Techniques for Radiographic Images," *IEEE Transactions on Computers*, Vol. C-20, No. 9, pp. 1032–1044, Sept. 1971.

10. UHR, LEONARD, ed., *Pattern Recognition*, Wiley, New York, 1966.

11. HUBER, WILLIAM A., "MINOS III—Adaptive Learning/Digital Computer Data Classifier," *U.S. Army Electronics Command R&D Technical Report ECOM-3135*, Fort Monmouth, W. Va., June 1969.

12. NELSON, G. D., and D. M. LEVY, "A Dynamic Programming Approach to Selection of Pattern Features," *IEEE Transactions on Systems Science and Cybernetics*, Vol. SSC-4, pp. 145–150, July 1968.

13. MUCCIARDI, A. N., and E. E. GOSE, "A Comparison of Seven Techniques for Choosing Subsets of Pattern Recognition Properties," *IEEE Transactions on Computers*, Vol. C-20, No. 9, pp. 1023–1031, Sept. 1971.

14. COOLEY, J. W., and J. W. TUKEY, "An Algorithm for the Machine Calculation of Complex Fourier Series," *Math. Comput.*, Vol. 19, No. 90, pp. 297–301, 1965.

15. NIEDERJOHN, RUSSELL J., and IAN B. THOMAS, "Computer Recognition of Phonemic Segments in Connected Speech," *Proceedings of the National Electronics Conference*, Vol. 26, 1970.

16. GOODMAN, JOSEPH W., *Introduction to Fourier Optics*, McGraw-Hill, New York, 1968.

17. GINSBURG, ARTHUR P., "Psychological Correlates of a Model of the Human Visual System," M.S. Thesis, School of Engineering, Air Force Institute of Technology, June 1971.

18. GOLOMB, S. W., et al., *Digital Communications*, Prentice-Hall, Englewood Cliffs, N.J., 1964.

19. ANDREWS, H. C., "Multidimensional Rotations in Feature Selection," *IEEE Transactions on Computers*, Vol. C-20, No. 9, pp. 1045–1051, Sept. 1971.

20. NILSON, N. J., *Learning Machines—Foundations of Trainable Pattern Classifying Systems*, McGraw-Hill, New York, 1965.

21. NAGY, G., "State of the Art in Pattern Recognition," *Proceedings of the IEEE*, Vol. 56, No. 5, pp. 836–862, May 1968.

22. FU, K. S., *Sequential Methods in Pattern Recognition and Machine Learning*, Academic Press, New York, 1968.

INDEX

253